AP

Advanced Placement

United States History

Duane L. Ostler, BA, MPA, JD
James Zucker, MAT
Nancy McCaslin, JD
Sujata Millick, PhD
Tomas Skinner, BA

XAMonline, Inc.

Copyright © 2017

All rights reserved. No part of the material protected by this copyright notice may be reproduced or utilized in any form or by any means, electronic or mechanical, including photocopying or recording or by any information storage and retrievable system, without written permission from the copyright holder.

To obtain permission(s) to use the material from this work for any purpose including workshops or seminars, please submit a written request to:

> XAMonline, Inc.
> 21 Orient Avenue
> Melrose, MA 02176
> Toll Free: 1-800-301-4647
> Email: info@xamonline.com
> Web: www.xamonline.com
> Fax: 1-617-583-5552

Library of Congress Cataloging-in-Publication Data
    Zucker, James

AP United States History/ James Zucker
ISBN: 978-1-60787-636-6

1. AP   2. Study Guides   3. History

Disclaimer:

The opinions expressed in this publication are the sole works of XAMonline and were created independently from the College Board, or other testing affiliates. Between the time of publication and printing, specific test standards as well as testing formats and website information may change that are not included in part or in whole within this product. XAMonline develops sample test questions, and they reflect similar content as on real tests; however, they are not former tests. XAMonline assembles content that aligns with test standards but makes no claims nor guarantees candidates a passing score.

Cover photos provided by © iStock.com/DanBrandenburg/556993, © iStock.com/SunChan/20751116, © iStock.com/Aneese/24187796, © iStock.com/cincila/54383864, © Can Stock Photo, Inc./billperry/13129480

Printed in the United States of America
AP United States History
ISBN: 978-1-60787-636-6

MEET THE AUTHORS

Mr. Duane L. Ostler

Mr. Duane L. Ostler has a BA (history), MPA and JD from BYU in Provo, Utah, and a PhD in legal history from Macquarie University in Sydney, Australia. He lives in Orem, Utah with his wife, 5 children and 2 cats.

James Zucker

James Zucker is a teacher at Loyola High School for Advanced Placement US History. He holds a Bachelor's degree in History and a MAT in History and Education. He is also a College Board Consultant in Advanced Placement US History. He read for the national exam from 2000–2005.

Nancy McCaslin

Nancy McCaslin is an attorney in Elkhart, Indiana. She has as B.S. in Education from Indiana University (Bloomington) and an M.A. in American History from Ball State University. Her J.D. in Law is from Valparaiso University. Nancy has taught history, government, and business law and has developed curriculum in those areas. She loves to read and travel in her free time.

Sujata Millick

Dr. Sujata Millick works at the intersection of the technology, education, security and privacy domains. She has over two decades of public sector executive and programmatic experience in science, R&D, and STEM education portfolios in the defense, commerce, and maritime organizations. She pursues work in the areas of education, internet connectedness, and emerging technologies.

Tomás Skinner

Tomás Skinner is an Irish archaeologist with interests in Chinese history and culture, the heritage of the Silk Road, tea, and travelling. He lives in The Hague, Netherlands, with his wife, and is currently pursuing his M.A. Asian Studies from the University of Leiden.

Table of Contents

SECTION I: About the Advanced Placement US History Program 3

    About the Advanced Placement US History Examination 5
    Historical Thinking Skills. 9
    The Make Up of the Exam 9
    How the AP US History Exam is Scored 9
    Hints for Taking the Test 11
    What To Expect In This Book 13
    College Board Websites 13

SECTION II: HOTs (Historical Thinking Skills) 15

    Cause and Effect 17
    Comparison and Contrast... 19
    Historical Argumentation 20
    Periodization. 21
    Document Based Questions and Answers 22
    Advice from an AP Reader 27

SECTION III: Time Period Summaries 35

    Summary of Period 1: 1491–1585................................. 36
    Summary of Period 2: 1585–1750................................. 44
    Summary of Period 3: 1751–1799................................. 52
    Summary of Period 4: 1800–1848................................. 63
    Summary of Period 5: 1844–1877................................. 74
    Summary of Period 6: 1865–1898................................. 86
    Summary of Period 7: 1890–1945................................. 97
    Summary of Period 8: 1945–1980................................. 106
    Summary of Period 9: 1980–Present 114

SECTION IV: Sample Test One 121

    Sample Test One 123
    Sample Test One Answer Sheet 157
    Sample Test One Answer Key..................................... 158
    Sample Test One Explanations.................................... 159

SECTION V: Sample Test Two 201

    Sample Test Two 203
    Sample Test Two Answer Sheet 235
    Sample Test Two Answers.. 236
    Sample Test Two Explanations.................................... 237

Appendix: Timeline of Important Dates, Key Figures, and Significant Events ... 275

SECTION I:
About the Advanced Placement US History Program

About the Advanced Placement US History Examination

The Advanced Placement® (AP) program is designed to offer students college credit while they are still in high school. There are more than 30 AP courses culminating in an intensive final exam given every year in May.

The AP US History Examination tests your knowledge of several key periods of American history centering around various themes. The course covers historical periods from about 1491 to the present.

About the Exam

Students taking the AP US History exam should have a good understanding of US history, and be able to describe significant events, individuals, developments, and processes across nine historical periods using critical thinking skills and methods. Short descriptions of each of the nine time periods follow:

Period 1: 1491–1585

Key Concept 1.1: As native populations migrated and settled across the vast expanse of North America over time, they developed distinct and increasingly complex societies by adapting to and transforming their diverse environments.

Key Concept 1.2: Contact among Europeans, Native Americans, and Africans resulted in the Columbian Exchange and significant social, cultural, and political changes on both sides of the Atlantic Ocean.

Period 2: 1607–1750

Key Concept 2.1: Europeans developed a variety of colonization and migration patterns, influenced by different imperial goals, cultures, and the varied North American environments where they settled, and they competed with each other and American Indians for resources.

Key Concept 2.2: The British colonies participated in political, social, cultural, and economic exchanges with Great Britain that encouraged both stronger bonds with Britain and resistance to Britain's control.

Period 3: 1754–1799

Key Concept 3.1: British attempts to assert tighter control over its North American colonies and the colonial resolve to pursue self-government led to a colonial independence movement and the Revolutionary War.

Key Concept 3.2: The American Revolution's democratic and republican ideals inspired new experiments with different forms of government.

Key Concept 3.3: Migration within North America and competition over resources, boundaries, and trade intensified conflicts among peoples and nations.

Period 4: 1800–1848

Key Concept 4.1: The United States began to develop a modern democracy and celebrated a new national culture, while Americans sought to define the nation's democratic ideals and change their society and institutions to match them.

Key Concept 4.2: Innovations in technology, agriculture, and commerce accelerated the growth of the American economy, precipitating profound changes to US society and to national and regional identities.

Key Concept 4.3: The US interest in increasing foreign trade and expanding its national borders shaped the nation's foreign policy and spurred government and private initiatives.

Period 5: 1844–1877

Key Concept 5.1: The United States became more connected with the world, pursued an expansionist foreign policy in the Western Hemisphere, and emerged as the destination for many migrants from other countries.

Key Concept 5.2: Intensified by expansion and deepening regional divisions, debates over slavery and other economic, cultural, and political issues led the nation into civil war.

Key Concept 5.3: The Union victory in the Civil War and the contested reconstruction of the South settled the issues of slavery and secession, but left unresolved many questions about the power of the federal government and citizenship rights.

Period 6: 1865–1898

Key Concept 6.1: Technological advances, large-scale production methods, and the opening of new markets encouraged the rise of industrial capitalism in the United States.

Key Concept 6.2: The migrations that accompanied industrialization transformed both urban and rural areas of the United States and caused dramatic social and cultural change.

Key Concept 6.3: The Gilded Age produced new cultural and intellectual movements, public reform efforts, and political debates over economic and social policies.

Period 7: 1890–1945

Key Concept 7.1: Growth expanded opportunity, while economic instability led to new efforts to reform US society and its economic system.

Key Concept 7.2: Innovations in communications and technology contributed to the growth of mass culture, while significant changes occurred in internal and international migration patterns.

Key Concept 7.3: Participation in a series of global conflicts propelled the United States into a position of international power while renewing domestic debates over the nation's proper role in the world.

Period 8: 1945–1980

Key Concept 8.1: The United States responded to an uncertain and unstable postwar world by asserting and working to maintain a position of global leadership, with far-reaching domestic and international consequences.

Key Concept 8.2: New movements for civil rights and liberal efforts to expand the role of government generated a range of political and cultural responses.

Key Concept 8.3: Postwar economic and demographic changes had far-reaching consequences for American society, politics, and culture.

Period 9: 1980–Present

Key Concept 9.1: A newly ascendant conservative movement achieved several political and policy goals during the 1980s and continued to strongly influence public discourse in the following decades.

Key Concept 9.2: Moving into the 21st century, the nation experienced significant technological, economic, and demographic changes.

Key Concept 9.3: The end of the Cold War and new challenges to US leadership forced the nation to redefine its foreign policy and role in the world.

Themes

The exam also tests on seven themes that students use to make connections among historical developments in different times and places. The themes focus on major historical issues and changes, helping students connect the historical content they study to broad developments and processes that have emerged over centuries in what has become the United States. The seven themes are:

1. American and National Identity: This theme focuses on how and why definitions of American and national identity and values have developed, as well as on related topics such as citizenship, constitutionalism, foreign policy, assimilation, and American exceptionalism.
2. Politics and Power: This theme focuses on how different social and political groups have influenced society and government in the United States, as well as how political beliefs and institutions have changed over time.
3. Work, Exchange, and Technology: This theme focuses on the factors behind the development of systems of economic exchange, particularly the role of technology, economic markets, and government.

4. Culture and Society: This theme focuses on the roles that ideas, beliefs, social mores, and creative expression have played in shaping the United States, as well as how various identities, cultures, and values have been preserved or changed in different contexts of US history.
5. Migration and Settlement: This theme focuses on why and how the various people who moved to and within the United States both adapted to and transformed their new social environments.
6. Geography and the Environment: This theme focuses on the role of geography and both the natural and human-made environments in social and political developments in what would become the United States.
7. America in the World: This theme focuses on the interactions between nations that affected North American history in the colonial period, and on the influence of the United States on world affairs.

Historical Thinking Skills

Another important part of the AP US History Exam is to show evidence of use of historical thinking skills. There are nine key historical thinking skills listed by the College Board for this exam across four categories, as depicted in the table below.

Analyzing Historical Sources and Evidence	• Analyzing evidence: content and sourcing • Interpretation
Making Historical Connections	• Comparison • Contextualization • Synthesis
Chronological Reasoning	• Causation • Patterns of continuity and change over time • Periodization
Creating and Supporting a Historical Argument	• Argumentation

The Make Up of the Exam

The AP US History Exam is 3 hours and 15 minutes long and includes both a 105-minute multiple-choice/short-answer section and a 90-minute free-response section. Each section is divided into two parts, as shown in the table below. The AP US History Exam is administered every May.

Section	Question Type	Number of Questions	Available Time	Percentage of Total Exam Score
I	Part A: Multiple-choice	55	55 minutes	40%
I	Part B: Short Answer	4	50 minutes	20%
II	Part A: Document-based question	1	55 minutes	25%
II	Part B: Long Essay Question	1	35 minutes	15%

How the AP US History Exam is Scored

The multiple-choice part of the test is scored by machine and the free response portion is scored by hand (every summer hundreds of professors, content specialists, and AP History teachers meet to grade the exams that are taken). There is no penalty for guessing or for wrong answers on the multiple-choice portion. Once both scores have been tallied, they are combined and then scaled. This raw score is then changed into a composite score ranging from 1–5.

The College Board proposes the following qualifications for each of the potential score:

Exam Grade	Recommendation
1	Extremely Well Qualified
2	Well Qualified
3	Qualified
4	Possibly Qualified
5	No recommendation

The minimum score required for college credit to be granted is a 3. As mentioned above, many schools require scores of 4 or 5 in order to grant credit. For comparison, the College Board makes the equivalents of the AP Exam scores at follows:

AP Exam Grade	Letter Grade Equivalent
5	A
4	A-, B+, B
3	B-, C+, C
2	None
1	None

For reference, the 2015 administration of the AP US History Exam had this score distribution:[1]

Exam Score	Percentage of Students
5	9.3
4	17.8
3	23.6
2	25
1	24.3

---

[1] http://www.totalregistration.net/AP-Exam-Registration-Service/2015-AP-Exam-Score-Distributions.php

Hints for Taking the Test

Section I, Part A: 55 Multiple-Choice Questions (55 minutes)

Multiple-choice questions can be tricky. A lot of times it is possible to eliminate one or two of the answers right away, but then get stuck with the others. On the exam there is no penalty for incorrect answers, so be sure to record an answer for every question, even if it is a complete guess.

It is also very important to know what the question is asking of you. The College Board is notorious for saying things like, "All of the following are examples, EXCEPT…" or, "Which of these is NOT…" These words can change the entire meaning of the sentence. Be on alert for qualifiers like this.

You will be using a number 2 pencil to bubble in your answers on an answer sheet. At this stage in your academic career you have taken enough tests of this type that hopefully you know how to properly fill in the circles. If you need to erase an answer, be sure to do it completely.

Remember how much time is allotted for each section. 55 minutes might seem like enough time, but be aware of your progress, and track your time, so you get to the end of the section.

Section 1, Part B: 4 Short Answer Questions (50 minutes)
Section 2, Part A: 1 Document-based Question (40 minutes)
Section 2, Part B: 1 Long Essay Question (35 minutes)

The free response questions are usually the items that give students the most difficulty. This is not because they do not they know the answers. The problem usually results from not organizing one's thoughts sufficiently and then getting them down on paper fast enough. The three free response sections account for a whopping 60% of the total score for the exam. So, don't take this lightly.

There are three type of free response questions: (1) four short answer questions, (2) one document-based question, and (3) one long essay questions.

Each AP Exam question will measure students' ability to apply historical thinking skills to one or more of the 9 thematic learning objectives. Both the multiple-choice and free-response questions on the exam require students to apply a historical thinking skill to a learning objective within a particular historical context. Additionally, the free-response section also requires students to provide specific historical evidence. So, make sure that you are using one or more of the historical thinking skills and referring to one of the themes and/or periods of the US History material.

One change that has occurred in the past years is the addition of a 15-minute preparation period before the start of Section 2. It is during this time that you can read the exam questions and start to put your thoughts in order. You can even make an outline if you wish. Be sure to write down any key terms that will be important.

The free response questions are graded on a point scale, with different key topics being worth different amounts. The maximum a question can be worth is 10 points (for example, of the question has two parts, each part is worth five. If the question has three parts, then each part would be worth three and the extra point would be given if all three parts are answered completely). In order to get full credit for each question, you must answer in sufficient enough detail that the reader believes you have a complete understanding of the topic.

Like the multiple choice, you do not lose credit for presenting incorrect information. However, you do lose time. Other things the readers do not care about including: spelling and grammar.

You will need to integrate knowledge and use analytic and organizational skills in writing your answer. You will also need to incorporate specific examples in your responses. Therefore, read each question carefully and answer the question in the way it was asked.

You may be expected to utilize provided charts, diagrams, and graphs to draw conclusions and relate those conclusions to general concepts and relationships.

The exam readers are not concerned about spelling, grammar, or penmanship because the answer is considered a draft. However, if a reader is unable to determine what it was you wrote, they cannot grade it, but they do their best to interpret a student's "chicken scratch."

Be certain your writing is in essay form (tell a story). Do NOT just list important concepts in an outline.

Also like the multiple-choice questions, the free response questions have key terms about which you should pay particular attention. These terms include, "Compare,' "Contrast," Describe,' and their favorite, "Explain." Pay particular attention to these terms and be sure to do what they ask.

Be aware of what you are writing. You do not want to say one thing in the first paragraph and then say the complete opposite in the second paragraph. If you do this, you will not get any credit, even if one of them is correct. This is because the reader does not know if you knew which was correct or just took a guess and got lucky.

Finally, the biggest piece of advice for answering the free response questions is to answer the question and then move on. Do not spend time going back over it (certainly reread it to make sure it makes sense) to edit it and turn it into a major piece of literature. You do not have time for this. Write what the question asks you to write and then move on.

What To Expect In This Book

As you move forward through these next pages, you will see a variety of information. The first section is a review of nine time-periods of US History that you should know, or be familiar with.

You will also find two sample tests at the end of this book. These are designed to give you hands-on experience that simulates the actual exam you will be taking. Each question on these tests has a detailed answer as to why it is correct and why the incorrect answers are wrong. Use this information to help guide your learning. The last section is an outline of important dates, key figures and significant events in the history of the United States. It is to be used as a supplement to the AP US History study guide and is not meant as a comprehensive list of material covered in the AP US History Course.

College Board Websites

https://advancesinap.collegeboard.org/english-history-and-social-science/us-history

https://secure-media.collegeboard.org/digitalServices/pdf/ap/ap-us-history-course-and-exam-description.pdf

SECTION II:
HOTs
(Historical Thinking Skills)

The College Board and Educational Testing Service recently created a new framework for the AP US History test. It is important for you, as a student, to know what has changed. The content largely remains the same, but the course is now more consciously emphasizing critical thinking skills.

The idea is that you, as a student, should become more like a historian in your study of American history. The College Board wants you to understand and articulate what it is that historians do, so they now emphasize the thinking skills pertaining to the discipline of historical study.

The historical thinking skills identified by the College Board and ETS include:
- Cause and Effect
- Comparison and Contrast
- Periodization
- Historical Argumentation
- DBQ analysis

This next section will discuss each of these thinking skills. This is really the heart of the new Advanced Placement class and exam. These skills are used in the multiple choice, short answer, DBQ, and Long Essay.

It is important for you to become conscious of each of these skills and how to strategically address them throughout the test.

Cause and Effect

One of the most basic truths about life is the relationship of cause and effect. It is common sense, so much so that we take it for granted. Let's look at a common example.

Imagine that you have a major test, such as an AP exam. And imagine that when you wake up in the morning, you choose to eat a donut and drink a cup of coffee to get you going. So you show up for the AP exam at 8:00 AM, ready to go. You fly through the first section of the test. You know every answer. You own this test. Then, the second hour hits. All of a sudden, you start to slow down. You notice that you are really tired. Now the questions seem to be harder. You are having a hard time focusing. What just happened?

The problem is obvious: You ate too much sugar, you experienced a sugar high and crash as you were taking the test. The cause is the sugar intake and the effect is exhaustion and collapse. If only we could go back and change that one element, then the test would have gone so much smoother. Or would it?

So, this is where cause and effect actually gets a lot more complicated. The cause and effect relationship that we described above is known as a mono-causal relationship.

A mono-causal relationship is when you have one cause and one effect. But that is not how life usually operates. In fact, even in this example, think of all the

other possible causes that could have derailed your efforts in taking the exam. You may have been affected by:
- The amount of homework the night before.
- A stressful conversation with a parent, friend, or significant other.
- You studied too much in the last few days and froze up.
- Or you just had a restless night filled with anxiety-causing nightmares.

The point is that most of human life is not conditional on one cause or one effect. Rather, there are multiple causes for any event, as well as multiple effects. Advanced Placement graders want to see you that you can develop a sophisticated and in-depth essay analyzing cause and effect. They want to see that you can provide multiple causes and effects with good analysis and reasoning.

Lets take a historical example that you could see on the AP test. What if the test asked you to discuss the Economic, Political, and Ideological reasons for the Americans' choice to sever their relationship with England during the American Revolution? How would you address this, since you don't want to end up describing a mono-causal or mono-effects relationship?

First, brainstorm all the possible causes and effects during the American Revolution. We could create a list of possible contextual causes like French-Indian War, war debt, the Stamp Act, the Proclamation of 1763, King George closing local assemblies, and the Intolerable Acts. Once we have this list, we have escaped from the mono-causal mistake.

Second, we don't want to just list these causes. We need to rank these causes and decide which ones contributed most to the American Revolution and desire to break from the British empire.

Third, we need to develop a reason for this cause being so important. A lot of students like to list off reasons for an event, but without an analysis statement, our argument is going to be very shallow and lack the depth that we need to get full points.

Fourth, we can actually overlap the top reasons with some of the subordinate reasons. This will provide more depth to our argument, and it will show the reader how much we know about the historical topic.

So lets see how you could create an in-depth and complex argument about the cause-effect relationships that led to the American Revolution.

First, lets look at a mediocre argument:

A student could argue that the American revolution was due to increased taxes and a lack of representation. Not bad for a first try. But there are a few problems. The argument is cliché, and it lacks a prioritization of complex causes. Also, the argument lacks evidence for the claim. So, how can we make it better?

Lets argue the following instead:

American colonists broke from England because they felt that they were treated as second class citizens, having had their rights to local representation violated by a monarch that was using them to pay off the empire's war debts.

Note that this argument provides a list of causes for the revolution including taxes, the lack of representation, the war debt, and the ending of local control.

But the argument also prioritizes the issue as one of violating British citizenship, and it overlaps the issues. It also provides a clear reason for the American Revolution.

So, the cause and effect relationship can provide multiple causes, connections between the causes, a reason for the causes, and a prioritizing of relationships.

Comparison and Contrast

One of the critical thinking skills that is necessary in developing historical argumentation is the ability to compare and contrast events, leaders, movements, ideas and even time periods. In many ways, this may be the most difficult skill that you as a student have to apply. Comparison and contrast allows us to see the parallels between different issues and time periods in American history.

So, why do we even study history? Many people offer the cliché that we study history because it helps us to not make the same mistakes of the past. However, this actually does not make a lot of sense when you think about it. The past is very foreign to us, including leaders who thought and acted differently from us. The problems that people faced in the past are not the same problems that we face today.

We study history to understand what has led up to this moment. We study history to understand the roots of our problems, and to understand our identity. Take, for example, yourself. Think of when you were a 5-year-old, a 10-year-old, or any younger age. Did you face the same problems that you face today? Probably not. But you can see patterns from the time you were a child that helped create who you are today. Understanding your identity will help you to approach your problems with a greater appreciation for its context.

So how do we apply this to history? You are going to be asked this year to complete comparison/contrast essays. And you are going to be asked to make synthesis statements that compare the issues in one time period to the issues in another time period.

1. First, you want to decide what the primary theme or issue is on a particular topic. For example, lets say that you are asked to compare the American Revolution to the Vietnam War. You could see that the two issues have a common theme about people's self determination.
2. You must provide a reason for the similarity between the two issues. In our example, you could argue that both the leaders

of the American Revolution and the Vietnam War favored self-determination because they were being ruled by a distant country.

3. You then need to choose the most direct and significant difference between the two issues. In the case of the American Revolution and the Vietnam War, we can argue that the Cold War makes the two different. While the American Revolution was fought over principles of natural rights, the Vietnam War was fought in the context of capitalism vs. communism.

4. Lastly, we need to create a significance statement about the two issues. We can argue that the American Revolution established the belief in natural rights and self-determination. But the Vietnam War has challenged these beliefs due to the need for Western powers to protect against communism.

Compare and contrast skills are absolutely necessary for good historical thinking and writing skills. They are necessary because they are at the root of why we do history. The difficulty is in making strong compare and contrast statements. We can do this by finding the most significant similar issues between what is being compared and contrasted.

Historical Argumentation

One of the key skills required in any Advanced Placement class is the ability to develop an argument. Most students think that regular classes are about memorizing facts, Honors classes are about memorizing more facts, and AP classes must be about memorizing a ton of facts. This is a misconception. Advanced Placement classes are about learning historical thinking skills so that you can provide an interpretation based upon original thinking. But how do you do this?

There is a popular model for argumentation called the Stephen Toulmin model. Stephen Toulmin was a British philosopher who developed a system for organizing your thoughts to develop complexity and support.

Every argument has to have the following elements:

1. Claim
2. Warrants
3. Impacts

First, a claim is a statement of opinion. For example, you can argue that America is an exceptional country. Many people think that simply making that claim is enough because it sounds so intuitive, but the claim is only the start of any argument.

Second, you need to provide support or warrants. One type of warrant is an analytical warrant. These are abstract reasons that support your original claim. For example, you could argue that America is exceptional because we have a written constitution that tries to limit the potential abuse of power by the government. Notice that this piece of support is abstract and very opinion-based. It is like a claim supporting a claim. A second type of warrant is an empirical warrant. This is a concrete and specific example or statistic. For example, you could claim that America is an exceptional country because our Declaration of Independence explicitly states that everyone deserves natural rights. Note that this is a specific and concrete example and reference.

Third, your argument needs to state why the point you are making is significance. This is called an impact. So, you could claim that the point of arguing that America is exceptional is to demonstrate that our tradition and identity is based upon individual freedom.

Why do we need to go through all of these steps to make an argument? An argument has to provide the grounds for answering the question. When you are offered a writing prompt for an essay, you need to show that your answer is relevant to the prompt. That is the point of the claim. The warrants provide complex support for your argument, and the impact of the argument reminds your audience (teacher or grader) how you are responding to the initial question or prompt.

A few final notes on writing a good argument: Make sure that your argument is well organized. Readers need to know what the main point is so that they can follow how you support it. Also, you need to provide multiple warrants to show that your argument is complex. Also, don't be afraid to overlap issues to show a complexity of thought.

The point of a good argument is to demonstrate unique thinking, so be creative in connecting information. But make sure that your argument is concise and direct in regards to the prompt.

Periodization

The next historical thinking skill is very similar to that of cause and effect. It is called Periodization. Historians use Periodization to define the differences between historical time periods. This is important because historians often disagree about the significance of issues and how they define the uniqueness of different time periods.

Lets start off with an example in your own personal life. When were you a child, and when did you become an adult? At first glance, this probably seems obvious. No one would claim that you were ready to be an adult when you were learning to crawl or walk at the age of two or three. But this becomes more difficult when you try to define the difference between childhood and adulthood in your teenage years. When are you responsible to drive? When are you responsible to have your own checking account? Should you be drafted into the military at the age of 17? What is an appropriate age for you to get married?

What defines you becoming an adult and being both free and responsible for your decisions?

In your own life, you choose to believe that there is a turning point when you become an adult. For some people, that turning point is the graduation from high school and moving on to college. That is what you are preparing for right now when you take the AP test. But that is not so clear either. You are making pretty big adult decisions about college even before you leave home and go to college, and these decisions will affect you for the rest of your life. So are you an adult when you are making these decisions or when you literally leave home for college?

Let's say that you decide to argue that you are an adult when you make the decision for college. This means that adulthood is based upon mature decision-making. And, you are now responsible for the consequences of your decisions as well.

The point is that you are defining the different periods of your life based upon your definition of what it means to be an adult. The process is the same for historians trying to define time periods. A historian is going to set up a reason for that definition, and that reason now becomes the basis for their arguments over different reasons for defining these periods.

Let's take a historical example. Say we are trying to define the Civil Rights movement. We could argue that it began with the choosing of Martin Luther King, Jr. as a civil rights leader and ended with his death. However, this means that we are defining historical periods by great leaders. What if we instead defined it by the movement of people who influenced great leaders? Now, the Civil Rights movement would have begun with the migration of African Americans from the South to the North in the 1920s. The point is that we can argue over the turning points, and our different reasons for privileging one definition over the other.

So, how do you approach this skill if you are asked about it?

First, identify the time period that is being discussed. Brainstorm all of the major examples, themes, and issues that you think are the most important to the time period.

Second, establish a reason for your definition of the time period. Make sure it is unique to other time periods.

Third, pick out a clear turning point that led to the time period based upon your previous two steps. Provide a clear reason for this definition of the turning point and time period.

Document Based Questions and Answers

Before beginning to write any essay for Document Based Questions, remember that there is no one answer that is correct. The focus of the essay is for you to create a thesis, support your thesis with historical evidence, and to reach a conclusion about the argument(s) you have presented. You will have a certain number of minutes allotted for reading the question, preparing, and writing the answer. Spend approximately 1/4 to 1/3 of your time reading the question and documents and organizing your answer. You should spend the remaining time writing your essay. As you take practice tests, use an alarm clock or other timing device to monitor your time and to pace yourself.

Good organization is one key to writing a good essay. You need to understand the question being asked before you begin writing. Read the question very carefully, and re-read the question if necessary. As you read, jot down ideas that you think might help you answer the question. Use the margins of the page to make your notations. There are several ways to organize your notes and structure your argument(s) once you have completed the reading. Use columns to make an outline for each argument or make a grid to show the positive and negative aspects of information obtained from the primary source.

Reading the instructions very carefully will help you decide what kind of an answer is required. Will you be comparing two periods in history? Are you being asked to present a chronological argument?

After you have written down some ideas, read the documents that are provided as evidence. Use the same note-taking methods. (If you need to reread the question, this is the point in time to be sure you understand what is being asked.) Then, decide what you want to argue in your answer. The argument is your thesis, and you will support your thesis with information from the included 8 to 12 documents and from outside sources that you remember from studying US History.

The Answer Format

A good answer will usually contain between three and five paragraphs, whether you are writing an answer that includes arguments for your belief, an essay comparing two or more events or eras, an argument presenting chronological events, or an argument opposing the beliefs of another person.

Regardless of the type of argument you are presenting in your essay, you will identify your thesis and explain how you will address the question.

If you are presenting arguments to support a specific view, the second paragraph (and third and fourth, if you include more than three paragraphs) will contain arguments for your thesis. The arguments will be based upon content within the provided documents. Most of the evidence within the documents will not be familiar to you, but it is important to use all of the documents to support your argument. It is also important to present arguments from your own independent knowledge that relates to, or ties in with, the evidence in the supporting documents.

The first paragraph should, in addition to identifying the thesis, present background information about the issue. This will provide the overall context for the time period addressed in the essay. The other paragraphs should discuss the events, efforts made by individuals and groups to address the issue, and the results of such action. The final paragraph, as in other argumentative essays, will restate the question presented in the first paragraph and reach a conclusion.

In addition to taking a position, it is important to explain which opposing arguments you are destructing, and the reasons why you believe these arguments are incorrect. Consider writing a second short paragraph in which you state a possible alternative viewpoint. Then, broadly state why you think this viewpoint is incorrect relative to your thesis. This is called weighing the two arguments.

After this, write several body paragraphs. These paragraphs should have a topic sentence that makes an overall point that supports the thesis. Then, provide about 2–3 documents in each paragraph. Make sure the documents are analyzed using the author's point of view, audience, or purpose. Provide outside details about the time period that are not contained in the documents.

Finish the essay with a synthesis paragraph. This is where you provide a parallel or comparison between your argument and a time period outside the one in the question. Make sure that you describe the similarity and state why the two time periods share an issue.

Good Facts – Bad Facts

The primary sources that have been included for you to review will contain possibilities for arguments in favor of your position and arguments against your position. It is important to include views opposite to the position you take in your argument. Explain why those views are not valid or applicable to your thesis and why they should be discounted. Ignoring bad facts will not make the information go away or not be relevant. Structuring a strong argument includes recognizing that there are other points of view. Because there is no "right" or "wrong" essay answer, it is important that the reader be aware you are familiar with "both sides" of the argument.

Details of good writing for the Answers to Document Based Questions

Remember the term TOP SCORE and you will remember the following guidelines for better writing:

T: *Terms* need to be defined. Definitions are usually found in the first paragraph of an answer, and it is very important to define any terms that may be misunderstood or have more than one meaning. For example, if you are making an argument that Manifest Destiny was the basis for westward expansion, the term "Manifest Destiny" needs to be defined to show how the term differs from "westward expansion."

O: *Outlines* need to be followed. Keep your ideas on track. What is your argument? What is your supporting evidence? What is your conclusion? It is important to write as much about a topic as you can. However, the information you include in your essay needs to be relevant and applicable to the questions you are answering. The document-based question essay is NOT an essay in which you should include everything you know whether it is relevant or not. To earn a good score on the essay, you need to make use of relevant, important evidence to support your argument.

P: *Paragraphs* need to be organized and begin with topic sentences. Identify paragraphs by number or sequence. If you use "First, second, third" or "1., 2., 3." for paragraphing, your ideas should flow more logically. Another way to clearly identify ideas is by using introductory words such as "some/others" or "on one hand/on the other hand." For example, "Some historians, such as *** believe.... while others such as *** contend that...." is one way writers keep paragraphs organized. Topic sentences guide the reader and serve as transitions between ideas. The topic sentence will tell the reader what you will be discussing in the paragraph and will let the reader follow your ideas from paragraph to paragraph.

S: *Simplicity* can help increase scores. Basic sentence structure in the active voice is welcoming for the reader who has limited time to assess answers.

C: *Clarity* in ideas and in writing can improve scores. Writing neatly and clearly will show you understand the question and have taken time to logically reach a conclusion. If you find that you need to make changes to any of the sentences, do so neatly. Cross out what you need to delete but do it in a way that doesn't distract the reader or delete the quality of your essay.

O: *One* idea at a time. Each paragraph of the essay for a document-based question needs one, and only one, idea. The first paragraph is the introduction; the second paragraph contains an argument; and the final paragraph contains the conclusion.

R: *Review* your work before submitting your answer. Remember that the essay you are submitting reflects the quality of information you have about a subject and reflects the quality of work you do. Be sure your answer includes all possible relevant content. Also, be sure your answer presents an appealing appearance, free from unnecessary marks and distractions. If your answer exhibits quality in content and appearance, your chances of scoring higher are increased.

E: *Examples* support your argument. Use relevant examples as often as possible. If your question involves the Muckrakers and you are discussing examples of abuse the Muckrakers were attacking, cite the conditions of the meat packing industry, for example, and explain that Upton Sinclair wrote about the abuses of labor in the meat packing industry in The Jungle. Remembering details, such as the date of publication, is not necessary; however, remembering that the book was published in the early 1900s is added information that tells the reader you are familiar with the subject you are writing about. It is important to include information in addition to content provided in the primary sources to obtain higher scores. Include as many relevant historical facts as possible for the time period and issues that complement the primary source information.

To obtain a top score, follow the suggestions listed to increase the possibility of a higher score.

The Question

Primary Sources

You will interpret the content in various primary sources. Evidence provided to support your essay answer will be presented to you in several formats. If, for example, you are crafting an answer that involves community response to events, such as the Boston Massacre, perhaps some documentation will relate to that colonial time period. One of the documents may be a newspaper article written at the time the British soldiers confronted the crowd. As you read the document, consider whether the writer was an eye witness to the event, whether his own ideas about the British rule are evident in the article, and whether the writer was editorializing or presenting factual events. A second document may be the diary of a citizen who participated in Shays' Rebellion. Consider whether the writer supported or opposed the rebellion, and consider the reasons for the position the writer took. If you are presented with a speech delivered by a member of Parliament about the necessity of taxing the colonies to help pay for the war Great Britain was involved in against France, consider whether this speech may have had an effect on events taking place that were referred to as the Boston Tea Party.

You should real all documents with the idea in mind that the documents will support or oppose your thesis argument. Consider the person making the statements, the events to which they relate, the connection (if any) to the question and your thesis, and the time period in which the primary source was created. It is important not to disregard opposing views. Reading and understanding opposing views can put your arguments into perspective. The primary sources that include views that are in conflict with your argument will be extremely important in explaining why an opponent's view is not valid. Although you need not use all documents in your answer, the more you use, and apply correctly, the more likely your score will be higher.

Scoring

Answers are not scored on the basis of being correct or incorrect. The focus of document-based questions is on eras, major time periods, and important issues that have arisen in the history of the United States. As a writer of answers for Document Based Questions, it is your responsibility to present a thesis for your answer. You will develop your thesis after you have read the primary source documents relating to the question. You will use the resources to argue your thesis. Your essay answer will be graded on the argument(s), strength of arguments, analysis, and conclusion. The answer to the document-based question will count toward 25% of the total exam score. Organization is important. The total number of points available for the answer is 7. The breakdown for scoring is as follows:

1 point – Thesis
4 points – Analysis and Support
1 point – Contextualization
1 point – Synthesis

Regardless of the type answer that is required, all answers should consist of a thesis, arguments to support the thesis, use of primary source documents within the arguments, outside historical evidence that shows your understanding of the period, and a conclusion/synthesis.

As you write your first practice answer for a document-based question presented as an example in this book, take as long as you need to work through the question/answer correctly and completely. After completing the first question, begin using a timer so you can pace yourself on the exam. For each question you answer, adhere to the following procedure to gain the maximum advantage of practice exams:

1. Read the question carefully.
2. Note information you have about the subject.
3. Read all primary source documents and apply the information to your answer.
4. Organize your answer.
5. Structure your answer.
6. Begin writing.
7. Use the format designed for the type of response required.

After you have completed the practice exams, you should feel comfortable in taking the actual AP US History Exam and by following the recommendations presented in this book, you should be able to obtain a TOP SCORE on the exam.

Advice from an AP Reader

This section of the review book is meant to be a question and answer section. The individual providing the answers is James Zucker, a teacher for AP US History. He has also graded national exams for fifteen years. The questions and answers are meant to be helpful hints and strategies for attacking the test. They are also meant to be ways for you to think like the national graders.

1. Who is the most important person in the room?

This is probably a strange question. I am sure that you are thinking that the most important person room is you. Because you, the student, are taking a very important test. You have spent the whole year working extremely hard to prepare for that moment. You are anxious, hopeful and exhausted. And you probably cannot wait for lunch right after the test. However, the answer is not you...

The most important person is not really in the room physically. He/she is in a room about month after the test in the convention hall where people are grading national exams.

About a month after the exam, in early June, teachers from around the country fly to a particular destination chosen by the College Board and the Educational Testing Service. All of the teachers teach either Advanced Placement United States History or teach a survey course in US History at the college level. This means that you have a very large group of very intelligent, well-educated, and enthusiastic proponents of education in US history.

This group of teachers sit in a convention hall for one week. They grade about 1200 to 1500 essays during this time. They grade from about eight in the morning to five in the afternoon. They get very few breaks during this time, and the work is exhausting.

Now add on top of this the grade that most students end up earning. The AP essays are graded on a 7-point DBQ rubric and a 6-point Long Essay rubric. The mean score is about a 2 on each essay. So if you can just score at a 4 level, think of how well you are doing!

You want to make the experience of your grader as easy and interesting as possible. So, remember, the most important person in your audience is a high school AP US History teacher who wants you to be direct, concise, interesting, clear, and have good handwriting. This alone will put you far above the majority of students.

2. Okay, how do I attack the multiple choice questions?

Before we get to the essay questions and how to impress your grader, lets talk about the multiple choice section. This section is a great place to pick up points. I would suggest that you think of the multiple choice section as a big game board. If you just know the rules of the game you can start to pick up points. Don't get me wrong. I teach history because I am passionate about the subject matter. But on the day of the national test, I want my students to think strategically. The point is not to be perfect. The point is to pick up points. You can do this via Process of Elimination, or POE.

You are going to look to the questions first. Scan the questions, and you'll learn what to look for in the reading.

Each multiple choice question will have what is called a stimulus and then about 3–5 multiple choice questions. Approach each stimulus with speed in mind. It is not important that you read over every word in each passage. This is a waste of your time. Instead, look to the author and date. Often, you can guess at what the reading is about solely because you know the author and date and its context. For example, if you see George Washington in 1793 giving his Farewell Address, you probably know that this reading is about the Neutrality Proclamation. In a way, you are already done with the reading. By identifying the author, date and context, you can now scan the passage.

This is what you do next. Scan the passage. Do not read every word. Try to figure out the gist of the reading, then take quick notes on the side about the main points illustrated. Do not write extremely neatly or in full sentences. Remember, you are not being graded on this part. Abbreviate a few words that will remind you about the ideas and themes of the reading. This will help to narrow down the information of the text.

Now, go back to the questions. As you read each question, underline the key terms. This will remind you what you are looking for. If you don't do this, you risk picking answers that are true to history but not directly related to the question.

Next, predict the answer in the margins. Don't write out a full sentence. Put down one or two words. Abbreviate them. This will help to focus your attention and force you to look for a particular answer.

The next move is to eliminate answers that don't fit with your predictions. Scan through the answers and get rid of the distracting ones that don't fit. Hopefully, you can narrow down the answers to two. Then, choose the best of the two that fit with this question.

The point of the multiple choice section is to approach it like a game. If you see it as a game of POE, there are two advantages. First, you will be more energized throughout the process because you will approach it as a competitive game. Second, you will be more careful to get rid of answers that don't fit with the question.

3. What about the Short Answer questions?

So, I can imagine that the Short Answer section might appear overwhelming at first. You have to address 4 different questions in 50 minutes. And, you are required to both read and analyze a stimulus. Then you have to address three different sections to each question. This gives you less than 12 minutes per section. This is a lot to do in a very short period of time.

But, good news is here! This is an easy place to pick up a lot of points. Here is how you are going to do it.

First, remember that this is not an essay section. You are not expected to write full-length arguments. Rather, you are directly answering the questions in a very concise manner. I would suggest that you write 1–2 sentences for each part of the question (A, B, C).

Second, when you read the passage they give, treat it like the multiple choice section. You are going to look at the questions first to determine what you have to focus upon. Then, look at the source. You will be able to get an idea of what is being argued if you recognize the author or title of the document. Scan the passage and get the overall idea of the passage.

Side note: sometimes you will get a cartoon, graph, or table. In that case, quickly jot down the details. Don't analyze them yet. You will get overwhelmed if you do. When you jot down a few details, ask yourself what the relationship between the details is. Then, ask yourself how this relates to the questions. Note that you are working your way up from basic description to analysis to significance.

Now, go to the questions and read them carefully to find out what they are asking for. Answer the question directly. Don't get flowery or add an English class flavor. Stick to the question. When the graders look at your answer, they will ask two questions. First, are you right? And second, did you answer the question? If you are direct, concise and simple, you can easily pick up some points.

There is no way to predict the questions. However, there is a basic pattern to expect. There are only so many questions that they can ask. So expect to see questions about a basic summary of the passage, provide an example that supports the passage, provide an example that contradicts the passage, or provide a connection or synthesis to another event like the one in the passage. Don't think that this pattern will necessarily be the case. But you can expect something like this and then react to any differences.

One more major point that is very important. They will provide you a box to write in for each answer. Do not go outside the box! This is very important. They will not grade anything outside of the box. Also, make sure to label each answer according to A, B, or C. They won't take points off if you don't do this. But it is a good way to make the grader's job easier.

If you stick to these guidelines, it will be much easier to finish the section. Remember that the section may appear to be overwhelming due to the amount of work and the small time frame. But keeping each answer simple, concise, and specific to the question will make your writing fast and will be what the graders are looking for you to do.

4. How do I do the DBQ?

The DBQ may appear to be very difficult. You have to read 7 primary source documents. Then you need to organize the material using the different techniques of document analysis. And, finally, you must write a persuasive essay using the documents as your evidence with a synthesis statement. And, you have to do this all in 55 minutes. Sounds very difficult. Good news! It is very manageable.

The first thing is to identify the type of question being asked. Remember, there are only so many types of essay questions that can be asked in a history exam. Basically, you can be asked to write a "change over time" essay (which includes change and continuity, cause and effect, periodization) or a comparison and contrast essay. It is good to identify this because that will allow you to set up your thesis as either a change over time or comparison and contrast essay.

Second, you want to read over the documents, like in the other sections. Just like the Multiple Choice and Short Answer, you are not reading the documents for every detail. You are reading them to get the overall gist of the document. This way you don't have to spend a long time in your preparation period for getting through the documents. Try to take down about 5 words or less for each document on the overall idea.

Third, you want to choose the type of analysis you are going to do for each document. I would suggest, as you are looking through each document and scanning ideas, you should scan the author or title as well. Based upon your knowledge of history, you can start to decide if you want to do a point of view, audience, or purpose statement for each document. I would label each document to remember what you want to do with them.

Fourth, make a quick bank on your paper of all the events you know in the time period. Don't worry about whether the events connect to specific documents yet. Just make a list of whatever you know. And trust me, once you put down one or two terms, you will remember a lot more about the period.

Fifth, make a quick outline of what you want to do. You should make a quick 2 to 3 word summary of your thesis. You should quickly make a few body paragraphs in a skeleton format and put the documents you want to use in each paragraph. Only put the numbers.

Now, start to write the essay. As you do so, think of doing the following:
1. Start your essay with an introduction that includes two parts. The first part is a brief 2–3 sentences about the context of the question. This is the background information and it provides the grader with a clear way to give you the contextualization point. Then provide a 2–3 sentence thesis statement. Make sure it is concise, clear, and answers all parts of the question.
2. After the introduction, you are going to write a 2–3 sentence 2nd paragraph. You need to state what someone might say that disagrees with your argument. Then state why your argument is still more correct. The reason for doing this is the 2nd point of the thesis statement. You have to show how someone would disagree with you and how you would answer the point.

3. As you use the documents, make sure to state the number of the document. This will make it easier on your reader to see which document you are analyzing. Also, specifically identify the type of skill that you are using for the document. For example, you could state the following, "The purpose of Document 1 was to establish..." The reason for doing this is to signal to the reader that you are using one of the analysis techniques.
4. Frame your documents. I would suggest trying to view your documents like a picture. Provide an outside detail before and after the document. This will frame your document with outside details and make it easy for your grader to give you that point.
5. Finish the essay with a concluding paragraph that is a synthesis statement. Think of another period in US history that is similar to your argument. Make sure the underlying principle is similar. Explain the similarity and its significance.

5. How should I approach the Long Essay? And, is that different from the approach to the DBQ?

Most students will say that they like the DBQ in contrast to the Long Essay. That is because, with the DBQ, you get documents to instigate thought. With the Long Essay, all you get is a prompt. Then you have to build an essay relying only upon your memory from the class. This can cause a lot of anxiety for students. But the good news is that you can feel confident about your ability to attack the Long Essay based upon your prior knowledge from the class. Here is how you instigate your thought on this.

Remember that the brain is like a computer. The point is how to bring up both your short term and your long term memory of issues. If you are overly anxious or concerned, you will have a hard time remembering information. But if you can calm down your brain, you will be able to recall information. The more information you bring to the surface, the more you will make connections with new information.

First, read the question. Then, identify two things. You want to identify the time period for the question and the thinking skill that you are being asked to tackle.

With the time period, you will need some issues to consider. Make a list. Don't hold back. Remember you can always pare back later after the notes. Once you make a list of a few issues that you remember, you will trigger your brain to remember other issues as well. For example, lets say the question is asking about the period right before the Civil War. You might be nervous and only remember the issue of slavery. But as you list slavery, you will probably remember that this was about a regional fight between North and South. Then, you will remember that Northern and Southern people expanded west under Manifest Destiny, and this led to compromises over the issue of slavery. And these compromises led to problems like the gag rule or the fight over fugitive slavery. We can continue to do this because we are making connections in our brain between issues.

Now you must identify the thinking skill that is being asked. There are about 4 that are possible. These include cause and effect, periodization, argumentation, and comparison and contrast. So, if you get a cause and effect or a periodization essay, you will talk about major turning points. If you get a comparison and contrast, you need to use the template for major comparisons and contrasts. And if the essay is a straight forward argumentative essay, you can apply the same types of rules that you would for any argument. These include a direct and concise thesis, well-organized body paragraphs, at least 5 major pieces of evidence and a synthesis statement at the end in the final paragraph.

One last comment to help take away anxiety. I want to see you shoot for the best possible score. On the rubric, this means a 6 for the Long Essay. However, keep in mind what most students score on the Long Essay. The median score is a 2. So, if you can score a 4 on the essay that puts you in the top group in the nation. This means that you do not have to be perfect. You just need to take the skills that you have learned all year and apply them. Make sure your essay is clear, well organized, answers the question and thinking skill, and hits all the major points on the rubric. You will do great by following those practical pieces of advice.

6. What should I do the night before the test?

Great question. I know a lot of students and parents want you to stay up all night cramming information and worrying. I always joke with my students the day before the test. I tell them I have a serious assignment for them. Then, I mention whatever is the hot new television series of the year and tell them tonight is the night to get caught up. I know. You must think I am crazy. But here is why.

Like I said earlier, the brain is like a computer. If you overload it with information, it will shut down on you. You probably have heard of that problem, "brain freeze". This happens when the brain is given too much data and cannot process it. This is what will happen if you try to cram the night before. Yes, it is good to study the night before. But you want to keep it to a minimum. Maybe one or two hours at the most. And you want to relax afterwards so that you can rest and keep your brain fresh. Get a lot of sleep. Tomorrow will be tough for about 4 hours. You will need your energy.

On the morning of the test, make sure to get to school a little earlier than usual. You want to show up relaxed. You don't want to worry about traffic or anything else that might make you late on that morning. If you are late or even right on time, you may be anxious. And the proctor could be angry at you for showing up late. You don't want the emotions of dealing with an angry proctor to get in the way of focusing on the test.

Make sure you bring all the things you will need for the test. I suggest bringing three pens, three pencils, and a big eraser. The pencils will be for the scantron portion. The big eraser is just in case you change your mind. Don't rely on the eraser on the pencil. It is too small. You will want several pens for the essay section just in case one breaks or goes out. Yes, you can ask the proctor for pens and pencils. But again, you don't want to worry about whether a proctor could be annoyed about this.

In the end, remember the following. You have worked hard all year. You have learned about content and skills. You have all the information and skills you need. Now just feel confident that you can express this on the test. As long as you have prepared during the year and you have a strategy for each section of the test, you can conquer it. Most importantly, remember that you don't have to be perfect. You just need to take your knowledge and apply it. I know you will do great!

SECTION III:
Time Period Summaries

Summary of Period 1: 1491–1585

What You Should Know Before Reading This Chapter

- Large numbers of natives occupied almost all parts of North America when European colonists arrived.
- European colonists came to America for a large variety of reasons.
- Natives fluctuated between cooperating with the Europeans, or fighting them.

What you Will Learn By Reading This Chapter

- Native populations in the territory that would become the United States developed over time into distinct societies and groups, many of which were quite complex.
- Predominant in the northeast was the Iroquois confederation of five tribes who formerly were enemies, but united together for purposes of trade.
- In the southwest were hunters and gatherers who ranged over large areas of the arid, desert land in order to sustain life. Farther south were the great nations of the Aztecs and Incas.
- The European nations which sought to gain power over North America each created different relationships with the natives they found there.
- The French sought to establish a trading empire up the Mississippi River, and allied with many native Indian groups to assist them in doing so.
- The Spanish sought to establish Catholicism among the natives, while at the same time exploiting their labor in silver mining.
- In contrast, the late-coming English consisted of transplanted family groups who came to the continent to stay.
- The English colonists viewed the natives as an annoyance, while natives were naturally alarmed at how the English newcomers were taking land. This lead to conflict between the two groups.

Many students may feel that the beginning of the United States is more connected to the colonization by the English and the political upheaval that led to the Declaration of Independence and the Constitution. However, a good understanding of the different nations, kingdoms, and tribes of the Native Americans is essential in gaining a fuller view of US History. This historical period shows how multiple complex civilizations developed across the globe, came into contact, and formed relationships on the North American continent.

Native American Nations

One of the mistakes found in previous interpretations of United States history is to combine all Native American people under one label, such as "Indian". A better way to approach this time period is by referring to groups of Native Americans who lived in tribes, confederations, kingdoms and empires.

We tend to stereotype Native Americans as hunters and gatherers who lived peacefully in simple communities. This assumption likely originated with Christopher Columbus, who met a group of Native American, known as the Arawaks, living in such a manner on the Caribbean island we call San Salvador today. This provided them with isolation from competing tribes, resources to support their population, and a climate that was favorable to their community throughout the year.

However, if we go to the Northeast, we find a different type of society. A group of Native American tribes allied into a confederation called the Iroquois. This confederation included Mohawk, Oneida, Tuscarora, Onondaga, Cayuga, and Seneca nations. The Confederation had been formed because the groups had warred with each other over resources. The creation of this alliance was done in the context of competition over resources and a complex agreement amongst political nations.

In the Southwest, Native American tribes were nomadic groups and kingdoms. There, groups like the Pueblo moved from place to place due to the lack of resources in the desert. However, they did establish an enormous kingdom, hewn entirely out of rock. This massive city was carved by hand out of the rock faces and included thousands of dwelling places for families. These communities thrived for thousands of years, until resources became scarce.

Then, to the South in Mesoamerica, we have the legendary empires of the Aztecs. The Aztecs filled in the power vacuum left by the original kingdoms of the Toltecs and Olmecs. Keep in mind that the Aztecs formed their capital city of Tenochtitlan in the middle of today's Mexican desert. There they formed a central capital city that at one point housed 140,000 people. Contrast that to the European cities that had about 50–100,000 people in their cities during the same period. And remember that the Aztecs had to create their own form of irrigation

Key Concept 1.1

As native populations migrated and settled across the vast expanse of North America over time, they developed distinct and increasingly complex societies by adapting to and transforming their diverse environments.

systems called Chimpanas. These were storage facilities for rain water that would be kept above ground to keep their civilization supported.

The Aztecs were a strong and centralized empire. There was a clear hierarchy, with an emperor who was advised by religious leaders. And the local areas of the city were governed by familial groups called calpulli. The Aztecs conquered hundreds of tribes in the area. Then, they forced these groups into a tributary relationship. The local tribe could keep its own culture, political system, and religious beliefs if they paid a tax to the Aztecs each year in produce.

Aztecs are also known for their practice of human sacrifice. Some estimates suggest that Aztecs sacrificed 200,000 people over their time. They did this out of the religious belief that they were returning human blood back to the gods to satisfy them and to continue the cycle of seasons.

A similar type of system can be found further South in Mesoamerica in the Incas. The Incan Empire arose out of the different religious and tribal movements in the Peruvian mountains. The Incans formed an empire with its capital at Twantinsuyu. The empire was based upon farming, tributary systems, and the use of resources in a difficult mountainous terrain. The Incans also created an incentive for their emperors to expand the empire. New emperors could not inherit the land of their ancestors. They had to go out and conquer new land for their namesake. This grew the Incan empire in the very difficult terrain of the Andean mountains.

Native American or Native American(s)

It is important to understand, the notion of a single Indian, Native American or American Indian group makes little sense. It is like reducing all of Europe into one people. We know that Europe at this time was broken into mercantile nations competing against each other. The same was true of the Native Americans. They included farming groups, hunters and gatherers, nomads, confederations and kingdoms/empires. The European nations are often considered to have been larger, in scale, but this is misleading. Their urban centers, for instance, were much smaller than those of the American Natives.

Both the Old and New Worlds saw the birth of new nations that competed with each other over resources, trade, and alliances in order to increase the extraction of resources and labor for the development of the empire.

Frontier Meetings/Wars

This leads to the next issue: the encounter between the Native groups and the Europeans. The Europeans eventually emerged as the dominant force, but at the time, it was not clear who would end up being the victors of this cultural clash. This was due to a variety of factors, such as superior technology, the spread of disease, religious beliefs, and shifting alliances.

Hernan Cortez, a Spanish conquistador, conquered the Aztec empire. Records of his first interactions with the empire suggest the Aztec Emperor, Montezuma, welcomed Cortez, believing he was the Priest Quetzelcoatl who had come back to save the Aztecs from the spread of diseases at the time. This allowed Cortez to infiltrate the Aztecs and conquer them from within. Cortez also allied himself with local tribes that had been forced to give tribute to the Aztecs. So, shifting alliances, combined with disease and religious beliefs, led to the Aztecs' fall.

In North America, the relationship was far more complex. The English formed family-based settlements on the East coast for long term settlement and extraction of resources, such as timber, tobacco, cotton, and rice. Differing English groups settled on the coast. In Massachusetts, New York, and Connecticut, a variety of religious groups came to the area to set up economic colonies, as well as faith-based communities that sought to avoid English oppression. In the Chesapeake, or what became Virginia, noblemen settled to find riches and land. They found tobacco, and began to sell it back to England. Thus, their colonies became established for economic gains, with a strong hierarchy of land owners who employed cheap indentured servant labor.

This led to conflict with the Native American tribes and confederations. In the Northeast, the Pequot Indians came into conflict with the Puritans over land rights. Eventually, the Puritans allied with the Pequot Indian rivals, the Mohegans and Narragansets, to wipe out the Pequots. Puritan leaders argued the Pequots had to be destroyed because they threatened the religious mission of the community.

In the Chesapeake, the colonists came into conflict with the Wampanoags on the issue of land. The king of the Wampanoags, Massasoit, had formed an uneasy relationship with the pilgrims. However, his son Metacom was upset by the increasing encroachment on the land of the natives. So he organized an alliance with the Narragansett Indians and attacked the English colonies along the coast in the Chesapeake. He eventually lost the war, though he did create in European settlers a fear that the Natives could eventually wipe out the colonies.

In response, the Governor of the Virginia colony, William Berkeley, formed a treaty with the local tribes to limit the colonies' land possessions. This angered the indentured servants who saw their land rewards being threatened by the agreement. A landowner, named Nathaniel Bacon, saw an opportunity to raise a revolution of the indentured servants against the landed elites. Bacon died during the revolution from dysentery. But the fear of a possible future uprising that could succeed led to the search for a "less troublesome" form of labor for tobacco production. This opened the door for African slavery, while also creating an incentive to seek out land possessions for the production of tobacco.

In the Ohio River Valley, Native tribes used a variety of political and economic tools to keep the European powers in check. The Native groups had already formed an alliance of trade before the Europeans arrived called the Iroquois

Key Concept 1.2

Contact among Europeans, Native Americans, and Africans resulted in the Columbian Exchange and significant social, cultural, and political changes on both sides of the Atlantic Ocean.

confederation. This group of Natives included the Cayuga, Oneida, Mohawk, Onondaga, and Seneca. They had at one time warred with each other. But, for economic trade reasons, they joined together to create a peaceful relationship. When the Europeans arrived, the Iroquois tried to use their group of countries to negotiate trade and land disputes. Eventually, the Iroquois would create an alliance with the British while the Ottawas, Mississaugas, Wyandots, and Potawatomis, and Delawares joined with the French. These groups hoped to both check the Europeans and their Native enemies. However, once the French lost the French-Indian War and were kicked off the North American continent, British and American expansion into the Western territories began to uproot the Natives and stop their ability to check back the advance of European powers.

Trade Networks

The primary activity that took place between the different kingdoms and nations was trade. However, this took on different formats depending on the contexts and the motives of each of the European and Native groups.

The original trading relationship created after the European "discovery" of the Western hemisphere is called the Columbian exchange. The Europeans received important agricultural products from the Native tribes, including maize, potatoes, tobacco, coffee, and tomatoes. The Western Hemisphere saw European introduction of horses, cattle, sheep, pigs, goats and chickens. The most important, and most destructive, exchange was disease. Europeans brought diseases from the Eastern Hemisphere including influenza, measles, mumps, malaria, and smallpox. Most of these diseases were not especially destructive in Europe and Africa because people had contact with each other for centuries and had developed immunities. But the people of the Americas had not had contact with Europeans, Africans, or Asian groups. So these diseases caused mass deaths.

The Spanish conquered the region stretching from modern day California into Mesoamerica and South America. Spain was the leader of the Catholic world in Europe, and it saw itself as under siege by the Protestant movement in Northern Europe and the Islamic world in Northern Africa. Spain began to view the Western Hemisphere as a place to provide new converts to Catholicism and new resources for fighting their enemies at home. They established New Spain to solve these problems.

New Spain took the Aztec and Incan survivors and placed them in regions for resource extraction. The primary resource in Mexico was silver. Aztec descendants were placed on haciendas, or large plantations, where they either farmed produce or mined for silver. The resources were then sent back to Spain. This system was called the encomienda system, and it was disastrous to the Natives. The labor was essentially slavery, and disease often swept through the community of Natives due to their lack of immunological defenses, weaknesses from working, and close proximity to one another. Eventually, this was criticized from a very unlikely A Catholic monk and slaveholder named Bartolomeo de Las Casas, who had originally supported the encomienda system as a way to convert Aztecs to Catholicism. However, when he observed the treatment of the Natives, he called for an end to the encomienda system.

Still, the Spanish treated the Natives like children who needed to be converted. In California, a system of missions was created. Here, Natives were often separated from their families and converted. The system of discipline at the missions tended to be harsh. The eventual result was the Pope rebellion in the Southwest that kicked the Spanish out of the region. The Spanish were able to return and create a local hierarchy to keep order. But the region was always tense in the relationships between the Spanish and local native population.

In the Louisiana territory, the French established New France as a way to create trade along the Mississippi River and the Great Lakes. The French explorer Jacques Cartier discovered what he would call the St. Lawrence River. Then, Samuel Champlain discovered its connection to the Great Lakes and Ohio region. Jacques Marquette and Louis Joliet then discovered that the Mississippi flowed out into the Gulf of Mexico. These discoveries created a massive trade route from the Atlantic, down the Mississippi and out into the Gulf of Mexico and Caribbean. France saw a huge potential for trading massive amounts of resources and gain the upper hand in its mercantile competition with Britain.

So, New France became a trading colony, and France controlled a huge tract of land. But most of it was settled very sparsely by military outposts and traders. The main trade was fur with the Native American tribes. France tended to treat the Native American tribes with tolerance. The reason was to keep peaceful relations for trading purposes. The advantage of this was a constant flow of resources out to France. The disadvantage was a lack of permanent or secure long term settlements.

And this is where New England gained an upper hand. The original colonies in New England seemed to be in a vulnerable position. They were on the Eastern Coast of the North American continent. They ranged over a very small portion of land. And, they were surrounded by their French enemies in the Great Lakes region and the Spanish in Florida and the Caribbean.

However, the method of settlement for New England actually gave the colonists the upper hand. The Pilgrims at Jamestown and the Puritans in Massachusetts came to the North American continent to establish religious colonies in order to reform England from afar. This meant that their colonies were based upon family settlements. And, whether they were established directly through the King or through joint stock investments, the colonists had a vested interest in seeing that their colony succeed spiritually, financially, and for security. This ensured that the English colonies had long-term stability and success. In fact, the notion of "grandparents" were first established in the Puritan colonies because the people there started to live longer due to the higher standards of living.

New England did grow and become stronger due to their stable foundations. However, their relationships with the local Native tribes was very tense. This was largely due to the religious beliefs that the tribes needed to be converted or moved out of the way. This led to a series of wars. The most significant and destructive were the Pequot wars and King Philip's War. The Pequot Wars ended with the mass destruction of the Pequot Indians at Mystic River. At the time, the Puritans justified this as necessary in order to stop the threats against God's colony. However, the long term effect was a questioning of the Puritan identity. Some internal dissenters, like Roger Williams, had to leave the colony because he criticized the Puritan leadership for its ill treatment of the Natives. King Philip's War ended with the English defeating the Natives. But the war created mass hysteria as Metacom and the Wampanoag tribe was able to devastate many settlements. The English colonists always had a very tense relationship with the local Native tribes.

Slavery

This leads up to one of the most important and most controversial aspects of early colonial history: the beginnings of African slavery. Two questions arise over this issue. First, why did African slavery begin in the colonies? And second, was slavery about race or economics when it got started?

Slavery has been a part of almost all major civilizations since the beginning of human history. For most of human history, slaves were either people captured in war or people who sold themselves to pay off debts. It is also true that Africans held slaves in the major kingdoms on the Northwestern coastline. And the largest number of slaves were transported through the Trans-Saharan trade route from Western Africa into the Middle Eastern Muslims empires.

However, European slavery did take a different turn from historical roots of slavery by making African slaves property. Slaves in most societies could eventually become a part of the kingdom, tribe, or nation. Slaves or their descendants would eventually join the group gaining all of the same rights and privileges as everyone else. But not in European slavery. In European slavery, African slaves were changed into property for ideological and for property reasons.

Europe developed a mercantilist economy. The mercantilist economy relied upon merchants and military to go out and conquer lands for colonies. The colonies were used to extract resources and send them back to the mother country for mass production. Then the mass produced items were sold to other countries with the hope of using that money to invest in the military for further conquering of colonies. Every nation competed to grow its military. The eventual goal was either to beat other countries or at the least check a growing country.

African slavery ended up being a key piece of this equation. The primary resources in the Western Hemisphere were sugar, cotton, and tobacco. These were rich products for mass production and sale, and they were labor intensive. Having a cheap form of labor like slavery reduced costs for extracting these resources. And since Africans were resistant to most European diseases, there was an even greater incentive to use their labor versus that of the Native American.

However, there was a huge ideological consequence to this. In order to maintain continued use of African slave labor, Europeans had to change Africans into objects so that they and their descendants could remain available for exploitation. This made it even easier to dehumanize African laborers into inferior objects that could be treated in such an inhumane way.

Africans were transported from Western Africa to the Caribbean by Spanish, French, and English ships. This voyage is called the Middle Passage. For many Africanists, it is viewed as a Diaspora or even a Holocaust because so many Africans lost their lives due to poor treatment, disease, or even being thrown overboard during the journey. The Europeans would then return their wealth from selling slaves to Europe. Then they would sail back to Western Africa. This three-legged trip is called the Triangle Trade.

It is true that African Kingdoms participated in this trade. African Kings saw this as an opportunity to get guns from Europeans. They used these guns to conquer local tribes in Western and Central Africa. For most African Kings, slavery was simply a part of human nature and human civilizations. In fact, when the British outlawed international slavery, African kings asked why they would do this.

Summary of Period 2: 1585–1750

What You Should Know Before Reading This Chapter

- Pilgrims settled in New England in the early 1600s, seeking religious freedom.
- British colonies were established from New Hampshire and Massachusetts on the north to Georgia on the south.
- Tobacco was the main southern crop in the colonial era.

What you Will Learn By Reading This Chapter

- Jamestown was the first permanent English colony in the New World, in 1607. The goal of this group was to gain gold and silver, and to quickly return profits to England. The goal was never met, and the colony only survived because of the discovery of tobacco, which quickly became popular in Europe.
- Puritan groups seeking religious freedom were the primary British colonists in the north. The pilgrims settled in Plymouth, while other distinct puritan groups went to Massachusetts Bay. Some dissenters who were cast out from the puritans settled in Rhode Island.
- Settlers seeking profits from the land settled in the southern colonies, particularly Virginia and North Carolina.
- Settling in the middle colonies were religious dissenter groups such as Catholics and Quakers who settled Maryland, Pennsylvania, Delaware and New Jersey.
- British control over the colonies was lax for over 100 years, which encouraged home rule and a strong sense of independence among the American colonists.
- Labor in the north was supplied primarily by indentured servants, and in the south by a growing number of transplanted African slaves. Rice and tobacco were the main southern crops.

Colonization: Different Goals Led to Different Outcomes

In the colonial era, the driving force behind the conquest of the Americas by European nations was the concept of mercantilism. Under the mercantilist mode of thinking, trade generated wealth (preferably in the form of gold and silver), and a favorable balance of trade would generate more wealth. Colonies were but one link in the chain that European nations would use to achieve such wealth.

However, mercantilism can be achieved in many different ways. Each of the four main European colonizers of the Americas approached their colonizing effort with different goals in mind, and therefore with different results. The Spanish goal was mainly to extract wealth from the land and from the natives. Initially, this goal was accomplished with ruthless disregard for the natives, and in time it was discovered that domination of the Indians was most easily accomplished if they were converted to Catholicism, and thus assimilated with their captors.

The French and Dutch focused more on trade with the natives as a source of wealth, such as trapping for furs, particularly since they were less successful at attracting settlers from the mother country willing to come to the Americas. Favorable trade relationships were often accomplished by forming alliances with the natives, and sometimes even by way of intermarriage between the colonizers and the natives.

And what of the English? While initially slow to become involved in the business of founding colonies to pursue mercantilist goals, two significant events set the stage for marked change in the 1600s. First was Henry VIII's break in the 1530s with the Roman Catholic Church, which led to the Protestant Reformation. The growth in divergent and sometimes unpopular religious ideas under the new banner of Protestantism in England would ultimately lead to the creation of a number of colonies in the new world based on a quest for religious freedom. The second event was the 1588 British defeat of the Spanish Armada. With Spain no longer capable of controlling the seas, British efforts to acquire wealth in North America in the 1600s could now more easily take place.

Accordingly, two divergent themes for British migration to the Americas in the 1600s evolved: religious freedom, and the mercantilist goal of improved trade between the colonies and the mother country based on producing and shipping products that each could specialize in which the other wanted. As will be seen, each of the colonies which eventually became the original 13 states got its start with one of these two goals primary in mind.

The First English Colonies

One of the first attempts at colonization occurred in 1585 under the direction of Sir Walter Raleigh. However, this first colony, the Roanoke Colony on the coast of what would become North Carolina, mysteriously disappeared during

Key Concept 2.1

Europeans developed a variety of colonization and migration patterns, influenced by different imperial goals, cultures, and the varied North American environments where they settled, and they competed with each other and American Indians for resources.

one of the long breaks between supply ships arriving from England. One of the disappeared colonists was Virginia Dare, said to be the first British baby born in the New World.

It was not until the founding of Jamestown in 1607 that a permanent British colony was established in the New World—more than 100 years after the Spanish had done the same farther south in the Americas. Jamestown was initially founded on greed. King James I granted a charter to the Virginia Company, which was a "joint stock" company in London, comprised of investors looking for a quick return on their money. Roughly 100 settlers formed the first settlement in Jamestown, with the goal of quickly finding gold and riches to pay the stockholders in England for their investment.

The goal was not achieved, and the settlement struggled. Large numbers of the original settlers died, as did many of the new settlers that came to join them. The vigorous leadership of Captain John Smith saved the colony from starvation in its beginning, as he insisted that only those who worked should eat. Smith was also firm in demanding that the Virginia Company send skilled and willing workers to the colony from England, rather than the gold-seeking, lazy settlers who had come first. Smith was later captured by natives and rescued by the princess Pocahontas.

But Smith was soon forced to return to England, and the settlement struggled once again. The colony probably would have died within a few years if not for the discovery and cultivation (initially by John Rolfe, who later married Pocahontas) of a noxious weed known as tobacco. In a few short years this weed became extremely popular in England and throughout Europe, providing a lucrative source of trade for the colonies. It was not long before much of Virginia and North Carolina were devoted to tobacco farming, which at first made use of indentured servants and later African slaves for labor. Slaves were preferred because they did not need to be replaced or given land after a certain number of years of work, as indentured servants did. Tobacco farming was labor intensive, requiring many workers. Unfortunately, tobacco cultivation was destructive to the soil, leaving the land badly depleted after only a few years of tobacco crops.

A few hundred miles to the north, British settlement in the Americas began with a very different basis. Puritans in England objected to certain rites of the Church of England which resembled those of Catholicism. Persecuted and driven temporarily to Holland, one of these groups of puritans (who have since come to be called the "pilgrims") eventually migrated to America and settled in Plymouth, Massachusetts in 1620. They wrote a document called the "Mayflower Compact," which established a "civil body politic" to govern the people. All adult males were participants in this "body politic," thereby highlighting a new democratic spirit of government in America.

But the pilgrims of Plymouth were not alone in Massachusetts for long. Because of persecution by Charles I of the many divergent puritan groups in England, the first pilgrims were soon joined by another, distinct puritan group who settled the Massachusetts Bay area under a royal charter in 1629. While both Plymouth and the Bay colony were founded by puritans, they held distinct religious beliefs and tended to be suspicious of each other.

One of the chief leaders of the Massachusetts Bay settlement was John Winthrop. Trained as a lawyer in England, Winthrop was governor of the Bay colony for a number of years. Winthrop sometimes disagreed with the stricter version of religious puritanism espoused by newcomers to the colony. He favored diplomacy toward the Indians, but was not afraid to support war with them when he felt it was justified, and to sell captured Indians into slavery.

As new groups of puritans arrived in the Massachusetts Bay colony, conflicts increased over differing religious beliefs. Dissenter Roger Williams was sufficiently disliked that he was exiled from the northern Bay colony in 1636. His unpopularity was due in part to his criticism of the puritans in Massachusetts for their poor treatment of the Indians. He cited as examples the brutal wars the Massachusetts Bay puritans fought against the Pequot, Narragansett and Wampanoag tribes. He also criticized the Massachusetts puritans for not adequately separating church and state. After being driven out, he ultimately settled in Rhode Island, which eventually received its own royal charter.

Other religious dissenters in Massachusetts also made Rhode Island their gathering place. For example, Anne Hutchinson was another puritan dissenter who was driven out of Massachusetts by the puritan majority due to her divergent religious beliefs. She also settled in Rhode Island, although she later moved to New York where she was killed by Indians.

One of the most notable aspects of life in New England was the extent to which Democratic principles of government flourished in the many self-governing small towns, and in the colonial legislatures. For example, the Massachusetts Assembly (known as the "General Court" even though it was a legislative body) included a lower house whose members were popularly elected. Rhode Island and Connecticut developed similar institutions.

In terms of economics, the settlements in New England focused primarily on small scale farming and commerce. There were only a small number of slaves, but quite a few indentured servants working for a set number of years in farming, sometimes in order to learn a trade. Indentured servants were able to pay for passage to the Americas by agreeing to work for a certain number of years. These servants were sometimes treated poorly, and some died, but usually such servants were treated with relative fairness, even if work expectations were much more intense than today. At the conclusion of their contract, the former servants were free to establish their own business, or to become independent farmers. A significant number of the population in the colonies started out as indentured servants.

Civil unrest in England in the 1640s resulted in fewer supply ships coming to the colonies. Rather than merely complaining to the home government, the colonists started to open trade with other colonies in the Americas, including some non-British ones. Because Britain was absorbed in civil war between 1642–1651, this colonial practice of free trade was largely ignored by the mother country, even though it was not strictly in keeping with British laws applicable to the colonies. No wonder, then, that much later, the colonists chafed at efforts by the British to restrict free trade that the colonists had carried on for decades without hindrance.

To the severe disapproval of the Massachusetts settlers, a royal charter was granted by the British crown in 1634 for a Catholic settlement in what became known as Maryland. Under the "head right" system, settlers in Maryland were given 50 acres for every new settler, indentured servant, or slave that they brought to the colony. Tobacco became the main colonial crop in Maryland, as it was in Virginia to the south.

Meanwhile, the region of what was to become Pennsylvania, New York, Delaware and New Jersey was originally mostly settled by the Dutch, who vied for control of the area with settlers from Sweden. However, this territory was eventually taken over by the British. Among the British settlers in this area was William Penn, who obtained a large land charter from King Charles II, partly as repayment for a debt Penn was owed. Pennsylvania was named after Penn, who encouraged friendly relations with the Indians. Penn was a Quaker, so it is no surprise that Pennsylvania was initially settled by members of this religious group, who preferred to avoid conflict with the natives. One of Penn's main goals was to provide a haven of religious freedom where those with different views could worship in peace.

Indeed, there was far more religious diversity among the first settlers of all of the "middle" colonies of Maryland, Pennsylvania, Delaware, New York and New Jersey. While religious tensions occasionally flared up, these regions were havens for Catholics, Quakers and other nontraditional settlers whose religious beliefs differed from their neighbors. In addition to growing tobacco in Maryland, these middle colonies focused on growing and exporting cereal crops and grains to Europe.

The primary cities in the middle colonies were Philadelphia and New York. The original settlement of New York City occurred in 1625, with the Dutch settlement of "New Amsterdam" which was strategically located in a natural harbor. It was partly because of the fact that this location was coveted by the British that they wrested control of the area from the Dutch in the 1660s. The city was renamed "New York" after the brother of King Charles, James the

Duke of York. However, conflict between the Dutch and the British had not ended. Battles continued for a number of years as the Dutch attempted to regain control of their original settlements, and especially their favored city of New Amsterdam. They even succeeded at regaining the city for a brief time, but in the end succumbed to the British.

Settlement in the far south took longer to eventuate. Georgia was established as a penal colony in the early 1700s. By this time, slaves from Africa were being imported to the Americas in ever growing numbers. While most slaves were transported initially from Africa to the West Indies, many were taken from there up to Georgia and other southern states to provide labor for the growing plantation system that was developing, which at that time primarily grew rice or tobacco. Since the climate of these southern regions was milder than New England and the growing season was longer, increased agricultural production was possible. This in turn required a greater labor force, which came to be filled more and more by African slaves.

Indian Relations

Native Americans did not fare well in any of the British colonial settlements. While colonists at Jamestown and Plymouth initially attempted peace with the Indians, the situation in both locations quickly deteriorated into one of frequent conflict. Indians were resentful of the settlers over the loss of their land, and jealous of the deadly European weapons. Far more lethal than European weaponry however were the foreign diseases brought to the new world by the settlers, for which the native population had little immunity. Massive numbers of Native Americans died from the spread of these new illnesses.

For those who survived, European goods forever changed their culture, as the natives came to rely on commodities from Europe. This was particularly true of gunpowder and guns, which the Indians coveted. European migrants and Indians often fought (usually over land), but also would form alliances with each other to oppose their respective enemies. For the British, the enemy was primarily the French, and also to a lesser extent the Spanish and Dutch. For the Indians, the enemies were other tribes with which they had warred for decades.

In the colonial era, the various political, social, cultural and economic exchanges between Britain and the colonies achieved mixed results. Sometimes these exchanges led to stronger bonds between the two locations, while they led to greater resistance by the colonies. Much of this had to do with Britain's inconsistent policy toward its colonies. Prior to the end of the French and Indian War in 1763, British control of the various American colonies was erratic and tended to be rather lax. While there were some very strict laws in place, such as those requiring the colonists to only conduct trade through England, enforcement of these laws was largely ignored.

Key Concept 2.2

The British colonies participated in political, social, cultural, and economic exchanges with Great Britain that encouraged both stronger bonds with Britain and resistance to Britain's control.

Notwithstanding occasional tension between Britain and the colonies, the commercial, religious, philosophical and political views of the colonists more closely resembled those of England than any other place. The colonies were closely tied to Britain and to each other, whether they wanted to be or not. But the American colonists were an independent group to begin with, who had demonstrated their independence by leaving England to brave the rigors of the New World. After arriving in the colonies they grew accustomed to home rule in their various local governments. From the Virginia House of Burgesses to the democratic town meetings of Massachusetts, local government tended to have more of the respect of the people and more of a local impact than rule from overseas. Again, this was because Britain was very erratic in enforcing its imperial and mercantilist policies. With this background, it is not surprising that stronger attempts by the British to control the colonies resulted in resistance in the 1760s and 1770s.

The economy of the colonists was focused primarily on satisfying the desires of Europe. Tobacco was a prime export, and the abundant timber available in the north also made shipbuilding quite lucrative. But the Americans did not produce all of their own goods. European luxury goods were highly prized in the colonies. Indeed, this was in keeping with the mercantilistic goal of mutual interdependence, by which the colonists would have a continuous desire for European goods, and those in England and Europe would require raw materials from the Americas. Satisfying the labor supply in America were slaves from Africa in the south and indentured servants in the north.

Despite the firm belief by most colonists that they possessed all the rights of Englishmen, in the mid-1700s there was growing tension between the colonies and the British. Most of the conflict had to do with frontier defense, trade, and home rule. Levels of conflict greatly increased upon the end of the French and Indian War in 1763, when England's lax policy toward the colonies came to an end.

Colonial Slavery

The "triangle slave trade" described the passage of Europeans traveling to Africa to take slaves, then taking them to the Caribbean, then traveling back to Europe to bank the profits before starting the process over again. Most slaves were taken first to the Caribbean, with some being brought up to the Atlantic coast of North America thereafter, primarily to Georgia, the Carolinas, Virginia and Maryland. Approximately 18% of transported slaves died during the journey across the Atlantic Ocean from Africa due to the horrible conditions of their transportation.

The British practice of obtaining large numbers of slaves from Africa to supply labor in the Americas had a lasting and profound impact on the New World. All of the American colonies initially participated in the slave trade, some more than others depending on their labor needs and economies. The demand for slaves in each colony was simply a reflection of the differing economic, demographic, and geographic aspects of the various colonies. Some in the colonies greatly disliked the practice of slavery, but had no way to resist it since it was a practice implanted by the British.

Unlike British immigrants however, slaves were unwilling participants in the economy. Forced against their will to migrate as they were captured and transported like cattle, slaves came up with a number of overt and covert ways to preserve their identity. Much of this had to do with their music and their food. This fostered a strict racial system of separation between the whites and the blacks—leaving scars that remain to this day. Unlike the Spanish, the British and colonials also maintained strict segregation from the natives as well.

Summary of Period 3: 1751–1799

What You Should Know Before Reading This Chapter

- The Revolutionary War was fought because colonists resisted the passing of tax laws in England where they were not represented.
- "Loyalists" were colonists in America who supported the British.
- The federal constitution created three distinct branches of government and numerous checks and balances between the branches.

What you Will Learn By Reading This Chapter

- The French and Indian War between 1754–1763 removed the French from North America, but resulted in increased efforts by the home government in England to tax and control the colonies.
- The Americans had been accustomed to being left alone, and resented these controlling efforts. Many taxes were passed, and many repealed. A tax on tea led to the Boston Massacre and then to the Boston Tea Party.
- The breach between the colonists and England grew into open conflict with the firing of shots in Lexington and Concord in April, 1775.
- The first Continental Congress met in 1774 and continued to meet as the new nation came into being.
- The Declaration of Independence and Articles of Confederation were formed in 1776, and the nation was born. Each state quickly drafted its own constitution, and many also drafted a state bill of rights.
- After the colonists' victory and the end of war in 1783, political and economic unrest in America created ongoing turmoil. Many came to see that a stronger central government was needed.
- A Constitutional Convention met in Philadelphia in 1787, and the new Constitution they created came into effect in 1789 after it was ratified by a sufficient number of states. Finally the nation had a strong federal government.

- The first presidents--George Washington and John Adams--established many precedents for the nation, and political parties were born as the Federalists opposed the Democratic-Republicans.

The French and Indian War

In the 1600s and 1700s, the rivalry between England and France led to war on several occasions. For the American colonists, the most significant of these conflicts was the French and Indian War, much of which was fought in North America. Both Britain and France had grown increasingly suspicious of the intentions of the other regarding control of the interior of North America between the Appalachian Mountains and the Mississippi River. Each country claimed this territory, and each ultimately determined that the only way to prove this claim was through demonstrations of force which resulted in armed conflict beginning in 1754. This war later expanded to Europe and became known there as the "Seven Years War."

Because the French were badly outnumbered to begin with, they resorted to treaties with a number of Indian tribes to supply much of their fighting force. Their main ally was the Huron tribe. While the British had some tribal allies (particularly the Iroquois), they relied more on British soldiers, with some additional support from the American colonists. George Washington gained his reputation as a tenacious and capable military leader in this war, although he was never granted the official British officer status he desired.

The war was mostly fought in the interior regions of what was known as Ohio Country, which was sparsely populated by anyone other than Indians. The British initially suffered a number of defeats, beginning with the defeat of George Washington in 1754 at Fort Necessity, and General Braddock's 1755 defeat and death at Fort Duquesne. Gradually however the tide of war turned in favor of the British. But the real victory of Britain over France occurred in Europe in the early 1760s. The war ended most of the French presence in North America.

Britain attempted to tighten control of the American colonies after the war ended in 1763. Particularly distasteful to the colonists was the British attempt to have the Americans pay (through taxes) for increased British debt caused by the war. Another disliked British policy was the prohibition of emigration to the fertile lands to the west in the Ohio Country, which the Royal Proclamation of 1763 said was reserved for the Indians. The war had just won large quantities of interior lands from the French, so the colonists were resentful of the British effort to prevent them from taking over these open lands, regardless of the Indians. Indeed, because these laws were so deeply resented and were hard for the British to enforce, they were often ignored entirely. Daniel Boone and other explorers and settlers opened roads to the west which resulted in increased numbers of Anglos in the interior.

Key Concept 3.1

British attempts to assert tighter control over its North American colonies and the colonial resolve to pursue self-government led to a colonial independence movement and the Revolutionary War.

British control over the American colonies

The British effort to impose and collect taxes on the colonists without direct colonial representation, as well as British efforts to assert greater authority and control in the colonies, served to unite many of the colonists against England. Many colonists felt they were being constrained in their economic activities and their political rights.

A number of British laws were enacted after 1763, largely to obtain tax money to pay war debts. The first of these was the Currency Act of 1764, which made it illegal to use colonial paper money to pay British creditors. Only gold or silver or British currency could be used. The Sugar Act in the same year increased British efforts to collect a tax on molasses which had previously existed for some time, but had been largely ignored. These were followed in 1765 with the Stamp Act, which imposed a direct tax on all paper products, even playing cards. No documents were legal without the stamps. The Quartering Act followed, which allowed for British soldiers to be lodged in public inns and empty houses and barns, but did not authorize direct quartering of troops in colonial homes without the homeowner's consent. The "Sons of Liberty" was formed in 1765 as an organized movement to oppose these efforts by the British to more tightly control the colonies.

Colonial leaders relied on a variety of arguments to justify their state of conflict with England. Among these were the sense that they should possess all the rights of Englishmen (such as representation when taxes were laid); new and liberal ideas about the rights of individuals to be free from governmental tyranny; local traditions of self-rule which had served the colonies well for over 100 years; and new ideas of the Enlightenment, particularly about the laws of nature and how England was abusing those natural laws and rights. British authorities gave little credence to these arguments.

While most of the troubling acts were repealed in 1765 because of American complaints, the British did not back off for long. Parliament passed the Townshend Act in 1767 which created a new wave of American resistance. The Townshend Act placed tax duties on a variety of popular items, such as paper, glass and tea. Bad feelings ensued, leading in 1770 to the Boston massacre in which an angry mob confronted a number of British soldiers who ended up firing into the crowd. While the soldiers were ultimately acquitted (due in part to the able defense they received in court from John Adams), bad feelings remained. In 1770 Parliament repealed all of the Townshend duties except the one on tea.

As relations with Britain deteriorated, the resistance movement gradually shifted from a call for change and restoration of the rights of Englishmen, to a call for total independence. Several charismatic and gifted leaders came forward to champion this cause, including Benjamin Franklin in Pennsylvania, Samuel

Adams in Massachusetts, and Patrick Henry and Thomas Jefferson in Virginia. Added to this were a number of popular movements calling for change, which included the political activism of laborers, artisans, and women.

Samuel Adams began the establishment of "Committees of Correspondence" or revolutionaries in Massachusetts. The committees became so popular they soon spread throughout the colonies. These committees provided an important organizational structure of resistance. While tension between the colonists and the British was abated in most places, the ongoing tax on tea was a continuing sore point. Ships loaded with tea were successfully turned back from Charleston, New York and Philadelphia during this time. But Governor Hutchinson in Boston refused to yield to such colonial rebel demands, insisting that the tea be unloaded and the tax paid. The Boston Tea Party in late 1773 was the result, in which the tea was dumped overboard by rebels dressed as Indians.

The Boston Tea Party enraged British officials, who saw American resistance as a direct defiance of British authority. The "Intolerable Acts" were thereafter enacted by Parliament, which closed the port of Boston and forced quartering of troops in private homes regardless of the objection of homeowners. In 1774, the first Continental Congress met in Philadelphia, at which the delegates agreed to boycott British goods, starting in December. Tensions mounted until shots were fired between colonials and British troops in Lexington and Concord, Massachusetts, in April of 1775. The Battle of Bunker Hill followed in June, outside Boston. British troops only succeeded at taking Bunker and Breed Hills from the rebels upon the third attempt, and suffered significant loss of life in spite of their apparent victory.

Once the war commenced, local economies in the colonies were greatly impacted. There were shortages of many basic commodities, while at the same time British troops were consuming goods in greater numbers. Notwithstanding these shortages and difficulties, those who favored the patriot cause mobilized in large numbers to provide financial and material support to the movement.

Not all of the colonists were in favor of the cause of independence, however. There were large numbers of "loyalists" who felt the patriots were overly zealous and were needlessly fighting their British benefactors. The loyalists hoped for a reconciliation with the mother country, and tended to agree with the British that the zealot patriots needed to be taught a lesson. In response, patriot legislative assemblies in all the colonies passed laws divesting loyalists of their property and usually also calling for them to be thrown in jail or executed. These legislative acts were known as "bills of attainder."

When the war commenced, most observers in Europe and many in the colonies predicted that Great Britain would easily win. After all, it was one of the strongest nations on earth, and controlled the seas with the strongest navy. There were many loyalists in America which undermined the patriot cause, and even among patriots there was enough divergence of opinion that it was not clear they would stick together and see the conflict through to victory. Financially, the colonists lacked the ability to sustain a prolonged conflict, and militarily they lacked a sufficiently trained and large enough army to win.

However, the patriot cause ultimately succeeded to the surprise of many due to a number of factors. Chief among these was the financial and military help of France, which jumped at the chance to cause trouble to its old enemy England. Another helpful factor was the inspiring and selfless leadership of George Washington, and his political genius at keeping the army together while prodding the Continental Congress to supply the army with sufficient provisions and soldier pay. Indeed, Washington's skill as a military leader—while commendable—was second to his tremendous talent at political leadership. In addition, the patriots' ideological commitment and resilience was greater and more enduring than many had suspected, and this zeal carried them through hard times to ultimate victory.

The Revolution was inspired by new beliefs about Politics, Religion, and Society

Enlightenment ideas and philosophy served as great inspiration to the American patriots. Many in America came to believe it was not right to uphold hereditary privileges as in England. Indeed, since the Americas were only recently settled, there simply was no deeply entrenched aristocracy in the colonies as there was in England. The Americans held a greater sense of equality, at least between white males. Many of these beliefs were preached from the pulpit, and indeed religion played a significant role in the independence movement. Many in America viewed themselves as a people blessed by God with inherent liberty, which they felt no government had the right to remove.

Almost all of the patriot leaders of the independence movement were well read in the enlightenment writings of John Locke, Samuel von Pufendorf, Hugo Grotius, and Montesquieu. These writings emphasized the natural rights of all mankind, including the right to rebel against a tyrannical government that failed to honor individual liberties. The superiority of a republican government of the people, based on the natural rights of man, was eloquently expressed in Thomas Paine's "Common Sense." This pamphlet was widely read throughout the colonies, and incited many to join the revolutionary cause. Following close on its heels, and also extolling principles of natural law and the rights of man was the Declaration of Independence, penned largely by Thomas Jefferson. The ideas in these and similar documents in the revolutionary era have continued to resonate through American history to this day. They have shaped Americans' understanding of the ideals on which their country is based.

During and after the American Revolution, an increased awareness of inequalities in society motivated a call by some for the abolition of slavery and greater political democracy in the new state and national governments. Likewise, the significant contribution of women in the Revolution fostered a greater sense of an expanded role for women in the new country. Women taught republican ideals and values in the family, which both fostered a new generation of freedom-loving Americans, and also gave women a new and greater importance in American political culture.

The American Revolution and the ideals on which it was based as described in the Declaration of Independence were noted throughout the world. Not long after, similar revolutionary movements copying many of these principles took place. While most of these independence efforts were not as successful as the American one, all of them concentrated on the rights of man as the mainstay of the movement with the United States as their primary example. Significant among these new revolutions was the one in France between 1789–1799, and many in Latin America.

The new political landscape—state and federal constitutions and Bills of Rights

During the War for Independence, most of the former colonies became self-governing and independent states, and thus they set about to craft their own constitutions. As such, the states assumed governmental powers previously held by Parliament in England. Along with their new constitutions, most states also adopted a declaration of rights which described the individual liberties of the people. These state constitutions instilled power primarily in the hands of the legislative branch, which usually consisted of two houses. The executive branch (the governor) and judicial branch were weaker. Property ownership was also usually required by the constitution in order to vote.

The newly independent states were unwilling to yield too much control to a central government. While the states were forced to cooperate with each other in order to fight the British, they saw themselves as independent within their geographic boundary, and were very reluctant to yield any of their sovereign power to a centralized government. Therefore, during the Revolution only a very loose and weak federal government structure was put in place, in the form of the Articles of Confederation. These Articles unified the newly independent states, but specified that the federal government would have only limited powers. In particular, the federal government under the Articles could request money from the states, but could not levy taxes. Major decisions could only be made with the unanimous consent of all the states, which was nearly impossible to attain.

After the Revolution was officially ended by the Treaty of Paris of 1783, the states continued to go their separate ways. While the Articles of Confederation were still in operation during this period, they did not provide adequate federal control over international trade and foreign relations, taxation and finances, or

Key Concept 3.2

The American Revolution's democratic and republican ideals inspired new experiments with different forms of government.

over interstate commerce. Lack of a coherent national policy led to economic hardship for many, and internal unrest. Shays' Rebellion in Massachusetts in 1786–1787 was a prime example of such unrest. Daniel Shays was leader of a group of farmers who were unhappy with state supported seizures of land and bankruptcies. They marched on the armory at Springfield, but were repulsed by the state militia.

Because of the growing problems and unrest, many of the leaders of the day felt there was a need for a stronger central government. A convention of delegates from five states met in Annapolis, Maryland, in September, 1786 in an effort to resolve some of these problems. Little was accomplished other than reaching an agreement to call for a better-attended convention to be held the following May in Philadelphia.

In late May 1787, delegates from 12 states gathered in Philadelphia for the convention which was originally intended to "revise" the Articles of Confederation. Rhode Island sent no delegates, since it was distrustful of the entire affair. Over the ensuing hot Philadelphia summer, the delegates met in secret. In the first few days, and over the objections of many, the delegates agreed that it would be more fruitful to completely abandon the Articles of Confederation and create an entirely new federal government. The "Virginia Plan" of government was taken as the primary guide in the ensuing debates. Although a few alternate plans were presented during the convention, none were debated for long, and the convention continued coming back to the original Virginia Plan. The original draft of the Virginia Plan was written by James Madison, and was presented to the convention by Virginia Governor Edmund Randolph.

Through hard fought negotiation, collaboration, and compromise, the convention hammered out a proposed constitution which contained many checks and balances specifically designed to prevent any one person or governmental body among its three distinct branches from assuming too much power. The federal government was to have powers limited solely to what was stated in the constitution itself, unlike the state governments which were assumed to possess all power in their domain unless limited by their state constitution. Hence, the presumption of power in the federal government was opposite to that of the states. In spite of this however, the new federal government would have dynamic powers, including control over interstate commerce, foreign policy and foreign trade, and taxation/financial matters. One of the most significant aspects of the new arrangement was the concept of "federalism," in which the state governments and the federal government both would contain extensive powers, and both would co-exist with each other.

One of the most hotly debated compromises during the Constitutional Convention had to do with slavery. While the institution of slavery was repulsive to many northern delegates, the majority of southern states made it clear they would not confederate unless slavery was allowed to continue. A compromise was ultimately reached regarding how to count the population of slave states, since the number of Congressional representatives a state could have was based on its population. Under this compromise, slaves would count as 3/5s of a person. The importation of slaves was allowed through the end of 1808, and not thereafter. For many in the north, these concessions demonstrated that the federal government had authority to both regulate slavery and the slave trade. Many in the south disagreed with this, however, viewing slavery as solely within the decision-making power of the states.

The proposed constitution was sent to the states in the fall of 1787 for a ratification vote. It was hotly debated by many, who felt it was a dangerous document. In these debates over ratifying the Constitution, so-called "Anti-Federalists" expressed concern that the federal government had been given too much power, in spite of the significant limitations of power expressed within it. Rising in defense of the constitution were the "Federalists," who argued that it should be adopted. Three Federalist leaders—James Madison, Alexander Hamilton and John Jay—wrote and published a series of articles about the constitution designed to answer the numerous Anti-Federalists arguments which were circulating in the newspapers. These writings in favor of the constitution were then compiled in book form known as "The Federalist Papers." To this day, these essays are the best descriptive source about the meaning of the constitution.

One of the chief complaints against the constitution was that it did not contain a bill of rights which would describe individual rights and restrict the powers of the federal government. Ultimately, Federalist supporters of the constitution promised that a bill of rights would be quickly added to the Constitution if it were ratified. This promise was one of the key reasons some of the states voted for ratification. Indeed, either as part of their ratification vote or by way of a separate document produced thereafter, many states proposed a list of rights they felt should be included. In the first session of Congress in 1789, James Madison made good on the promise of introducing a bill of rights, by proposing twelve new rights-based amendments. Ten of these were ultimately adopted at that time, and became the federal Bill of Rights. One of the two proposed amendments which failed at that time—regarding compensation for Congressmen—was ratified over 200 years later, and became a part of the constitution in 1992 as the 27th Amendment.

The emerging political culture of the United States

The presidential administration of George Washington created a number of precedents intended to put the principles of the Constitution into practice and to clarify how the office of the president was to function. Perhaps most significant of these was formation of the President's "cabinet," consisting in that day of six persons—the Secretaries of State, War, Treasury and Foreign Affairs, as well as the Attorney General and the Postmaster General. By contrast, the president's cabinet today has fifteen members. Washington also established patterns of behavior that most of his successors have followed, such as limiting his direct contact with all of Congress when it is in session, and serving only two terms as President.

While the governmental structure of the country was clarified by the new constitution, many significant problems still needed to be resolved. These included issues such as the relationship between the national government and the states, economic policy, foreign policy, and the balance between liberty and order. Political leaders in the 1790s often took opposing views on how to resolve these matters, which led to the creation of political parties. The two major parties of that era were the Federalists, with Alexander Hamilton as its primary leader, and the Democratic-Republican Party, with Thomas Jefferson and James Madison as its primary leaders.

One of the greatest challenges faced by the fledgling country had to do with foreign trade and foreign affairs. Trade relations with Europe were vital to the economic well-being of the country, but powerful nations such as Britain and France frequently made trade difficult by seizing American merchant ships and American sailors. The new war between France and Britain in the 1790s that resulted from the French Revolution also presented other challenges to the United States. For example, during Washington's administration there was pressure by many in the Democratic-Republican Party to go to the aid of France, the country that had helped the United States so much during its own recent revolution. Later, during John Adams presidency, there was pressure to go to war with France, due to its actions against American shipping on the high seas. Fortunately for the new nation, which lacked the resources at that time to handle another conflict, Presidents Washington and Adams resisted the pressure and pursued a course of neutrality. Indeed, George Washington in his Farewell Address warned of the danger of becoming entangled in foreign alliances.

Some of the measures pursued by the different political parties sparked debates so intense that many feared they would lead to conflict within the country itself. One such matter was the "Alien and Sedition Acts" of 1798, during the presidential administration of John Adams. These acts, passed by a majority of federalists in Congress, gave President Adams the power to deport persons identified as dangerous aliens. The acts also stated that persons who made certain negative public statements against the United States government could be prosecuted for having committed a criminal act. Because of this, the Alien and Sedition Acts appeared to defy the first amendment guarantee of free speech. In response, Jefferson and Madison drafted the "Virginia and Kentucky Resolutions," in which they urged the other states to join Virginia and Kentucky in a declaration that the states considered the Alien and Sedition Acts to be unconstitutional. None of the other states joined in this declaration, however.

The "Virginia and Kentucky Resolutions" would later play a leading role in debates over slavery in the south. This is particularly true of the Kentucky Resolution written by Thomas Jefferson, which many interpreted as describing a right of the states to "nullify" federal laws they did not like. Even in this early period of the 1790s, regional differences had an impact on national politics. Some in the South argued for expansion of slavery into adjacent western lands. This contrasted with a growing antislavery sentiment in the North, where such expansion was generally opposed.

Meanwhile a distinct national identity began to take shape in the new country of the United States, which found expression in works of art and architecture. This included a design for a new capital city on the Potomac River which divided Maryland and Virginia, named "Washington D.C." In art, the famous portrait of George Washington, which is now used on the one-dollar bill, was painted by Gilbert Stuart.

Dealings with Indians and European Nations

The relationship between the federal government and American Indian tribes continued to be problematic in the decades after American independence. Native Americans continued to assert their claims regarding wrongful seizure of their lands, in violation of several treaties. Some native tribes formed alliances with foreign powers—particularly the British—who they saw as a more favorable ally. These alliances with American Indians further increased the tensions between the US and Britain. One of the primary goals of the Indian groups was to limit migration onto their lands. However, they were not able to prevent the tide of American settlers migrating to the west.

Due to increasing westward migration during the 1780s, the Northwest Ordinance was passed in 1787 which pertained to the Ohio region. This act was created by the Confederation Congress which existed prior to adoption of the new federal constitution. The Act specified the procedure for admitting new states, promoted public education and the protection of private property, and established a ban on slavery in the territory.

It did not take long for new states to seek entrance into the union. By the turn of the century the original group of 13 states had been joined by Vermont, Kentucky and Tennessee, with Ohio following soon after in 1803. As increasing numbers of migrants moved westward, frontier cultures continued to grow and expand. Sometimes this growth fueled social, political, and ethnic tensions between people of different backgrounds who were thrown together on the wild frontier.

Key Concept 3.3

Migration within North America and competition over resources, boundaries, and trade intensified conflicts among peoples and nations.

Meanwhile, the continued presence of European powers in North America challenged the United States to find ways to safeguard its borders, maintain neutral trading rights, and promote its economic interests. The new nation struggled to forge diplomatic solutions dealing with the continued British and Spanish presence in North America, as US settlers migrated farther and farther west, and sought free navigation of the Mississippi River. Meanwhile, the Spanish expanded their mission settlements into California which provided opportunities for social mobility among Spanish soldiers, and led to new cultural blending between these soldiers and Native Americans. In a few short years, this uniquely blended culture would be inherited by the United States.

Summary of Period 4: 1800–1848

What You Should Know Before Reading This Chapter

- The "Louisiana Purchase" greatly in increased the territory of the United States.
- The War of 1812 was essentially a second war of independence between the United States and England.
- A "tariff" is a tax on imported or exported goods.
- The United States fought a war with Mexico in the 1840s.

What you Will Learn By Reading This Chapter

- In 1803 with Thomas Jefferson's Louisiana Purchase, the geographic size of the United States doubled. The new area extended from present day Louisiana and Arkansas all the way up to Montana.
- Later territorial additions occurred when the United States obtained Florida from Spain, and when independent Texas was annexed in 1845.
- The War of 1812 solidified the United States as a nation able to stand on its own, and greatly reduced the trade pressures that had been put on the country by the British for the last decade.
- The industrial revolution began with the invention of the weaver's loom and cotton gin, and the establishment of textile mills. The growth of factories created a new group of workers, many of whom were Irish immigrants.
- Supplying the mills were large cotton plantations in the south, which relied on slave labor.
- Farm products and other goods were shipped on canals and by a growing network of rapid train transportation which was spreading over the nation.
- Tension between the southern and northern regions increased in the decades before the civil war. One reason had to do with tariffs. High tariffs

were disliked in the south since it hurt their cotton sales. However, high tariffs were desired in the north as a protection of new industries.

- South Carolina "nullified" the tariff of 1832 and threatened to secede from the union. Crisis was averted when a new tariff was passed, but the seeds of secession were sown.

- "Manifest Destiny" became the philosophy of the nation as settlers expanded ever westward.

- War with Mexico starting in 1846 resulted in acquisition of significant portions of the Southwest including present day California, Arizona and Utah. This greatly increased the size of the nation.

Developing Relations and Conflict with other Nations

War of 1812

In the early 1800s, the United States faced an international crisis as it attempted to maintain its neutrality. England and France fought in Europe, but the United States continued to trade with both nations. The British issued the Orders in Council, a series of measures that prohibited American ships from entering French ports in Europe, India, and the West Indies. Likewise, the French issued orders that prohibited the Americans from trading with the British. The British were also stopping American ships and pressing American seamen into service on their own vessels. In 1807, Congress passed the Embargo Act that prohibited American ships from sailing into foreign ports. Eventually, the Embargo Act was repealed.

In 1812, Britain and America entered into a war that eventually eliminated the threats to American neutrality. The Native Americans aligned themselves with the British and there were several skirmishes in the Ohio River Valley to prevent American settlers from continuing to encroach upon their lands. Native American leader Tecumseh, and his brother, called the Prophet, were defeated by American troops around this time. William Henry Harrison, the victor at the Battle of Tippecanoe (in Indiana) later became president.

The only clear-cut victory of the war was at New Orleans in 1815, which finally ended the war. News of the Treaty of Ghent (Belgium) had not been received, and Andrew Jackson became the hero of the Battle of New Orleans when he defeated the British. The victory, and his continued popularity, led him to the presidency in 1828.

The war proved to be a turning point in American history. America's position of neutrality was recognized. Also, America's business sector realized it did not need to be as dependent on imports as it had been. As a result, America entered the manufacturing arena.

Monroe Doctrine

In 1823, President James Monroe delivered a speech in which he informed the powers of the world that the American continent was no longer open to European colonization and that any effort to extend their political influence into the New World would be considered dangerous to the peace and safety of the United States. The policy became known as the Monroe Doctrine.

Westward Movement

Manifest Destiny

In 1803, the United States purchased the Louisiana Territory from France. Adventurers Meriwether Lewis and William Clark led an expedition into the area to determine what had been purchased. Their two-year journey led the way for future explorers to learn more about the territory and resulted in the doctrine that became known as Manifest Destiny, which was the belief that it was America's destiny to explore and settle the west. The goal of westward expansion was to complete settlement of America from the Atlantic Ocean to the Pacific Ocean.

In 1818, the Red River Basin area was added to finalize the Canadian-US border after the War of 1812. The area opened the way to further settlement in the North Dakota and Minnesota areas.

The following year, east and west Florida were acquired from the Spanish through the Adams-Onís Treaty.

The Second Great Awakening also encouraged westward expansion. The Native Americans were thought to need Christianizing, and missionaries began moving west to spread Christianity.

The Red River Cession was an acquisition of land that came about as part of a treaty with Great Britain in 1818. The acquisition included parts of what later became North and South Dakota, and Minnesota. In 1819, Florida, both east and west, was ceded to the US by Spain along with parts of Alabama, Mississippi, and Louisiana. The Republic of Texas was annexed in 1845, and in 1848, the US paid Spain for the areas that would later become California, Utah, Nevada, and part of western Colorado.

The Oregon Territory was shared by the United States and Britain for several years. In 1846, the United States claimed the Territory and signed a treaty with Britain, dividing the land at the 49th parallel. The treaty opened Oregon for further settlement.

Economics played a role in Manifest Destiny because the land of the trappers and traders became open to settlement. Wagon trains and groups wanting to establish communities in fertile river valleys took up the call to venture west. The 1848 California Gold Rush beckoned those who wanted to become wealthy and start a new life in the west. Planters who needed more and better land moved west, taking slaves with them. The westward movement required the federal government to address the issue of slave-holding states versus free states.

Treatment of Native Americans

As settlers moved into the Northwest Territory in the late 1700s and beyond, they settled in areas that had been inhabited by Native Americans. Usually, the Native Americans moved to other lands, but at times they fought back against the Americans. Battles in the Ohio River Valley, as well as up north in Illinois and Indiana, pitted Americans against the native people. Tecumseh, a Shawnee, and his brother, The Prophet, wanted to remove the Americans from their land but were unsuccessful. The Native Americans in the Ohio River Valley and Northwest Territory had many skirmishes and battles with the Americans. William Henry Harrison, who was elected president in 1840, had defeated the Indians at the Battle of Tippecanoe in present-day Indiana and became famous as a result. The battle had provided him his campaign slogan of "Tippecanoe and Tyler, too." John Tyler was his vice-president.

Andrew Jackson had a definite plan during his tenure as president to remove the Native Americans to the area west of the Mississippi River and eliminate their land claims east of the Mississippi. In 1830, Congress passed the Indiana Removal Act.

Most of the Native Americans living in northern parts of the US had moved, or been removed. Jackson did not consider the Native American tribes to be foreign nations, but rather to be groups subject to United States government control. Congress passed legislation during Jackson's administration that would permit the Native Americans to retain their tribal governments if they relocated to west of the Mississippi River to lands set aside by the federal government. Some of the Creek Indians refused, and the government forcibly removed them from where they were living in Alabama.

The Cherokees who lived in Georgia also resisted removal. Gold had been discovered on their lands, and since they considered themselves an independent nation, they filed suit in federal court, asking the Supreme Court to issue an injunction to prevent the state of Georgia from taking their land. Chief Justice Marshall's court ruled that the Supreme Court did not have jurisdiction over the Cherokees because they were not a "foreign nation" as intended by the framers of the Constitution. Although the Supreme Court found in favor of the Cherokees, eventually some of them entered into a treaty with the government. Those who did not were forcibly removed by the military. In a three-year period, thousands of Cherokees walked to Oklahoma. This removal is known as the Trail of Tears.

Settlement of Texas and Conflict with Mexico

After the Louisiana Purchase, Americans began moving into Spanish territory. A few hundred American families in what is now Texas were allowed to live there but had agreed to become loyal subjects of Spain.

In the 1821, Americans began settling in Texas, once Mexico had gained independence, from Spain and decided to be more tolerant toward the American settlers and traders. Mexico banned slavery in the area, but the southern planters who moved west were taking their slaves with them. Technically, slavery was illegal in Texas, but the Mexican government looked the other way. With the influx of so many Americans and the liberal policies of the Mexican government, concerns grew over the possible growth and development of an American state within Mexico. Settlement restrictions, cancellation of land grants, the outlaw of slavery, and increased military activity brought this conflict to a head. In 1836, a group of Mexicans defeated a small gang of Texans at the Alamo Mission in San Antonio. All of the Texan defenders were killed, and the Alamo defeat became a battle cry for Texan independence. Texas became an independent republic in the same year and Sam Houston became the Republic's first president. Later, Texas became a state in 1845.

Growth of Political Parties

Federalist Party

The Federalist Party controlled the House of Representatives at the time of the 1800 election. Aaron Burr was the Federalist candidate and Thomas Jefferson was a Democratic-Republican. Neither of the men received a majority of votes from the Electoral College and the decision was left to the House of Representatives. After more than 30 ballots, Jefferson was chosen as president. The power had transferred from the Federalists to the Democratic-Republicans without bloodshed or violence. For that reason, Jefferson referred to the transfer as a "bloodless revolution."

Republicans (Democratic-Republicans)

Thomas Jefferson was the first Democratic-Republican president. He refused to accept the "midnight appointments" that Federalist John Adams had made before leaving office.

One of the appointments involved William Marbury's appointment as justice of the peace. James Madison, Secretary of State for Jefferson, refused to certify the appointment and Marbury sued for the certification. The lawsuit was heard by the US Supreme Court. The court's decision in Marbury v. Madison established the doctrine of judicial review. The court agreed that Marbury had the right to the appointment, but that the law under which he was appointed was

> **Key Concept 4.1**
>
> The United States began to develop a modern democracy and celebrated a new national culture, while Americans sought to define the nation's democratic ideals and change their society and institutions to match them.

unconstitutional. The law in question was the Judiciary Act of 1789 and it gave the court the power to hear different types of cases, including the type Marbury was litigating. However, the Constitution only gave the court the right to hear certain types of disputes involving original jurisdiction. Those cases involved disputes between states and cases involving ambassadors, foreign ministers, and consuls. Chief Justice Marshall wrote the decision for the court, denying the commission because the type of case was not one permitted by the Constitution. This helped to establish the court's right to judicial review, which let them decide whether acts of Congress were unconstitutional.

President Jefferson also purchased the Louisiana Territory from France in 1803. The purchase doubled the size of the United States, giving the country the port of New Orleans, and providing room for westward expansion. The Corps of Discovery was headed up by Meriwether Lewis and William Clark. During their expedition, the pair wrote many maps and journals about the existence of types of animals, birds, and vegetation in the area, as well as notes about the Native Americans living there. This was instrumental in assessing the wealth and economic opportunities that might exist in the area.

James Madison followed Jefferson as president. Madison had favored a strong central government and had written some of the Federalist Papers. He broke away from the Federalist Party, and he and Jefferson became Republicans. During Madison's presidency, the Republicans (Democratic-Republicans) had to deal with the British and French encroachment that threatened America's efforts at neutrality. The government also passed a series of acts collectively referred to as the American System. The National Bank was re-chartered, the National Road was expanded, and protective tariffs were passed. Henry Clay, Speaker of the House of Representatives, favored the acts and lobbied for them. The American System is sometimes referred to as Clay's American System.

When James Monroe became president, the Federalist Party no longer existed. Because there was unity, and only one party, the time was referred to as the Era of Good Feelings. However, the Panic of 1819 resulted in mortgage foreclosures and business failures. Chief Justice Marshall's decision in McCulloch v. Maryland strengthened the federal government's position favoring a national bank. In McCulloch, the state of Maryland had attempted to tax a state branch of the National Bank. The bank refused to pay the tax and the state sued McCulloch, a bank officer. The high court supported the bank and established the principle that federal law took priority over state law.

There was still only one party when John Quincy Adams became president. However, each region of the country had its own choice for the office. Andrew Jackson had won the most popular votes and the most electoral votes but none of the four candidates had a majority of votes. The House of Representatives had to decide the election. Henry Clay, the Speaker of the House and a southerner who did not like Jackson, supported John Quincy Adams. When Adams became president, he appointed Clay Secretary of State. Jackson called the election a "corrupt bargain" and began making plans for the 1828 election.

Democrats

Andrew Jackson and his group of supporters became known as Democrats. He was thought of as a self-made man who favored western interests. He also favored the common man and, when it came to appointments, his friends and supporters. This system of appointments became known as the "spoils system" and his type of governing became known as "Jacksonian Democracy."

Martin Van Buren became president in 1836. He had been Jackson's vice-president and came into office just before the Panic of 1837, an economic downturn that lasted throughout his tenure as president.

After four years of Whig rule, the Democrats won the presidency in 1844 when James K. Polk was elected to office. Polk favored westward expansion and the annexation of Texas. Polk believed that all of Oregon should belong to the United States. He defeated the Whig candidate Henry Clay, who opposed westward expansion and the annexation of Texas.

Whigs

In the 1830s, the Whig Party was formed to oppose Jackson's policies. War-hero William Henry Harrison was the first Whig candidate elected (1840). He died after about a month in office and his vice-president John Tyler ascended to the office of president. Tyler, also a Whig, was a former Democrat. His support of states' rights led to his being a one-term president.

Development of Regional Interests

The economic interests of each region of the United States played an important development in the growth of the country. The South's economy was agricultural, and southerners exported cotton to Britain and other European nations. The northern manufacturers built ships that carried southern cotton to ports all over the world. Urban areas were becoming centers of industry. The west provided agricultural products and farming became the dominant economic factor in the west.

In the early 1800s, businessmen needed funding for their economic activities and borrowed from banks for the funding they needed. In 1818, the Bank of the United States and its branches stopped renewing personal mortgages and began requiring state banks to immediately pay their dues in silver, gold, or national bank notes. Most of the borrowers were unable to repay the banks, resulting in the closure of many banks. People lost their properties, and foreclosures were rampant throughout the county. Cotton prices fell and the demand for American manufactured goods declined.

In 1824, Congress passed a higher tariff that favored the financial interests of New England and mid-Atlantic manufacturers. The tariff bill that passed Congress had been proposed by Henry Clay and was called the American System. Its purpose was to fund road building and other infrastructure and to create a national bank. Southerners opposed the tariff because they believe it protected northern industry interests against their agricultural economy interests.

In 1828, before John Quincy Adams left office, Congress passed a protective tariff that had such high rates that it became known as the Tariff of Abominations. The repercussions from the passage of the legislation fell upon Andrew Jackson, the new president. John C. Calhoun was Andrew Jackson's vice president and was from South Carolina. He, along with other southerners, believed that the states could nullify the law because of the oppressive rates. Earlier, southerners had declared that if any state believed a federal law was unconstitutional, the state could nullify the act. South Carolina decided that the Tariff of Abominations was an act that should be nullified. In 1832, the state imposed the doctrine of nullification after Congress passed another tariff bill that, although lower than the earlier bill, was higher than southerners wanted. In addition to nullifying the act of Congress, the State of South Carolina threatened to secede from the Union. A year later Congress passed tariff legislation that the South accepted. A constitutional crisis had been averted but sectional divisions were growing.

The southern planters were focused on farming large areas of land. Cotton, in the south, and tobacco, in the Chesapeake region, were depleting the soil. As western areas opened, southerners moved west for better soil and more land. As they moved west, the issue of slavery became an issue for the region they moved to. Texas was one of the areas southern planters moved to. When they moved, they took their slaves with them to work on the new plantations.

Expanding Suffrage and Reform Movements

Horace Mann led a major effort for public education for all children in the 1830s and 1840s. He worked with school boards, and in 1848 was appointed to fill a term in Congress after John Quincy Adams died. Mann was from Massachusetts. He argued free public schools were essential for educating citizens who would be capable of sustaining American democracy, and would increase the wealth of individuals, communities, and the nation.

Reform movements resulted from the Second Great Awakening during the early to mid-1800s. Dorthea Dix was involved in prison and asylum reform in those years.

Elizabeth Cady Stanton and Lucretia Mott were interested in abolition and in women's rights. In 1848, the women organized a women's suffrage convention in Seneca Falls, New York. They modeled their Declaration of Sentiments after the Declaration of Independence and declared that all men and women were equal.

Religions and Religious Revival

Religious Revival

The Second Great Awakening began in 1790, and continued to gain followers until it peaked in 1850. This religious movement was revivalist in nature. It focused on emotion and salvation rather than the rationalism of the Enlightenment. Charles Finney was one of the evangelists of the movement. The movement is also remembered for tent meetings or camp meetings, where they shared the goals of reform. Temperance societies were formed to stop people from drinking alcohol and to close taverns. Other groups focused on the evils of gambling and poverty.

Utopian Societies

The first half of the 1800s saw the establishment of utopian societies. Some were religious and others were organized for economic purposes. The Shakers established utopian communities in the Northeast and believed in communal living, celibacy, and equality of the sexes. Their communities peaked before the Civil War. Brook Farm, in Massachusetts, was an example of communal living that was not based on religion but on transcendentalism and philosophical thinking. The Oneida community in the state of New York was based on religion and began around 1850. Its artisans were known from many types of manufacturing and production, the most famous of which was silverware. A group of Germans founded the Amana colonies in New York in the 1840s but the colonies were later moved to Iowa.

Mormons

Joseph Smith became a leader in the Church of the Latter Day Saints in the 1830s. This group, known as the Mormons, believed in polygamy, and had a settlement in Illinois. After Smith was killed, the group left Illinois and moved to the deserts of Utah. Their members had a strong sense of community and they transformed a barren area into a lovely oasis through their use of irrigation.

Innovations

In the early 1800s, interchangeable parts were used in the textile mills in New England, revolutionizing the industry. The power loom was invented about the same time. Before the invention of the power loom women would weave thread into cloth in their homes. The power loom made it possible to produce both thread and fabric more efficiently—and more quickly.

Several improvements and inventions in the area of transportation in the early 1800s improved commerce and made regions less isolated from each other. Travel was made easier by the building of the National Road. The road covered the distance between Maryland and West Virginia in its early years. Later it was

Key Concept 4.2

Innovations in technology, agriculture, and commerce accelerated the growth of the American economy, precipitating profound changes to US society and to national and regional identities.

extended into Ohio and Illinois. Today, Interstate 70 and US Highway 40 follow the route of the first National Road.

The 1820s and 30s were known as the Canal Era. In 1825, the Erie Canal was completed and ran between Albany and Buffalo, New York. Other canals, or internal improvements, were constructed. The goal of the internal water links was to aid transportation and to speed agricultural products from farms in the Midwest to markets in the East Coast area. Thousands of miles of canals were created, but none were as successful as the Erie Canal. By 1850, the canal era had ended. The Panic of 1837 and failures of banks led to the failure of the canals. Also, rail transportation was becoming the faster way to ship products across the various regions of the country.

Trains began running between major cities in the 1830s. However, cities could not be linked because the gauges of the tracks were not always the same size.

In the 1820s and 30s, Samuel Morse and other inventors had been working on a way to send electronic messages by wire. In 1844, Morse sent the first message across telegraph lines between Washington, D.C. and Baltimore, Maryland. He later developed the system of dots and dashes that is used today to send messages. The system became known as Morse Code.

Farming inventions of the period included the mechanical plow, the thresher, and baler. The cotton gin also made it easier and faster to remove seed from the cotton plant.

Industrialization

The War of 1812 had completely cut off the source of manufactured goods for Americans, and it became necessary to build factories to produce what was needed. To encourage the US to have its own industries rather than to be dependent upon Great Britain for supplying its goods, Congress passed the Tariff of 1816, which levied high duties on manufactured goods coming into the United States. Southern leaders, such as John C. Calhoun of South Carolina, supported the tariff and assumed the South would develop its own industries. In 1818, prices for American cotton fell and the demand for American manufactured goods declined, revealing how fragile the economic prosperity of the "Era of Good Feeling" had been.

Samuel Slater, who became known as the Father of the American Industrial Revolution designed the first textile mills in the early 1800s. Factories employed women, children, and immigrants. Wages were low, hours were long, and working conditions were not always sanitary. When Irish immigrants began arriving in the 1840s because of the potato famine in Ireland, they often took the place of existing factory workers because they would work even more inexpensively than the current factory workers. In the 1820s and 30s there were several violent strikes by workers hoping to improve working conditions and long hours. In 1842, a

Key Concept 4.3

The US interest in increasing foreign trade and expanding its national borders shaped the nation's foreign policy and spurred government and private initiatives.

Massachusetts court ruled that workers had the right to form associations. The case was the precedent that provided the path for union organization.

Slavery

Anti-slavery sentiment increased in the first half of the 1800s, and numerous organizations took up the cause. The American Colonization Society was founded in 1816 and promoted sending free black people back to Africa. William Lloyd Garrison, a Quaker and newspaper editor, founded the American Anti-Slavery Society. His newspaper, The Liberator, was an important voice for the abolitionist movement.

David Walker was a free black who became an outspoken abolitionist in the early 1830s. In the 1840s, Frederick Douglass, a former slave, began publishing The North Star, a newspaper that supported the abolition movement.

The slavery issue in Texas grew into a crisis when Texas petitioned Congress for statehood. Texas wanted to allow slavery but the Northerners in Congress opposed admission to the Union because it would disrupt the balance between free and slave states and would Southerners in Congress increased influence.

The issue of slavery also posed a problem when Missouri applied for statehood. Missouri was the first state in the Louisiana Territory to seek statehood. Its admission as a slave state would upset the balance of free and slave states in the US Senate. The constitution of the Missouri Territory allowed slavery, so a non-slave state was needed to balance numbers in the US Senate. The Missouri Compromise of 1820 resolved the conflict by approving admission of Maine as a free state along with Missouri as a slave state. The Missouri Compromise also designated that there would be no slavery north of latitude 36°30'. Southerners accepted this because it was not profitable to grow cotton on land north of that latitude.

The slavery issue became more controversial when abolitionist groups formed in the North. In 1831, Nat Turner, a slave, staged a rebellion that resulted in the killing of whites and blacks. When Turner was captured he was hanged. Women formed abolitionist organizations and an anti-slavery convention was held in Philadelphia in 1838.

Summary of Period 5: 1844–1877

What You Should Know Before Reading This Chapter

- Tensions between the north and south finally erupted into a bloody civil war. This was largely due to disputes over slavery.
- Slavery was banned at the end of the war by constitutional amendment.
- After the ward, the south was subjected reconstruction efforts by the north that were usually resented.

What you Will Learn By Reading This Chapter

- Sectionalism in the United States gradually increased. Slavery became a polarizing point of dispute, inflamed by such things as Harriet Beecher Stowe's anti-slavery book "Uncle Tom's Cabin," and the Supreme Court's Dred Scott decision which seemed to support slavery.
- Upon Abraham Lincoln's election in 1860, southern states started seceding from the union before he even took office.
- At its core, the civil war was a constitutional struggle about federalism, as to which government (federal or state) was superior. The federal prevailed. From the time of the civil war until now, states have not had as much power as they did before.
- War almost occurred in 1850 when California sought to be admitted to the union, since there was a serious debate about whether it would be a slave state or a free state.
- The crisis was prevented by a political compromise in Congress in which California came in as a free state, but residents in New Mexico and Utah territories were allowed to decide on slavery when they applied for statehood.
- The Kansas-Nebraska Act of 1854 was another compromise in which residents in these territories would decide for themselves whether they were slave or free upon applying for statehood. The contention was so

heated in Kansas that fighting broke out, resulting in what came to be known as "Bloody Kansas."

- War commenced shortly after Lincoln took office when a federal government effort to re-supply Fort Sumter, South Carolina resulted in bloodshed. While many thought the war would be quick and easy, the civil war ended up being extremely bloody and costly, taking more American lives than any other war, before or since.

- The Southern war strategy was simply to hold on to their territory and outlast the north, with the expectation the north would become exhausted and sue for peace.

- The Northern strategy was to blockade the south from trade with Europe, and to seize the southern capital at Richmond as well as the Mississippi River.

- With the end of the war came three new amendments to the constitution and the era of reconstruction. Some in the north sought for reconstruction to be a vengeful way to make the south pay for the trouble it had caused.

- Freed blacks continued to be oppressed in the south to such an extent that their condition was little improved above what it had been before.

Westward Migration

Westward expansion occurred for a number of reasons, the most important being economic in nature. Cotton was important to the Southern states. The effects of the Industrial Revolution, which began in England, were now being felt in the United States. With the invention of power-driven machines, the demand for cotton fiber greatly increased the amount of yarn needed for spinning and weaving. Eli Whitney's cotton gin made the separation of the seeds from the cotton much more efficient. This, in turn, increased the demand and more farmers became involved in the raising and selling of cotton.

The innovations and developments of better methods of long-distance transportation moved the cotton in greater quantities to textile mills in England as well as to mills in New England and the Middle Atlantic states. As prices increased along with demand, Southern farmers began expanding by clearing more land to grow more cotton. Americans headed west to settle and farm fertile soils. This, in turn, increased the need for a large supply of cheap labor. The system of slavery expanded, both in numbers and in the movement to lands "west" of the South.

Many people in other fields of economic endeavor began to migrate. Trappers, miners, merchants, ranchers, and others were all seeking their fortunes. The Lewis and Clark expedition had stimulated the westward push. Fur companies hired men, known as "Mountain Men" to go westward, searching for animal pelts to supply the market and to meet the demands of the East and Europe. These men explored and discovered the many passes and trails that would eventually be used by settlers in their treks west.

The California Gold Rush drew gold-seekers to the west. Missionaries who traveled west with the fur traders encouraged increased settlement and sent word back east for more settlers. The results were tremendous. By the 1840s, population increases in the Oregon country alone were at a rate of about a thousand people a year.

The fur traders and missionaries ran up against the Native Americans in the Northwest as well as the claim of Great Britain for the Oregon country. The United States and Britain had shared the Oregon country but by the 1840s, with increases in the free and slave populations and the demand of the settlers for control and government by the United States, the conflict had to be resolved. In a treaty signed in 1846 by England and the United States, the countries reached a peaceful resolution, with Britain giving up its claims south of the 49th parallel.

The movement west also involved control of land that was being claimed by foreign powers. Russia and Britain both claimed parts of what is today known as Oregon. Because people saw it as their destiny to settle all of North America, they also decided it was their destiny to see that other powers did not rule it. Manifest Destiny became a national goal, but with it developed issues that led to sectionalism and regionalism.

In the 1844 presidential election, the Democrats pushed for annexation of Texas and Oregon, and after James Polk won the election, they started the procedure to admit Texas to the Union. The Republic of Texas was annexed to the United States in 1845 and when Texas statehood occurred, diplomatic relations between the US and Mexico were ended. President Polk wanted the US to control the entire southwest, from Texas to the Pacific Ocean. He sent a diplomatic mission with an offer to purchase New Mexico and Upper California, but the Mexican government refused to even receive the diplomat. Consequently, in 1846, each nation claimed aggression on the part of the other and war was declared. After the war with Mexico in 1848, the US government paid $15 million for what would become the states of California, Utah, and Nevada, and parts of four other states.

In 1846, the Oregon country was ceded to the United States. The acquisition extended the country's western border to the Pacific Ocean. The northern US boundary was established at the 49th parallel. The states of Idaho, Oregon, and Washington were formed from this territory.

In 1853, the Gadsden Purchase rounded out the present southwest boundary of the forty-eight contiguous states when payment was made to Mexico in the amount of $10 million for land that makes up the present-day states of New Mexico and Arizona.

Congress encouraged westward migration by passing the Homestead Act of 1862. The act gave 160 acres of land to anyone over the age of 21 who had not "taken up arms" against the United States, and was the head of a household. The act required that the applicant live on the land for five years and improve it. After the requirements were met, the applicant would receive title to the property.

Immigration

Immigrants from western Europe began coming to America in large numbers during the 1840s. The Irish potato famine in the mid-1840s brought thousands of Irish to the East Coast. In 1846 there were approximately 92,000 arrivals, but by 1854, more than two million immigrants were arriving yearly. The German revolution of 1848 resulted in about one million German immigrants coming to America in a ten-year period. The French revolution of 1848 brought French immigrants to urban areas. German Jews began emigrating in the 1850s and most became involved in business.

The rising numbers of immigrants became a concern for many Americans. The immigrants lived in their own neighborhoods, spoke their native languages, and had their own stores and customs. The rise in number between 1840 and 1850 resulted in the development of the Know-Nothing political party. The purpose of the party was to curtail the power of the immigrants and the Catholics. Nativism also became popular during the time period. Nativism favored Protestant values and opposed the foreign-born and Catholics. One aspect of Nativism was to require that only people born in the United States could hold elected office.

Political machines became more powerful as a result of the increasing numbers of immigrants. Tammany Hall was one such political machine. Tammany Hall was formed as a political discussion group, but it became involved with patronage and associated with the immigrant vote. Boss Tweed was one of Tammany's most well-known leaders. The organization had a great amount of influence in New York City, both in the city's development and in the city's corruption. Its influence was at a peak during the 1850s and 1860s, but it continued to influence the politics of New York for several more years.

Sectionalism

By 1860, the country was made up of three major regions, and the people in all three regions had a number of beliefs and institutions in common. Each, however, had its own unique characteristics. The North had a great deal of agriculture, but it was also industrial with towns and factories growing at a very fast rate. The South was largely agricultural, and it was becoming increasingly dependent on one crop, cotton. In the West, restless pioneers moved into new frontiers seeking land, wealth, and opportunity.

Key Concept 5.1

The United States became more connected with the world, pursued an expansionist foreign policy in the Western Hemisphere, and emerged as the destination for many migrants from other countries.

Slavery and tariffs were two main issues relating to sectionalism in the pre-Civil War period. Many pioneers and settlers were from the South were slave owners, who brought their slaves with them. In different parts of the country the views on tariffs, public lands, international improvements at federal expense, banking and currency, and the issue of slavery were decidedly different. Sectionalism became stronger and more apparent each year, putting the entire country on edge. Sectionalism, especially in the area of politics, remained strong over the next century after the Civil War, but never to its pre-war level.

The North wanted high tariff duties to protect their industry and manufacturing. The South wanted low tariff duties because they were agricultural and purchased goods from European countries. Regardless of which tariff was passed during the pre-Civil War time period, at least one section of the country was not happy with the rates. This period in US history was one of compromises, breakdowns of the compromises, desperate attempts to restore harmony among the three sections, short-lived intervals of the uneasy balance of interests, and ever-increasing conflict.

Reform Movements

Temperance

Closely allied to the Second Great Awakening was the temperance movement. The temperance reform movement began before the Civil War, and Maine became the first state to ban alcohol in 1851. The WCTU, Women's Christian Temperance Union, was founded in 1874 and was the largest and most influential temperance organization. Under the banner of "home protection," WCTU members advocated not just temperance, but all kinds of reform that would protect women and children from the effects of men who drank alcohol.

Education

Horace Mann worked diligently to improve the poor quality education that was available to children in the United States in the mid-1800s. Schools were often one-room facilities where students of various ages learned together. As more and more immigrants came to America, the reformers realized that the quality of education needed to be improved. Horace Mann was involved in education in Massachusetts, and through his efforts new schools were built, teachers were better trained, and the school year was extended. Free public education became available in New England and later spread to other areas of the country. Girls were also given the right to equal education in New England as the result of Horace Mann's efforts.

Women's Rights

The women's suffrage movement gain momentum after the Civil War, and in 1869, Susan B. Anthony, Ernestine Rose, and Elizabeth Cady Stanton founded the National Women's Suffrage Association

Labor

As the number of immigrants increased, immigrant labor became commonplace, and reformers and workers began demanding better working conditions, shorter hours, and better pay. They also wanted rules relating to child-labor. Unions began developing in the 1830s and 1840s. In 1842, the Massachusetts Supreme Court hear a case involving the right of association and decided that so long as the association did not advocate illegal activities, or violence, they had the right to organize. The National Labor Union was formed in 1866, and the Knights of Labor came into existence in 1869.

Slavery

Abolitionists helped the slaves escape through the use of secret passages and routes to northern states and Canada. The network of getting slaves into freedom was called the Underground Railroad, and had been established early in the 1800s but reached its peak between 1850 and 1860.

The slavery issue flared up again in 1849 when California applied for admission to the Union and was not to be done away with until the end of the Civil War. It was obvious that newly acquired territory would be divided up into territories and would later become states. In addition to the northerners who advocated the prohibition of slavery and the southerners who favored slavery, a third faction arose supporting the doctrine of popular sovereignty. This doctrine stated that people living in territories and states should be allowed to decide for themselves whether or not slavery should be permitted.

The result was the Compromise of 1850, a series of laws designed as a solution to the issue of slavery in areas requesting admission to the Union. The Compromise of 1850 addressed the issue of slavery in the southwestern part of the United States in relation to admission to statehood and the number of free/slaves states in Congress. Concessions were made to the North and included the admission of California as a free state and the abolition of slave trading in Washington, D.C. The laws also provided for the creation of the New Mexico and Utah territories. As a concession to southerners, the residents in these two new territories were to decide for themselves whether or not to permit slavery when the territories applied for statehood. As a result, sectionalism became more intense.

Key Concept 5.2

Intensified by expansion and deepening regional divisions, debates over slavery and other economic, cultural, and political issues led the nation into civil war.

In 1852, Congress passed a Fugitive Slave Act, an act that had strict rules relating to the capture of runaway slaves, decreeing that such slaves must be returned to their owners. Northerners opposed the law.

The Kansas-Nebraska Act was passed by Congress in 1854 and allowed for the territories to decide for themselves as to whether the state would be slave or free. This concept was called "popular sovereignty." Violence increased and Kansas was referred to as "Bleeding" Kansas. The issue of sectionalism became more intense and the country headed toward a civil war.

In 1857, the US Supreme Court decided a case that had an important impact on the slavery issue. Dred Scott was a former slave whose master had taken him west, into areas where slavery did not exist. After he returned to a slave state, he sued for his freedom, alleging he had become free when he lived in a free state. The Supreme Court ruled that slaves were not citizens and that Scott did not have a right to sue in federal court. The South considered the decision a victory in the issue of slavery.

In 1859, abolitionist John Brown and his followers seized the federal arsenal at Harper's Ferry in what is now West Virginia. His purpose was to take the guns stored in the arsenal, give them to nearby slaves, and lead the slaves in a widespread rebellion. Colonel Robert E. Lee, of the United States army, captured Brown and his men. Brown was found guilty at trial, and he was hanged. Southerners assumed that the majority of Northerners approved of Brown's actions, but in actuality, most of them were shocked. Southern newspapers took great pains to quote a small but well-known minority of abolitionists who applauded and supported Brown's actions. This merely served to widen the gap between the two sections.

Lincoln-Douglas Debates

In 1858, Abraham Lincoln and Stephan A. Douglas were running for the office of Senator from Illinois. They participated in a series of debates that proved influential to the 1860 presidential election. Douglas, a Democrat, was up for reelection and knew that if he won this race he would have a good chance of becoming president in 1860. Douglas had originated the doctrine of "popular sovereignty" and was responsible for getting the Kansas-Nebraska Act through Congress. Lincoln, a Republican, was not an abolitionist, but he believed slavery was morally wrong and he firmly supported the Republican principle that slavery must not be allowed to extend any further.

In the course of the debates, Lincoln challenged Douglas to show that popular sovereignty reconciled with the Dred Scott decision (in which the Supreme Court ruled that Congress had no authority to prohibit slavery in federal territories). Douglas knew that any answer he gave would cause him to lose crucial support from one group or another. He responded to Lincoln that territorial legislatures could exclude slavery by refusing to pass laws supporting it. The answer gave Douglas enough support and approval to be reelected to the Senate but it cost him the Democratic nomination for the presidency in 1860.

International Relations

During the period of westward expansion, the American government negotiated with various countries to establish boundaries that resulted in the boundaries of today's continental United States.

In order to establish trade relations with another country, President Millard Fillmore sent Commodore Matthew Perry to Japan in 1852 to meet with the emperor in the hopes of opening up trade with the country. He arrived in Japan with four ships and was met, but not welcomed. He returned in 1854 with more ships and convinced the Japanese to enter into a treaty and accept America's proposed terms. The terms included protection for stranded American sailors, the opening of two ports to be used for refueling and provisioning of American ships, the appointment of two US consuls, and giving the US "most favored nation" trade status that would guarantee future trade relations between the countries.

Civil War

The North and South quickly prepared for war once South Carolina seceded and shots were fired on Fort Sumter in Charleston harbor. The North had more in its favor: a larger population; superiority in finances and transportation facilities; and manufacturing, agricultural, and natural resources. The North also possessed most of the nation's gold, had about 92 percent of all industries, and almost all known supplies of copper, coal, iron, and various other minerals. Since most of the nation's railroads were in the North and Midwest, men and supplies could be moved whenever needed and food could be transported from the farms of the Midwest to workers in the East and soldiers on the battlefields. Trade with nations overseas could go on as usual due to the North's control of the navy and the merchant fleet. The number of northern states (24) outnumbered the South's eleven.

Although the North outnumbered the South in population, the South was confident they would achieve victory. The southerners knew that all they had to do was fight a defensive war, protecting their own territory until the North, who had to invade and defeat an area almost the size of Western Europe, tired of the struggle and gave up. The South also had the advantage of a number of West Point's best officers who had long years of army experience, some even exercising varying degrees of command in the Indian Wars and the war with Mexico. The men from the South were also conditioned to living outdoors and were more familiar with horses and firearms than many men from northeastern cities. Southerners believed that the governments of Britain and France would help them because those countries were dependent on raw cotton that the South provided them.

The South had specific reasons and goals for fighting the war. Their major aim was to win independence, govern themselves, and preserve slavery. The northerners were not as clear in their reasons for conduct the war. At the beginning, most believed, along with Lincoln, that preservation of the Union was paramount. Only some of the abolitionists looked on the war as a way to end slavery. However, by war's end, more and more northerners had come to believe that freeing the slaves was just as important as restoring the Union.

Jefferson Davis was chosen as president of the Confederate States of America, but many did not consider him an effective leader.

Strategy

The war strategies for both sides were relative clear and simple. The South planned a defensive war, wearing down the North until it agreed to peace on southern terms. The exception was to gain control of Washington, D.C., go north through the Shenandoah Valley into Maryland and Pennsylvania in order to drive a wedge between the Northeast and Midwest, interrupt the lines of communication, and end the war quickly.

The North had three basic strategies. They intended to blockade the Confederate coastline in order to cripple the South; seize control of the Mississippi River and interior railroad lines to split the Confederacy in two; and to seize the Confederate capital of Richmond, Virginia, and drive south, joining up with the Union forces coming east from the Mississippi Valley.

Emancipation Proclamation

On January 1, 1863, President Lincoln issued an executive order that proclaimed the freedom of slaves in the Confederate states that were considered to be in rebellion. The proclamation did not apply to slaves in Union-held areas or states that were not in rebellion. Freedom for those slaves would be handled differently. The proclamation only freed the slaves. It did not make them citizens or declare slavery illegal, nor did the proclamation compensate slave owners.

The battle of Gettysburg was the turning point of the war. It had not been the intention of either side to fight at Gettysburg, but the fighting began when a Confederate brigade stumbled into a unit of Union cavalry while looking for shoes.

The day after the battle of Gettysburg, General Ulysses S. Grant took the city of Vicksburg. Vicksburg, Mississippi, was on the Mississippi River and was an important center for obtaining supplies. Grant's capture of the city severed ties between the western and eastern Confederacy.

The battle of Appomattox Courthouse was one of the last battles of the Civil War. Robert E. Lee had moved north from Richmond, the Confederate capital, to meet other Confederate troops in North Carolina. The Union troops cut off his path at Appomattox Courthouse, Virginia. On April 9, 1865, Lee formally surrendered to General Grant.

Effects of the Civil War and Reconstruction

Effects

The Civil War has been called the first modern war. Its effects were far reaching because the war introduced weapons and tactics that, after later improvements, were used extensively in wars of the late 1800s and the 1900s. Civil War soldiers were the first to fight in trenches, the first to fight under a unified command, and the first to wage a defense called the "major cordon defense," a strategy of advance on all fronts. Civil War soldiers were also the first to use repeating and breech-loading weapons. Submarines, observation balloons, ironclad ships, mines, telegraphy, and railroads were also first put to use in the Civil War.

The Civil War was considered a modern war because of the vast distribution it created and because it was a "total" war that involved the use of all the resources by opposing sides. There is was no way the war could have ended without total defeat and unconditional surrender of one side or the other.

More American lives had been lost in the Civil War than in any other war in history. The South lost one third of its soldiers, whereas the North lost about one sixth of theirs. More than half of the total deaths were caused by disease and the horrendous conditions of field hospitals. Both sections paid a tremendous economic price, but the South suffered more severely.

Destruction was pervasive with towns, farms, trade, industry, lives, and homes of men, women, and children destroyed. The entire Southern way of life was lost. The deep resentment, bitterness, and hatred that remained for generations gradually lessened as the years went by, but the legacies of it remain to this day.

After the war, the South had no voice in the political, social, and cultural affairs of the nation, almost eliminating the influence of the traditional Southern ideals. The Northern Yankee Protestant ideals of hard work, education, and economic freedom became the standard of the United States and helped influence the development of the nation into a modern, industrial power.

Reconstruction

President Lincoln did not want to punish the South. He was most concerned with restoring it to the Union in a program that was flexible and practical. His plan, announced before the end of the war, consisted of Southerners swearing an oath of allegiance to the Union, promising to accept all federal laws and proclamations dealing with slavery. Once an individual swore allegiance to the Union, the person would be granted a full pardon. High officials of the Confederacy and military leaders of the Confederacy were excluded. The plan also provided that states

Key Concept 5.3
The Union victory in the Civil War and the contested reconstruction of the South settled the issues of slavery and secession, but left unresolved many questions about the power of the federal government and citizenship rights.

would write new constitutions and include in the document an amendment providing for the freedom of the slaves. The states also needed to elect new officials.

After Lincoln's assassination in 1865, Andrew Johnson became president. Johnson, a moderate, was willing to allow former Confederates keep control of their state governments. A federal agency, the Freedmen's Bureau, was establish to provide help to the freed slaves, allowing them to become self-supporting and to protect them from being taken advantage of. Northerners looked on it as a real and honest effort to help the South out of the chaos it was in. Most white Southerners charged the bureau with causing racial friction, deliberately encouraging the freedmen to consider former owners as enemies. As a result, Southern leaders adopted a set of laws known as "Black Codes" that were similar to pre-war slave codes. The Black Codes denied voting rights to the blacks and granted them only limited civil rights. The Radical Republicans in Congress responded to the Black Codes by continuing their hard line on allowing former rebel states back into the Union.

In 1866, the radical Republicans won control of Congress and passed the Reconstruction Acts, which placed the governments of the southern states under the control of federal troops. With this backing, the Republicans began to implement their policies such as granting all black men the vote and denying the vote to former Confederate soldiers. Congress had passed the Thirteenth, Fourteenth, and Fifteenth Amendments that granted citizenship and civil rights to blacks. The former slave states had to ratify these amendments as a condition of readmission into the Union. The Republicans found support in the South among freedmen (former slaves), white southerners who had not supported the Confederacy (scalawags), and northerners who had moved to the south to benefit economically after the war (carpetbaggers).

Ku Klux Klan

Bitterly resentful of the federal troops that protected the Republicans who took over control of the states' governments, white southerners fought the system by joining a secret society, the Ku Klux Klan (or KKK). The Klan was a group mainly composed of Confederate soldiers who opposed the Reconstruction government and espoused a doctrine of white supremacy. The group used violence, intimidation, and fear tactics to keep black Americans from voting. In 1871, President Ulysses S. Grant took action to use federal troops to halt the KKK activities and to prosecute members of the group in federal court.

The Emancipation Proclamation in 1863 and the Thirteenth Amendment in 1865 ended slavery in the United States, but these measures did not erase the centuries of racial prejudice among whites that held blacks to be inferior in intelligence and morality. The rise of the Redeemer governments (Democrats that took control after federal troops and Republicans left at the end of Reconstruction) marked the beginning of the Jim Crow laws and state-sanctioned segregation. During Reconstruction the concept of separateness of the races increased. New schools were built for the blacks and they formed communities where they could share culture. Many of the former plantation workers became tenant farmers for the landowners. Jim Crow laws restricted the rights of the blacks, and poll taxes and literacy tests were imposed to prevent black voting. The concept of separateness continued and was approved in the "separate but equal" doctrine identified by the Supreme Court case of Plessy v. Ferguson in 1896.

Reconstruction was a limited success. Its goals had been both the reunification of the South and North and the granting of civil rights to freed slaves. In the eyes of the blacks, it was considered a failure. Although its limited successes included the establishment of public schools and colleges for blacks and the expansion of legal rights for black Americans, many former Confederates and slave owners regained power and the whites, once again, were in control.

Civil War Amendments

The Thirteenth Amendment (1865) outlawed slavery throughout the United States. The Fourteenth Amendment (1868) made former slaves citizens. It also incorporated the due process clause of the Fifth Amendment and made due process applicable to the states. The Fourteenth Amendment also provided equal protection under the law. The Fifteenth Amendment (1870) gave African Americans the right to vote, and made it illegal to deny anyone the right to vote because of their race.

End of Reconstruction

Interest began waning in Reconstruction. It had limited success because it had set up separate public schools for the freed blacks and expanded legal rights of black Americans. Nevertheless, white "redeemer governments" rapidly worked to undo much of the changes resulting from Reconstruction. One of the Radical Republicans who had wanted to punish the South, Charles Sumner, died. General Grant had been elected president in 1868 and had served two scandal-ridden terms. He was an honest, upright person but lacked political experience and extended blind loyalty to those who supported him. During his administration, there was also a rapid growth of business and industry by large corporations that were controlled by unscrupulous men. Reconstruction officially ended in 1877 when federal troops left the South.

Summary of Period 6: 1865–1898

What You Should Know Before Reading This Chapter

- Many new inventions were made during this period.
- Railroads spread quickly across the nation, and Railroad companies became very powerful.
- The circumstances faced by Blacks freed from slavery were still very difficult.

What you Will Learn By Reading This Chapter

- Reconstruction in the south officially ended in 1877 when the final northern troops were removed.
- Railroad lines were so extensively built during this period that most areas of the country were soon linked to the rest of the nation. In 1869 the railroad lines were linked from coast to coast with completion of the transcontinental line.
- As industrialism grew, so did labor unions. Union membership was fed by large numbers of immigrants which shifted during this period so that they now mostly came from Eastern and Southern Europe.
- Unions sought for improved working conditions. They initially had only marginal success, but kept trying.
- Government by and large remained aloof and sought to avoid involvement in the economy. However, the corruption of what Mark Twain called the "gilded age" grew bad enough that some action was required. The Interstate Commerce Commission was created in 1887, and Congress passed the Sherman Anti-Trust Act of 1890 to curb the power of monopolies.
- The homestead act of 1862 led to significant westward expansion, as poor settlers could gain 160 acres of land for themselves after 5 years of labor.
- Great advances were made in communication with growth of the telegraph and invention of the telephone.

- Women's organizations sought for increased rights for their sex, but met with resistance.

- Major conflicts with Native Americans largely ended with the Battle of Wounded Knee in 1890. Indians during this period were relocated to reservations on undesirable, barren land.

- Blacks continued to suffer, as the Supreme Court's Plessy v. Ferguson decision in 1896 allowed southern states to create "separate but equal" facilities that segregated blacks from whites, in facilities that were rarely equal at all.

Technology

More than anything else, technological innovation was the driving force for changes that occurred in America between 1865 and 1898. Following the destruction during the Civil War and the innovations of the global Industrial Revolution, a wave of reconstructive efforts swept the country, leading to the widespread use of machinery for both agriculture and industry. This was largely due to newly-discovered natural resources and new technologies to acquire them. Vast coal and oil deposits provided abundant cheap energy, which made steel cheaper to produce. These provided all the materials needed for the railroad expansion and urbanization that were characteristics of this time.

An improved communication network emerged across the country. Telephones, invented by Alexander Graham Bell and Thomas Edison in 1876, and telegrams, perfected by Samuel Morse in 1844, were available to many levels of society, and became particularly important for businesses. Urbanization accelerated during this period, especially in the Northeast and Midwest. For example, Chicago was the fastest growing city during the 1860s and 1870s, due largely to industrial expansion in the steel-industry and a growing population of migrants from the South. Despite a tremendous fire in 1871, the city made a range of modern installations, such as electric lighting, cable cars, and telephone switchboards. The first skyscraper was built there in 1885, and because of the invention of the elevator, it reached 12 stories by 1890.

Railroads

Representative of the nationwide impact of these new technologies was the expansion and use of a railroad infrastructure across the country. Railroads spread at a staggering rate during this time, especially in the South and to the West.

A number of factors led to the growth of railways. They were funded by large corporations from the Northern states, including the railroad and shipping businesses of Cornelius Vanderbilt. The use of assembly-line factories made building, repairing, and redesigning railroad parts simpler than ever before. A transition from whale oil to alternative fuel sources—coal in particular—solved

> **Key Concept 6.1**
> Technological advances, large-scale production methods, and the opening of new markets encouraged the rise of industrial capitalism in the United States.

the problem of dwindling whale schools and rising costs of whaling voyages. The extraction of lubricants from petroleum allowed the new machinery being used to run smoothly. Indeed, the demand for petroleum-derived products created the foundations upon which the oil industry would boom. Finally, the growth of the country's steel-refining industry provided ample supplies of material with which trains and railroads were constructed. Many immigrants from Europe and Asia worked on these railroad projects, providing a cheap labor force. However, many were subsequently laid-off due to a decrease in rail-expansion following the Panic of 1873 and Great Railroad Strike of 1877.

Other innovations made trains more comfortable and safe for passengers and cargo—especially those making the long journey to the Western frontier. Compressed-air brakes were manufactured according to a 1868 patent by George Westinghouse, making trains less likely to derail in the case of an accident. Track gauge width was a problem that had hindered attempts to use railroads for transportation during the Civil War. A railway gauge of 4 ft. 9 in. was being used by the Pennsylvania Railroad, and the Pacific Railway Act (1863) encouraged its use across the country, standardizing all track widths by 1886. Used for industry, trade, and migration, the railroad led to an accelerated exchange of people, goods, and ideas in the nineteenth and twentieth centuries.

Ideology

The last half of the Nineteenth century also witnessed the clash between a number of conflicting ideological stances. An early progressive movement was known as the Social Gospel, who believed solutions to society's problems could be found by applying the lessons of Christianity to improve peoples' situations. This religious movement believed that society as a whole must take responsibility for those less fortunate.

Charles Darwin's theory of evolution was published in 1859 with *On the Origin of Species by Means of Natural Selection*. This seminal text proposed that species change over time and creatures best suited to their environment will adapt and survive with more success. This formed the justification for a "survival of the fittest" mentality proposed by Social Darwinists, whereby individual intuition and economic success were considered to be the key factors in establishing one's position in society. Although both Social Darwinism and the Social Gospel attempted to address the social problems of an industrializing America, they did so in different ways. Andrew Carnegie's "Gospel of Wealth" (1889) stated that Social Darwinists supported philanthropy as a solution, maintaining that the wealthy have an obligation to distribute their wealth in order to aid people that are disadvantaged. However, it was often used by monopolistic corporate trusts to justify consolidating wealth and influence to a limited number of individuals.

Key Concept 6.2

The migrations that accompanied industrialization transformed both urban and rural areas of the United States and caused dramatic social and cultural change.

Improved literacy rates contributed to the spread of these ideologies. Illiteracy dropped by around 10% between 1870 and 1900, according to the decennial censuses starting from 1870. In 1862 the Morrill Act granted each state land to establish a public land-grant college. These grants of public land awarded up to 90,000 acres to the states, and the colleges that were established have grown to be some of the most successful in the world. For example, in 1885 Stanford University was founded by Leland Stanford—a railway tycoon and governor of California. In the Social Darwinist spirit of the times, John Hopkins University was founded by the philanthropist John Hopkins in 1876 as a land-grant college.

Government

This period was marked by the US government's generally laissez faire attitude towards corporate expansion. This meant that they would usually keep out of economic affairs by not regulating businesses. For example, the government did not implement regulations for a minimum wage, child labor laws, or many safety measures. This was to the benefit of businesses that were able to freely manage their industry without intervention.

However, on some occasions the government decided to take control. In 1886, the Wabash Case resulted in a Supreme Court decision that limited control of interstate commerce to Congress. It denied individual states the right to regulate interstate railroads in an effort to combat corruption. This resulted in one of the first federal regulatory bodies, the Interstate Commerce Commission, being established in 1887 to oversee interstate railway practices. These culminated with the Sherman Antitrust Act that was passed by Congress in 1890 to outlaw monopolies on the market, giving the government powers to investigate companies suspected of violating the act.

Reconstruction

The Thirteenth Amendment was passed in 1865, abolishing slavery. This initiated a period known as the "Reconstruction", which referred to attempts made to implemented anti-slavery laws in the South and generally incorporate the former Confederate states into the Union. The Republican Party was founded in 1854 by various groups that were either anti-slavery, anti-Whig, or both. The Republican Party was heavily concentrated in the North immediately after the Civil War, aligning their interests with many regional industrialists, whilst the Southern states remained mostly Democratic. According to Lincoln's 10 Percent Reconstruction plan any former Confederate state could be readmitted into the Union provided that 10 percent of its voters made a pledge of loyalty to the United States. The state also had to accept a ban on slavery.

Andrew Johnson became president in 1865 and continued Abraham Lincoln's policies of rebuilding the South. However, Reconstruction was not supported by many Democrats, and even radical Republicans opposed it—contributing to the chain of events that led to President Johnson's eventual impeachment. The Fourteenth Amendment was passed in 1868, protecting the rights of African Americans by confirming their equal American citizenship and their equal protection according to the Bill of Rights. The Fifteenth Amendment was passed in 1870, guaranteeing African American men the right to vote. However, the Southern states found ways to work around these laws, and discrimination continued in the region for at least another century.

Gilded Age

In 1873, Samuel Clemens, also known as Mark Twain, called this period the "Gilded Age" to describe the political and economic corruption that lay underneath the riches and expansion being enjoyed by corporations and a corrupt government marred by political scandals. In 1867 the Tenure of Office Act was signed to prevent Presidents from removing appointed cabinet members without the permission of the Senate. However, President Andrew Johnson fired Secretary of War Edwin M. Stanton, resulting in an impeachment of the President by the House of Representatives in 1868. Another example was in 1872, when Union Pacific were revealed to have hired Credit Mobilier to work on construction for a government contract to build a transcontinental railroad. Union Pacific attempted to bribe congress to stop any investigations, though were unable to prevent it from being hotly discussed. Finally, in 1875 the Whiskey Ring scandal was exposed, revealing tax revenues that were being diverted between government workers and whiskey distilleries. Some measures were taken against this corruption. The Pendleton Civil Service Reform Act introduced competitive examinations with the intention of employing federal officials based on merit rather than their wealth and connections to the political elite. However, it only applied to federal jobs, and therefore did not affect corruption in other sectors. The Act also made it illegal to fire government employees for political reasons.

Labor

Labor Unions

Beginning in the mid-Nineteenth century, labor conditions transformed as a result of technological and ideological developments. There were many different perspectives of these changes. The combination of unequal working conditions, a growing wage gap, and economic panics encouraged the growth of labor unions, such as the National Labor Union. Formed in 1866, it had nearly 600,000 members, including both skilled and unskilled laborers. They did not encourage recruiting African-Americans, Chinese or women. They campaigned in earnest for an eight-hour working day, and managed to have it granted for government employees.

The Knights of Labor were a secret society founded in 1869, but later became the first nationwide labor union. Membership was open to all skilled and unskilled workers, including women and African Americans, as part of their "one big union" ideology. They distanced themselves from political affairs, focusing their efforts towards social and economic reforms, such as the implementation of an eight-hour working week for all laborers. However, they fell from prominence following the Haymarket Square Bombing incident in Chicago, 1886.

The American Federation of Labor was a union that split from the Knights of Labor in 1886. They were relatively elitist, and restricted their membership to only skilled laborers. Their campaigns focused on acquiring better wages, working conditions, and an eight-hour working day. On May 1st 1890 the American Federation of Labor announced that the eight-hour working day would be compulsory, forming the origins for the May Day celebrations enjoyed today.

Industry

Between 1865 and 1898 the country gradually adopted an industry-based economy led by large monopolistic corporations and a pro-growth government. Monopolistic corporate trusts formed, in which power was consolidated to a limited number of individuals and companies. The most famous individuals associated with these monopolies include John Davison Rockefeller (oil), John Pierpont Morgan (corporate finance), Ivar Kreuger a.k.a. the "Match King" (global match production) and Cornelius Vanderbilt (railroads). Vertical integration strategies occurred when a corporation retained ownership of all stages of the company's work—resource acquisition, production, and distribution. Because of this, they could enjoy all of the profits. Horizontal integration, by contrast, occurred when companies only expanded within one industry, allowing them to develop particular niches of production.

During this period, laborers would work for extremely low wages and long hours, since they were easily replaceable by a growing immigrant work force. Although the Factory Act was passed in 1833 to limit the number of hours children over the age of nine could work, and making daily attendance in school compulsory, child labor was prevalent, with children working long hours in extremely dangerous conditions.

Increasing industrialization sparked an economic panic in 1873. The quick formation of too many railroads and factories couldn't be supported by existing markets. This combined with banks giving too many loans to developments to cause the nation to draw its attention away from the Reconstruction of the South, allowing Southern Democrats known as the Redeemers to restore control over state legislation in the region during the 1870s.

Agriculture

Industrialization brought some benefits to farmers, especially in the South. In the 1870s the "New South Creed" was promoted by Henry Woodfin Grady and other reformers interested in modernizing the Southern states. To attract funding from northern corporations, many states in the South offered tax exemptions to new businesses and extremely cheap labor. Southern resources were heavily exploited by those that took advantage of these offers, in particular iron and steel production.

The population of the South was predominantly rural, and suffered from high illiteracy rates and federal government policies that were damaging the South's economic aspirations. The McKinley Tariff (1890) triggered a rise in the price of most goods to their highest levels ever. Sharecropping was prevalent, forcing laborers to provide a share of the crops they farm on land granted by the landowner. These laborers and landowners were often former slaves and slave-owners, resulting in a situation not much better than before the Thirteenth Amendment.

In response to these conditions, farmers created a number of local and regional cooperatives. The Farmer's Alliance developed in the 1870s to end the crop-lien system of the South. In 1891, it became the People's Party, also known as the Populist Party, a political party that formed to demand inflation to raise the price of crops, a free currency of silver coinage, and the implementation of graduated income tax.

Cattle ranching became the economic basis of the West, where cowboys would round up the vast herds of wild cattle to be sold and transported across the country. Buffalo herds were decimated during this period, in an attempt to force Native Americans to abandon their economic opportunities and accept their migration to reservations.

Demography

This period brought changes that affected immigrants, women, African Americans, and Native Americans in particular.

Immigration

Urbanization in cities such as New York and Philadelphia—and even more rapidly in the West—provided employment opportunities and a standard of living that attracted people from many countries. During the Nineteenth century, around 20 million people travelled from Asia, Europe, and Africa to the USA. There were two waves of immigrants; before 1871, most immigrants came from northern and western Europe, including Germany, the UK, Ireland, Norway and Sweden. For

Key Concept 6.3
The Gilded Age produced new cultural and intellectual movements, public reform efforts, and political debates over economic and social policies.

example, the Irish potato famine (1845–1850) resulted in over one million Irish emigrating from Europe. The second wave of immigrants, known as the "New Immigrants", occurred between 1871 and 1921. These came mostly from southern and eastern Europe, including Italy, Greece, Poland, and Russia. Many also came from Asia, particularly Japan and China. They arrived on faster and cheaper steamships, attracted by employment opportunities such as the transcontinental railway, though the vast majority found that there weren't as many jobs available as they had hoped.

These immigrants were not entirely welcome in the country, as they were perceived to be stealing competitive jobs and to be too culturally different. The Chinese Exclusion Act became the first to forbid a particular ethnic group from immigrating to the USA. The Chinese were singled out as "aliens" that were ineligible for citizenship since they could not assimilate to American ways of life, and even resulted in many Chinese already residing in the USA to be forced to leave without any chance of re-entry. Assimilation was thus an enormous problem for those new to the country. Settlement houses were set up by Social Gospel volunteers to help immigrants survive and adapt to the new country and ways of life. For example, Jane Addams founded the Hull Settlement House in Chicago in 1889, aimed at helping the poor working class and immigrants residing in the city through education.

Women

In the early Nineteenth century, women could not vote or own their own property, and they had no control over their husband's property or their children. They could not ask for divorce and could not sign legally binding contracts. African American women faced all of these challenges alongside segregation and discrimination. Women sought greater equality with men, in terms of employment, education, and domestic expectations, but progress for most rights remained slow after the Civil War. Susan Anthony (1820–1906) was a women's rights advocate and supporter of the temperance movement. She formed the National Woman Suffrage Association in 1869. Elizabeth Cady Stanton was another women's rights advocate that organized conferences demanding the right to vote, attend school, enter professional employment, and participate in politics. Anthony and Stanton founded the Woman's National Loyal League in 1863 to campaign for women's suffrage, leading eventually to the Nineteenth Amendment being ratified in 1920—granting women the right to vote.

Not all activist women were involved in women's rights per se. Many instead chose to face what they perceived as larger issues of the time—such as an end to slavery and segregation, and increasing literacy rates through education. Over 500 women's organizations existed that were devoted to supporting libraries, hospitals, schools, child labor organizations, and temperance laws. Dorothea Dix (1802–1887) worked to improve the lives of the mentally ill in America by founding over thirty mental hospitals.

Prohibition and temperance in particular gained strength through the work of female activists. They identified alcoholism as the reason for social problems, especially amongst the working class. In 1869, the National Prohibition Party was organized as a single-issue party against alcohol consumption. In 1874, the Women's Christian Temperance Union was founded, and later grew into a national organization with Frances Willard as president. Their members would pledge to abstain from all alcoholic beverages and discourage their traffic and use by others. In 1893, the Anti-Saloon League worked to close bars and encourage prohibition in individual states. The efforts of these organizations and other individuals resulted in Kansas becoming the first state to outlaw alcohol in 1881, and provided the foundation for the temperance movement of the next century.

African-Americans

African Americans faced increasing segregation and discrimination during the second half of the Nineteenth century. The Reconstruction of the South had some successes, including improvements to the transport and banking infrastructures, and the development of a public school system as well as several orphanages. Frederick Douglass was a former slave, lecturer at the Massachusetts Anti-Slavery Society, and dedicated abolitionist whose autobiography was popular throughout the country.

The government made some steps towards enforcing universal freedom and suffrage in the South. In 1865 the Freedmen's Bureau was founded by Congress to help freed slaves, though they ended their efforts in 1869.

However, Reconstruction remained unpopular and for the most part unsuccessful in the South. The Black Codes passed in the Southern states immediately after the Civil War sought to limit the civil rights of African Americans. Many African Americans could not vote or take literacy tests without being harassed or impeded, and many more suffered under the ideological context of Social Darwinism and race theory, which was used to justify white supremacy. Northerners that attempted to start businesses in the South were labeled as "carpetbaggers", whilst white Southerners that cooperated with them were called "scalawags", discouraging economic investors in the region. The Ku Klux Klan formed in 1865, and by 1867 was reported to have been involved in murders and assaults against African Americans that would not slow down until the Klan disbanded in 1869.

In 1870, Congress passed the Force Acts which authorized military intervention to protect polling stations, especially for African Americans being harassed when they turned up to vote. The 1875, Civil Rights Act was a final attempt to reinforce racial equality in the South, but it was disabled by the Supreme Court in 1883, stating that it did not apply to individuals or businesses.

The Compromise of 1877 resulted in the last Union troops leaving the South, following the controversial presidential election of Rutherford Hayes. Segregation increased across the Southern States into the twentieth century following the Plessy v. Ferguson Case in 1896, where separate-but-equal facilities were announced as being constitutional. This would lead to the Jim Crow Laws, which restricted access of African-Americans to federal employment and public services.

Native Americans

The idea of Manifest Destiny continued into the late Nineteenth century, as the United States pursued their westward expansion in earnest. The California Gold Rush began in 1848 and resulted in hundreds and thousands of gold-seekers migrating to the West. By 1850, most of the gold had been collected, and between 1855 and 1857 the gold in the Sierra Nevada had essentially disappeared. Despite this, the long-term effects of the Gold Rush were significant, leading to California being admitted to the Union as a Free State and continued population growth in the region with the transcontinental railroad. Thanks to the merging of the Union Pacific and Central Pacific railroads in 1869, what was a long and dangerous journey of up to six months by land or boat was reduced to only a matter of days. The Homestead Act (1862) gave Americans an incentive to settle in the West by offering 160 acres of land and promising to build a house, farm acreage of crops, and reside there for five years. However, Westward expansion caused enormous disruptions for Native Americans, removing many from their homes and disrupting their traditional ways of life.

Those involved in the Americanization of the West saw the traditional tribal structures of Native Americans as an obstacle. The Treaty of Fort Laramie in 1851 set a precedent for Native Americans being moved to certain territories which would belong to them. The Dawes Act (a.k.a. General Allotment Act of 1887) divided the tribes into individual families, provided them with land and granted them United States citizenship. The intention was to assimilate Native Americans to the nation, rather than forcibly remove them from the country. However, there was much contestation and conflict associated with its implementation. Land provided to them was in the form of reservations, where Native Americans were expected to give up their traditional culture—including language and religion. Many Native Americans opposed these measures. The Ghost Dance Movement was a Native American religious movement that aspired to resist settlers that were taking their land.

Conflicts between settlers, the federal government, and Native Americans were provoked by frequent violations of treaties and accusations of federal corruption. In 1864, Col. John Chivington and his troops slaughtered hundreds of Native American men, women and children at the Sand Creek Massacre. In 1876, President Grant's Secretary of War, William Belknap, was caught taking bribes from suppliers to Native American reservations, resulting in a scandalous impeachment and resignation. At the battle of Little Bighorn Col. George Custer's cavalry fired upon hundreds of Sioux before getting massacred. Tensions peaked at the massacre of Wounded Knee (1890), the last showdown between Native Americans and the United States Army. Three hundred Lakota men, women and children were massacred.

Summary of Period 7: 1890–1945

What You Should Know Before Reading This Chapter

- Two world wars were fought during this time.
- The great depression of the 1930s had a great impact on the nation.
- Many new inventions were made, which transformed America.

What you Will Learn By Reading This Chapter

- Industrialization and the resulting labor movement continued, but government finally started cracking down and creating greater controls and protections for workers.
- Significant technological advances transformed the very nature of life, with the advent of the assembly line and automobiles, radios and movie theaters for entertainment, and the invention of the airplane in 1903.
- Imperialism, or the dominance of one nation over others, was a hotly debated topic. The United States had a flirtation with imperialism in the Spanish-American war of 1898 in which the U.S. took over the Philippines and Cuba. The U.S. also exerted its influence in Central America to create the Panama Canal.
- However, most Americans preferred to remain neutral and not interfere in international affairs. Hence, the U.S. delayed entering WWI for 3 years, and after the war ended refused to join the League of Nations.
- The 1929 stock market crash and ensuing great depression of the 1930s was one of the most transformative events in American history. Americans were desperate for relief, and saw the emergence of a limited welfare state as government took a far more active role in financial and economic affairs than ever before.
- The nation did not fully emerge from the depression until WWII, when a military-oriented economy bolstered production.

- During WWII women went to work in large numbers, since men were off at war.
- The war ended with the dropping of the atomic bomb on Hiroshima and Nagasaki Japan, and the United States emerged as the unquestioned leading nation on earth.

Technology

One of the largest influences on domestic and foreign policies that came into being between 1890 and 1945 was technological innovation.

Domestically, standards of living improved, due to the mass production of consumer goods. Modern transport became available to an increasing number of people. Henry Ford founded the Ford Motor Company in 1903. With his assembly line factories, he produced automobiles quickly and reliably, decreasing their cost and allowing more people to afford to drive. Great strides were made in wireless communications technology during the 1880s. Radio broadcasting, and eventually cinemas, contributed to a unifying sense of "American" culture. Public health campaigns and improvements to medical science resulted in the life expectancy of Americans rising from 47 years in 1900 to 63 in 1940. However, the stratification of urban centers into distinct upper, middle, and lower classes meant that everyone did not have equal access to these benefits. With changing labor demographics, women began earning wages as well. This provided extra spending money for commodities and leisure activities. America's foreign policies were also heavily influenced by motivations to find new markets abroad with which to trade excess commodities.

Science and technology became arenas of controversy as well, particularly with regards to the consequences of development and modernism. The environmental impact of resource acquisition for these new technologies sparked debate over preservation (protecting ecosystems and environments regardless of their utility value) and conservation (regulating the exploitation of a resource so that it does reach the point where it becomes non-renewable). In 1872, Yellowstone National Park became the first protected landscape in America, covering an area of exceptional geyser formations and hot springs within Wyoming, Montana, and Idaho.

Military Technology

New technologies alongside a growing labor pool contributed to a US victory in the First and Second World Wars. The Wright Brothers built and successfully flew the first airplane in 1903—an achievement that would lead to greater aviation technology. The Manhattan Project was a research program organized by the USA, Canada, and the UK. The research center at Los Alamos, New Mexico, produced and tested the first atomic bomb in July 1945 under the direction of

Key Concept 7.1

Growth expanded opportunity, while economic instability led to new efforts to reform US society and its economic system.

General Leslie Groves and the physicist Julius Robert Oppenheimer. These developments laid the foundation for the subsequent "atomic age," including the conflicts surrounding the Cold War.

Ideology

The early twentieth century was known as the "Progressive Era" due to the government's general abandonment of their laissez-faire position. Instead, they took a greater part in regulating the affairs of the nation. Urbanization, social stratification, segregation, government corruption, immigration, and corporate monopolies were the major problems that had been carried over from the "Gilded Age," though many of these became overshadowed by the World Wars. The Progressives were divided over many of these issues, such as segregation in the South and restrictions on immigrants.

Free Speech

Restrictions to freedom of speech besmirched this period, affecting the definition of what "being an American citizen" meant. During the World Wars, communication was particularly censored. The Sedition Act of 1918 made it a criminal offense to engage in any activity or communication that was contradictory to America's war efforts. In 1919, the Schenck v. United States case established the Supreme Court's position regarding free speech in response to Charles Schenck's anti-military pamphlet operations, stating that they could not protect speech that presented a "clear and present" danger to the safety of the nation. The Taft-Hartley Act came into effect in 1947, after the Second World War was over. It cracked down on the power of labor unions, allowed the government to postpone strikes through injunctions, and implemented a mandatory anti-Communist pledge for union leaders.

A discourse of freedom, security and democracy gradually formed, establishing a unifying "American" identity, with "fascists", "socialists", "aliens", and eventually "communists" being identified as threats to the American nation. The Red Scare was a period of fear and paranoia between 1919 and 1920, targeted towards socialists and leftwing radicalism. Eugene Debs was a popular presidential candidate in the elections between 1900 and 1920, yet was jailed due to his socialist views and campaigns against the Sedition Act. The Palmer Raids of 1920 were directed by Edgar Hoover, in which over 4,000 suspected anarchists and leftwing supporters were rounded up across America.

Imperialism vs. Anti-Imperialism

The expansion into the Western frontier of the later Nineteenth century was considered successful by the early twentieth century. New lands were sought by imperialists, who promoted the economic and cultural opportunities afforded by extending America's presence overseas. For example, Alfred T. Mahan's The

Influence of Sea Power Upon History (1890) advocated America's development of a strong navy and overseas bases to serve as "stepping stones" for economic and military purposes. He also encouraged the construction of the Panama Canal. This sentiment was shared by President Theodore Roosevelt. He expanded the Monroe Doctrine in 1904, which authorized American intervention in Latin American affairs to ensure regional stability. "Dollar diplomacy" was a policy advocated by William Taft to encourage joining business and diplomatic relations with other countries, rather than military treaties. For example, Henry Clay's "Open Door Policy" in the early twentieth century encouraged directing business interests towards China, as few other countries were enjoying economic treaties with Asia at the time.

Despite the isolationist and anti-imperialist sentiments promoted by the federal government, the period showed a number of attempts to expand America's overseas territories. For example, in 1867 the US purchased Alaska from Russia in an action known as "Seward's Folly" due to contemporary perceptions that it was an unprofitable exchange. America supported Panama's successful independence movement against Colombia in exchange for the land required for the Panama Canal. It was constructed between 1880 and 1914, and revolutionized travel between the Atlantic and Pacific. Finally, a US victory in the Spanish-American War (1898) allowed them to expand territories in the Caribbean and Pacific, most significantly in Cuba and the Philippines.

Anti-imperialists responded to these events by advocating self-determination. The Anti-Imperialist League was founded in 1899, with illustrious members including Mark Twain and Andrew Carnegie. They denounced the annexation of the Philippines by America and similar imperialist acts. However, due to the American victories in both World Wars they found that most of the population tended to support the imperialist government.

Labor

The Progressive era introduced legislation against monopolies, child labor and unsafe working conditions. In 1914, the Clayton Antitrust Act was passed by Congress, preventing companies from acquiring stocks owned by another company in an attempt to discourage monopolies. Interstate commerce was heavily regulated; the Elkins Act (1903) ensured that all railroad customers paid the same rates by fining railroad companies that accepted rebates, and the Hepburn Act strengthened the powers of the Interstate Commerce Commission to regulate companies engaging in trade between states. Despite these measures, the government was accused of social injustices and corruption. One notable example was the Teapot Dome Scandal (1921–1922), in which the Secretary of Interior Albert Hall became the first cabinet member to be convicted of bribery by allowing federal reserves of oil to be sold to a private company in exchange for a sizable cut.

The Great Depression

The period between 1890 and 1945 also displayed fluctuating economic growth. A politically conservative Republican administration dominated the countries affairs during the 1920s, pursuing pro-business policies and economic relations with foreign nations with minimal consultation or cooperation with their neighbors. Under this administration—in particular that of Calvin Coolidge (1923–1929)—the population experienced a widening wage gap alongside ceaseless overproduction of commodities. Meanwhile, extensive stock market speculation was taking place. The Wall Street Crash occurred on "Black Tuesday," October 29th 1929, when stock market prices plummeted. This caused rising unemployment, the failure of many American businesses, and American banks defaulting on their loans—a period known as the Great Depression. Whilst the country was experiencing this economic crash the Dust Bowl phenomenon occurred across the Midwest. Record high heats, almost no rainfall, and constant high winds destroyed huge quantities of farmland, forcing thousands out of their livelihoods and even homes. The World Wars had a tremendous impact in bringing the country out of the Depression, thanks to the mass-mobilization of all levels of American society—especially by offering employment opportunities to women.

The New Deal

In response to this economic instability greater efforts were made by the government to regulate the financial system. Between 1933 and 1937, President Franklin Roosevelt's "New Deal" formed the basis of many reforms in the country. This was a policy through which multiple initiatives would be taken to restore the US economy. The Securities Exchange Commission was created in 1934. Their role was to regulate abuses of the sale of stocks and monopolies on financial investment information. This was due to individuals who monopolized on financial information and contributed to the Wall Street Crash, such as J.P. Morgan. The Glass-Steagall Banking Act was passed in 1933, creating what became known today as the Federal Deposit Insurance Corporation. This organization was given powers to guarantee individual bank deposits, regulate and monitor banks, and it separated commercial and investment banking in order to restore American faith in the banking system following the Wall Street Crash.

Although these measures were generally more popular than Hoover's responses to the Great Depression, which involved the formation of the Reconstruction Finance Corporation and resisted the provision of federal aid to the unemployed affected by the Depression, there were mixed reactions to the New Deal. Many people believed that the New Deal was an attempt by Roosevelt to control judicial independence and remove the separation of judicial powers. Senator Huey Long and Upton Sinclair were particularly active critics of the New Deal.

The "New Deal" resulted in greater economic security and the US being transformed into a limited welfare state, with the federal government heavily involved in economic, military and social affairs. Early welfare programs continue to the current day, such as the social security, the Securities and Exchange Commission, and the Federal Deposit Insurance Corporation.

Demography

Labor demographics shifted during this period, with many immigrants, African Americans, women, and working-class laborers changing their social and labor roles, largely as a result of the two World Wars.

Immigration

Immigration peaked before World War I, as people rushed in from an increasingly tense Europe and conflicts that were taking place in Asia between Japan and China. However, ethnic groups and Americans of immigrant descent were threatened during the World Wars, due to radical fears of espionage and treason.

The fear and prejudice against Germans and leftists caused by the First World War and Red Scare expanded to include immigrants, triggering a rise in racism and nativism—the desire to protect the interests of "real" Americans against a perceived immigrant threat. Quotas and restrictions were implemented by the government during and between the Wars to limit immigration. Following the attack on Pearl Harbor in 1941, debates over the loyalty of Japanese-Americans resulted in the detainment of over 110,000 Americans of Japanese ancestry in internment camps. In 1944, the Renunciation Act was passed, allowing people to lose their American citizenship by choice, and resulted in over 5,000 Japanese-Americans losing their citizenship, with 1,300 of them being repatriated to Japan. Others decided to stay in America and strove to prove their loyalty by fighting for the United States army during the Second World War, though they were widely discriminated against and violently abused.

Despite these measures, immigrants arrived to the United States throughout the period, especially from Mexico. The Bracero Program started in 1942 due to a labor shortage America was experiencing from the War, enabling Mexican citizens to move to the USA to engage in temporary agricultural work. Despite awful working conditions and reported human rights abuses, around 5 million Mexicans moved to the US between 1943 and 1964.

African-Americans

Segregation increased across the Southern States following the Plessy v. Ferguson case in 1896, where separate-but-equal facilities were considered constitutional. This led to the Jim Crow Laws, which restricted access of African-Americans to federal employment and public services. The First Great Migration

---

Key Concept 7.2

Innovations in communications and technology contributed to the growth of mass culture, while significant changes occurred in internal and international migration patterns.

was a period between 1910 and 1930 when thousands of African Americans moved from these harsh conditions in the South to the North and West. Many African Americans settled in the Harlem neighborhood in New York City during the Great Migration. This gradually became the cultural center for many African American musicians, writers, poets, scholars and artists. The Harlem Renaissance Movement, also known as the New Negro Movement, was a period of cultural expression and a flourishing of the arts for many African-Americans. Jazz and blues were some of the products of this artistic melting pot.

African American rights activists worked tirelessly throughout this period. Booker T. Washington campaigned for vocational training and gradual rights for African Americans, whilst William E. B. Du Bois sought immediate education rights and equality for African Americans. Du Bois and his supporters founded the Niagara Movement in 1905, which became a cornerstone for desegregation and led to the formation of the National Association for the Advancement of Colored People (NAACP) in 1909—the organization that would work so hard to fight discrimination during the Civil Rights Movement of the 1960s.

Women

The World Wars transformed opportunities available to women, as well as their perceived roles in society. Conscription resulted in fewer men working in the country and women were targeted to fill up the gaps.

Much work was done by women to improve labor laws during this period. Florence Kelley founded the National Consumers League in 1891 to boycott consumer goods produced by child laborers, contributing to the Illinois Factory Act of 1893 which prohibited child labor under the age of 14. In 1889, Jane Addams founded the Hull settlement house in Chicago, aimed at helping the poor working class and immigrants residing in the city. She was a co-founder of the Women's Peace Party in 1915, and campaigned against both World Wars. In recognition of her actions she was awarded the Nobel Peace Prize in 1931—the first American woman to do so. Susan Anthony supported woman's suffrage through the National Woman Suffrage Association. The Nineteenth Amendment was passed in 1920, granting women the right to vote. Francis Perkins became the first female Cabinet member as the US Secretary of Labor from 1933 to 1945. However, African American women experienced roughly the same amount of discrimination as before. In 1890, the National American Woman Suffrage Association emerged to campaign for equal voting rights for African Americans.

Moral reforms concerning prohibition and temperance took place during this period. Susan Anthony continued supporting the temperance movement until her death in 1906. Carrie Nation was a particularly notable Kansas-based prohibitionist in the early twentieth century who would vandalize saloons and destroy alcohol bottles and barrels with a hatchet. In 1920, the Eighteenth Amendment was signed, prohibiting the production and sale of alcoholic beverages.

Foreign Policy

The events that took place between 1890 and 1945 established America's position as a key player in world affairs for most of the twentieth century.

First World War

America gradually abandoned its policy towards isolationism and non-involvement of European affairs during the First World War. When war broke out in Europe on 28th July 1914 between the Triple Entente (Britain, Russia, and France) and the German-Austro-Hungarian powers, the USA initially adopted a neutral and isolationist position that was supported by the American population. This allowed economic relations with countries involved in both sides of the conflict, and supported the democratic and peace-seeking rhetoric of the Progressives.

However, there was growing anti-German hysteria in America due to unrestricted German submarine warfare in the Atlantic. This culminated with the sinking of the Lusitania by German submarines in 1915. This British passenger ship was carrying Americans on board, turning the United States population against the Germans and their allies. In 1917, the Selective Service Act was passed, allowing the federal government the right to raise an army through conscription, enabling the USA to enter the war. Woodrow Wilson called upon Congress for the defense of humanitarian and democratic principles, and war was declared on Germany on April 6th 1917 and the Austro-Hungarian Empire on December 7th 1917. The contribution of America in the First World War was relatively small compared to the Second, though they still tipped the balance towards an Allied victory. In one case, American actions prevented the German occupation of Paris at the Battle of Château-Thierry in 1918.

Interwar Period

Despite supporting the victorious Allies, the USA distanced themselves from the aftermath of the First World War in Europe by refusing to ratify the Treaty of Versailles. Signed in June 1919, this peace treaty was supposed to prevent future wars in Europe. However, the terms of the treaty were particularly harsh for the Germans, especially with regards to reparations they had to pay, and was a factor that contributed to the Second World War. Furthermore, America did not join the League of Nations, which was set up to allow disputes between nations to be settled without resorting to war. American foreign policies between the Wars advocated overseas investment and peace treaties.

However, in response to growing tensions in Europe preceding the Second World War, the US government passed the Neutrality Acts (1935–1937) to position themselves as being firmly isolationist and non-interventionist. These acts restricted American trade, financial aid, and travel that involved countries that were at war. The America First Committee started in 1940 to discourage American involvement in the Second World War.

Second World War

Although America generally opposed any direct military involvement against the Nazis in Europe, on December 7th 1941, a Japanese attack on Pearl Harbor resulted in America being drawn into the Second World War. The American navy was stationed at Honolulu when the Japanese attacked, and suffered over two thousand casualties. The next day, America declared war on Japan.

During the War America tightened relations with the European Allies. The Lend-Lease Act of 1941 allowed the US to sell arms, ammunition, and other military products to the UK, USSR, China, and France. In August 1941, President Roosevelt and Winston Churchill (Prime Minister of the UK) met near Newfoundland to draw up the Atlantic Charter. This postwar plan advocated disarmament, a permanent global security system, and giving each nation the free right to choose their own type of government. It solidified relations between the USA and the UK, and indicated that both countries were looking ahead to postwar global affairs.

This conflict saw the United States involved in multiple theatres of war. The Office of War Mobilization was created in 1943 by President Roosevelt to organize the wartime mobilization of labor and conscription. Some of the fiercest battles fought include the Allied invasion of Normandy (aka. Operation Overlord, June 1944) and the Battle of Iwo Jima (aka. Operation Detachment, March 1945). With the Allied powers closing in on Germany's west, and the Russians in control of the east, Adolf Hitler committed suicide and on May 8th, 1945, Germany surrendered. In August 1945, the United States dropped atomic bombs on Hiroshima and Nagasaki, Japan, resulting in between 129,000 and 246,000 casualties over the following decades. Japan announced their surrender on August 14th, the day after the bombing of Nagasaki. On September 2nd, 1945, Japan formally signed their surrender aboard the USS Missouri, ending America's involvement in the Second World War.

Postwar

After the war, the Marshall Plan was put into place to help rebuild Western Europe. America sought to be a key player in global human rights and values by promoting democracy and peace with countries that exhibited similar values, whilst at the same time uniting against those that do not support these values.

Key Concept 7.3

Participation in a series of global conflicts propelled the United States into a position of international power while renewing domestic debates over the nation's proper role in the world.

Summary of Period 8: 1945–1980

What You Should Know Before Reading This Chapter

- The Korean and Vietnam Wars occurred during this period.
- The civil rights movement finally brought better treatment for Blacks and other minorities.
- Many social changes occurred in the 1960s and 1970s, and moral values were questioned.

What you Will Learn By Reading This Chapter

- Never in American history has there been a period of growth and prosperity to equal the boom after the end of WWII. Returning GI's took advantage of the GI bill to get an education. Home building and buying was on the rise, as was the use of credit cards and consumer spending.
- The TV changed the face of entertainment, and the "space race" ended up putting an American on the moon.
- Internationally, the U.S. took a different approach to post-war involvement after WWII, to avoid sowing the seeds of another war. The U.S. implemented the "Marshal Plan" to assist the recovery of war torn Europe and Japan, and took a more active role around the globe.
- The "cold war" evolved in this period, in which the U.S. pursued a policy of "containment" of the spread of communism across the world.
- This "containment" effort led to the Korean Conflict in the early 1950s, and the highly controversial Vietnam War of the 1960s and 1970s.
- After 100 years of oppression, blacks finally started gaining their civil rights. In Brown v. Board of Education in 1954, the Supreme Court ruled that "separate but equal" policies of discrimination are unconstitutional. Other changes followed, culminating in the Civil Rights Act of 1964.
- Women also gained greater rights, including laws mandating equal pay. The Equal Rights Amendment was proposed, but failed to receive enough ratifying votes to be added to the Constitution.
- A "revolution" of social morals in the 1960s changed the fabric of America.

Many in the rising generation questioned existing moral standards.
- The 1970s finally saw a slow-down of economic growth, as inflation and joblessness increased and OPEC shut off oil shipments to the U.S.
- The combination of the Vietnam War and Watergate scandal increased popular distrust of government. The 1970s was a discouraging time.

Postwar

The period following World War II is termed by many historians as the "Golden Age", when an economic boom brought unparalleled prosperity to the United States. In 1945, the US was a far different country. "Nearly a third of Americans lived in poverty. A third of the country's homes had no running water, two-fifths lacked flushing toilets, and three-fifths lacked central heating. More than half of the nation's farm dwellings had no electricity." Racial segregation in schoolhouses, restaurants, and public services was required by law. Immigration was favored for Europeans and limited for migrants from the rest of the world.

Over the next four decades, a series of domestic improvements—such as highways, job training, housing assistance, and education programs—would bring opportunities for many Americans. The Civil Rights Movements would change the status quo for African Americans, and changes in immigration law would remove preferential treatment for Europeans, allowing immigrants to come from all over the world. The Cold War, the Vietnam War, and the Korean War would continue to shape the nation's foreign policy. It would be an exciting and challenging time for America, and in the four decades following World War II, the country would sow the seeds for the 21st century.

The Cold War was a geopolitical, ideological, economic, and cultural battle fought between the United States and the United Socialist Soviet Republic (USSR). It started in 1945 and had two epochal endings—the tearing down of the Berlin Wall in 1989 and the dissolution of the Soviet Union in 1991. Through the five decades of the Cold War, the United States sought to stamp out communism overtly and covertly, by engaging in international treaties, funding anti-communist actions, and sponsoring regimes to overthrow dictators. The Cold War was also fought culturally and economically, in events like the Olympics, trade sanctions, embargoes, and boycotts. On the United States domestic front, the Cold War policies led to anti-nuclear weapon protests, budget battles in Congress, and increased spying on United States citizens believed to be communist sympathizers.

Cold War—International

The Iron Curtain

One of the earliest events in the Cold War arose from the anti-Communism remarks of British leader Winston Churchill. On March 5, 1946, in a famous speech characteristic of the political climate of the time, he said: "From Stettin

Key Concept 8.1

The United States responded to an uncertain and unstable postwar world by asserting and working to maintain a position of global leadership, with far-reaching domestic and international consequences.

in the Baltic to Trieste in the Adriatic an 'Iron Curtain' has descended across the continent. Behind that line lie all the capitals of the ancient states of Central and Eastern Europe. Warsaw, Berlin, Prague, Vienna, Budapest, Belgrade, Bucharest and Sofia; all these famous cities and the populations around them lie in what I must call the Soviet sphere, and all are subject, in one form or another, not only to Soviet influence but to a very high and in some cases increasing measure of control from Moscow." The Iron Curtain included the construction of the Berlin Wall, dividing East and West Berlin. East Berlin, under the control of the Soviets and part of the German Democratic Republic, and West Berlin part of the Federal Republic of Germany.

Philosophies

Several philosophies ruled the Cold War, and drove US engagement internationally. The Marshall Plan, implemented after the war in 1946, provided more than $12 billion to reconstruct bombed-out Europe. The expectation was that Europe would become an American ally, and that the United States could forestall another world war by helping Europe rebuild. The US also reconstructed Japan under the same plan. The Truman Doctrine coined by President Truman, articulated that the US must support people all around the world that are attempting to resist "subjugation by armed minorities or outside pressures." Essentially this meant, that the United States would come to the aid of any country in danger of Soviet invasion. Proxy wars were skirmishes, or full-out wars, where the United States supported a nation that was being invaded or occupied by communist forces (Soviet, Chinese, Korean). The Korean War, the Vietnam war, and the Cuban missile crisis were extensions of the Truman doctrine and the containment approach. In the Eisenhower era, mutually assured destruction became the philosophy that prevented either the Soviets or the United States from launching their arsenals of nuclear weapons. If the United States launched, then the Soviets launched, and vice-versa. During the Nixon era, communism was still going strong, but now times had changed and called for openness, an approach called détente. The Nixon doctrine posed that the United States would withdraw its troops from overseas, relying instead on alliances with the governments of the countries, to stop the spread of communism.

Over the next four decades, the Cold War also extended to United States interventions in Latin America and Africa, with US involvement in Guatemala, Nicaragua, Cuba, and Egypt, and East Africa.

Cold War—Domestic

The Cold War had perceptible domestic impacts. In the late 1950s, Senator Joseph McCarthy, started to "root out" communist sympathizers. He used many hardline tactics and held hearings over the course of several years, subpoenaing witnesses and invading privacy, all to little avail. Citizen's civil liberties and privacy were trampled on in the name of security during this time.

However, it was the drawn-out US engagement in Vietnam that brought a rash of anti-government and protest activity domestically. America's involvement in Vietnam began after World War II, and was precipitated by the desire to root out communism in the Third World. The United States, under President Lyndon Johnson, decided to support a coup in South Vietnam, and to overthrow despotic leader Ngo Dinh Diem, whom the United States had previously installed. From 1964 to 1968, United States troops landed in South Vietnam, and it became "America's War." Back home, ambiguity over the purpose of the war, the mounting losses of American lives, and the draft of young men to join the Army drew increasing opposition from the people. Rallies, protests, and draft-dodging increased during the Vietnam War years. Finally, a beleaguered Johnson announced that he would begin negotiations with the North Vietnamese and also stated that he would not run for reelection.

Organizations established during the Cold War included the North Atlantic Treaty Organization (NATO) a European alliance to safeguard Europe from future occupations. In the United States, the National Aeronautics and Space Administration (NASA), the Peace Corps, the Agency for International Development (USAID), the National Security Agency (NSA) and the Central Intelligence Agency (CIA) were created under the auspices of the Cold War, and remain in operation today.

Oil Crisis of the 1970s

Reliance on oil grew in the United States during the 1950s through 1970s, and assurances by the government that the United States would always have access to Middle East oil came crashing down in the mid-70s when the OPEC (Organization of Petroleum Exporting Countries) alliance embargoed oil supplies to the United States. Increased fuel prices and shortages changed the lives of most Americans, who had become accustomed to a steady supply of gas. This was coupled with inflation and increasing unemployment. The 1970s were a tough decade domestically, and resulted in greater oversight of the United States foreign relations and resource dependencies. As a result, in 1977, President James Carter created a new governmental Department of Energy to oversee America's energy needs and explore alternative forms of energy.

Civil Rights Movement

The modern day civil rights agenda began with Truman, who convened the Committee on Civil Rights in 1948, which called for an end to segregation, poll taxes, and an aggressive enforcement of anti-lynching laws. Truman also issued an executive order banning discrimination in federal government hiring and desegregating the Armed Forces. But much more action and government intervention would be needed through the 1950s and 1960s to get to the landmark 1964 Civil Rights legislation.

During Eisenhower's term, the Supreme Court ruled on Brown v. Board of Education of Topeka, and decisively clarified that "separate but equal" did not apply to educational facilities, putting into play a key decision that would lead to greater political and activist push for civil rights. Events like the Montgomery bus boycotts after the Rosa Parks incident, the Birmingham riots, and the rise of Martin Luther King Jr. as a spokesman and leader for the non-violent civil rights movements all fueled the fire for equal rights. President Kennedy embraced the civil rights movement late in his term, and after his death, Lyndon Johnson pushed the Civil Rights Act of 1964 through Congress. The infamous act outlawed segregation in all public facilities, and holds even today in civil rights discrimination lawsuits.

In the 1950s and 1960s, Martin Luther King Jr., the charismatic leader of the civil rights movement, mobilized non-violent protests, boycotts, and sit-ins through a variety of mechanisms, including the Southern Christian Leadership Conference, the Freedom Riders, and the Student Nonviolent Coordinating Committee. Martin Luther King was awarded the Nobel Peace Prize in 1964 for his work. In 1968, Martin Luther King was shot and killed by James Earl Ray, shocking the nation and his followers.

The civil rights advances did not come without confrontation by pro-separatists. The Ku Klux clan carried out several violent and punitive acts against blacks in the South. In response, Malcolm X, a leader and minister of the Nation of Islam, advocated a stronger uprising for black power. After King's assassination, civil rights activism started to slow down, and focused on righting specific wrongs and self-empowerment for African Americans.

Through the civil rights period, the Supreme Court played an important role in enforcing the rights of African Americans. Several landmark rulings under Chief Justice Earl Warren enforcing equality and civil rights, cemented his role in the changing times. It included voting rights for blacks, redistricting in minority-populated areas so they received representation, the right to have a state-appointed defense counsel for those who couldn't afford their own counsel (Gideon v. Wainwright), and the right to be advised of your right to remain silent when arrested, until you consulted with a lawyer (Miranda v. Arizona).

The Growth of Liberalism in the 1960s

The 1960's signaled a shift in culture and social mores. Important changes were beginning to sweep the nation. The civil rights movements were part of a larger social shift in America towards empowerment and self-determination of

---

Key Concept 8.2

New movements for civil rights and liberal efforts to expand the role of government generated a range of political and cultural responses.

one's future. Citizens took to protests, lobbying, and activism to force government to improve their living conditions and the environment.

Women wanted to end job discrimination and to challenge assumptions about their role in society. Betty Friedan formed the National Organization for Women (NOW) to fight for legislation geared towards women's equality. Feminist movements attacked discriminatory practices in pay, hiring, and college admissions. Roe v. Wade granted women the right to choose to have an abortion in all 50 states. Despite challenges to Roe v. Wade in the 1980s and 1990s, it still represents a landmark win for women's rights.

The first gay pride march occurred in 1969, after the Stonewall riots, where gays fought back against police raiding a bar in New York.

Other groups fought against poverty, for a cleaner environment, and banning pesticide use. The Clear Air Act was passed in 1955, the first one to limit industrial pollutions into the air.

Perceptions of Role of Government

The US government remained an active participant in foreign policy through the Cold War. Domestically, several Presidents left their mark during this time. The post-World War II economy required that funds be redirected towards growing the infrastructure, jobs, and economy. The roads (Eisenhower's Great Highway programs), education (the GI Bill for returning veterans); unemployment benefits, minimum wage increases and farmer aid program (Kennedy's New Frontier programs); housing assistance, job training, and poverty relief (Johnson's Great Society programs) all helped improve domestic life after the War.

The public's perceptions of government were shaken by the Vietnam War and the Watergate crisis. Watergate brought to the forefront the power of the media and investigative journalism. In 1971, Watergate started with the "Pentagon Papers", a top-secret government study of the US involvement in Vietnam. Nixon tried to block the release of the document, but failed. In an effort to prevent further classified leaks, Nixon approved the burglarizing of the Democratic Committee's office in the Watergate Hotel in Washington D.C., recorded phone calls from the White House, and tried to gather incriminating evidence on the whistle-blower who leaked the Pentagon Paper. All this came to light, when the burglars were caught, and Washington Post's reporters Bob Woodward and Carl Bernstein uncovered the connections to Nixon. Nixon resigned after the Watergate scandal to avoid being impeached, and turned the wheel over to his Vice President Gerald Ford, who finished out the remainder of Nixon's term.

Ford's term was dogged by his presidential pardon of Nixon, and a drawn out crisis with OPEC on oil. Carter followed Ford, and struggled with a comatose economy with inflation exceeding 10 percent, and unemployment at 20 percent.

Key Concept 8.3

Postwar economic and demographic changes had far-reaching consequences for American society, politics, and culture.

Economic growth

After the end of WWII, the various Presidents set about to the task of growing the domestic economy. While the Cold War consumed resources, each President tried to invigorate the economy through social programs. Truman created GI bills to help returning veterans re-integrate into society, and Eisenhower initiated highway projects, which promoted travel by car and created more suburbs around cities. Kennedy promoted social programs to increase unemployment benefits, social security, and the minimum wage, while Johnson tackled poverty relief, education, job training, and housing assistance. Towards the end of the 1960s, war bills, inflation, and oil crises were taking a toll on the economy, and America entered 1980 with lackluster economic predictions.

Migration and Immigration

As the country grew, its education and industrial growth continued to draw large populations of immigrants looking for better opportunities. The Immigration and Naturalization Act of 1965 replaced a varying system of quotas for ethnic origins with a system that focused on skills and family connections. Over the subsequent decades, this allowed for greater immigration from Asia than had happened prior to the Act. In the first five years, since the passage of the Act, immigrants fleeing war-torn Southeast Asia, and the oppressive communist regimes in Europe grew at large rates. In the three decades following passage of the Act of 1965, more than 18 million legal immigrants entered the United States, more than three times the number admitted over the preceding thirty years.

Social Movements

The social movements of the 1950s, 60s, and 70s were important in shaping future leaders of American industry (who would lead companies in the 80s and 90s). The counterculture of hippies, the feminist perspectives, and the non-conformists all came together to challenge government policy and push for legislation. The Equal Rights Amendment was passed by Congress in 1966, but not ratified by the states. But, this along with Roe v. Wade pushed the women's movements into the limelight. Colleges also became the breeding grounds for rebellion, and the counterculture of non-conformism became the norm for artists, hippies, and musicians of the period.

Not everyone in America embraced the new culture, and religious conservatism started to reappear at the grassroots levels around issues like abortion, tradition gender roles, affirmative action, and the nuclear family. Southern segregationists like the Ku Klux Clan rejected the civil rights movements, and continued to terrorize individuals.

By 1980, the Communists had come and gone. While communism still existed in several countries, it no longer had the ability to spread. The Cold War had ended and people's attention shifted to a domestic agenda. The 1980s ushered in a new conservatism, and a chance to beat back inflation and other missteps of the previous decade.

Summary of Period 9: 1980–Present

What You Should Know Before Reading This Chapter

- Ronald Reagan was a conservative president in the 1980s.
- The "cold war" ended when the Soviet Union disbanded in the 1990s.
- The War on Terror began after the 9/11 attacks on the Pentagon and World Trade Center.

What you Will Learn By Reading This Chapter

- Ronald Reagan came to the White House in 1980, bringing a sharply conservative view to government. Taxes were cut and industries were de-regulated. At the same time, he sought to increase the strength of the military.
- With the tumbling of the Berlin wall in 1989 and the end of the Soviet Union in 1991, the "cold war" was finally over. The purpose of military spending was then put in question.
- The cold war was replaced a decade later by a new and insidious enemy--terrorists. With the 9/11 attacks on the World Trade Center and the Pentagon, America launched into a war on terror that continues to this day. Troops were sent to Afghanistan and Iraq.
- Advances in technology have been tremendous, as the internet came into being during this period.
- The 1990s savings and loan crisis highlighted shady mortgage lending practices.
- In 2008, dubious mortgage lending practices by banks were again the target of attention. Many land speculators losing their entire investment. Recent economic improvements have given hope to many, and the future looks brighter than before.

Unprecedented growth in information technology and social media have transformed not only the United States but the entire world. Truly the world has shrunk, as nearly instantaneous communication anywhere in the globe can occur for free on the internet, and the masses freely buy and sell en masse on Ebay and Amazon. From 1980 onwards, the United States saw enormous economic growth in its industry, a growing population, and an increased standard of living for most. Around the world, more nations saw domestic uprisings within its borders for greater freedom and rule of law. Much of both the economic growth and the rebellions against entrenched governments came due to the availability and access to information technology and social media. While the last global age that changed the world had to do with mechanization and industry, the 21st century's growth and lifestyle impacts seemed to come from Information Technology and the democratization it enables.

The 1980s ushered in an era of conservative political administrations. The policies of President Reagan, and of President Bush senior and junior, dominated government action in the economy and defense. Clinton removed trade barriers in North America and attempted to create a universal health care program. The political actors of the 1980s and 90s laid many of the seeds for the technological revolution of the 21st century.

Ronald Reagan came into office in 1980, running an "outsider" campaign against Jimmy Carter. A conservative, Reagan emphasized that America was inherently good and stable, but needed a new direction and leader. Carter meanwhile, seemed to run a campaign blaming Americans for their self-indulgence and selfish attitude.

Carter and Reagan were opposite personality types. While Carter seemed to complain about the state of the country as a by-product of the self-empowerment movement, Reagan marched into the primaries, with a can-do attitude, and a charismatic presence. The following passage is considered a key event from their debates that stands out as one example of their approaches, and is sometimes credited with Reagan's landslide victory in November:

"…many observers thought Carter was the better of the two, but Reagan was more relaxed and confident. When Carter accurately pointed out Reagan's record of opposition to the Medicare program in the hopes of portraying his opponent an extremist, Reagan ignored the charge and softly replied, "There you go again," a line he had rehearsed in debate practice. He wound up the debate with an effective iteration of his basic campaign theme asking Americans to make their decision on the basis of the Carter administration's record: "Are you better off than you were four years ago? Is it easier for you to go and buy things in the stores than it was four years ago? Is there more or less unemployment in the country than there was four years ago? Is America as respected throughout the

Key Concept 9.1

A newly ascendant conservative movement achieved several political and policy goals during the 1980s and continued to strongly influence public discourse in the following decades.

world as it was?" For voters who answered "no" to these questions, Reagan was the clear alternative." Reagan came into office on a landslide vote.

Finally, it was the economic challenges of the 1970s—the high inflation, the high unemployment rates, the oil crisis, and to some a lackluster foreign policy that ended the decade with the taking of American hostages by Iranian rebels. Held for over a year, it was an epic event that ended with the release of the hostages on the first day of Reagan's presidency.

Reagan's eight years in office from 1980 to 1988 included his push for supply-side economics, which translated into tax cuts for companies, whereby the companies would turn around and invest that money into growing their company (hiring more employees, investing in research, new equipment, etc.). Reagan also deregulated several government functions into private industries (telecommunications, the airlines, banking, and the environment). Not all of this worked immediately, and it would take another 10–15 years with the advent of the Information Technology revolution, before the US rose out of the economic doldrums of the 1970s.

Reagan was a big believer in defense, creating the SDI initiative—Strategic Defense Initiative, a space-based missile shield system. A huge financial investment of billions, it was heavily criticized. It eventually became the theater missile defense system that the US now has with its NATO allies. Reagan was also criticized for the Iran-Contra affair, a plan to funnel funds to the Contras in Nicaragua, by evading Congressional approval.

George H. W. Bush followed Reagan as president, and lasted one term. He is most remembered for saying this during his campaign: "Read my lips. No new taxes." It was a promise he had to renege on, as the Persian Gulf War, which was required to oust the Iraqis from the Kuwaiti oil fields, drained America's coffers.

After Bush, William Clinton came into office, and remained in office for two terms. He has been remembered for the Monica Lewinsky affair, where he was impeached by the US House of Representatives for perjury, obstruction of justice, and abuse of power, but acquitted by the Senate, allowing Clinton to finish his second term in office. Clinton failed at creating a universal health care plan, but did pass the North American Free Trade Agreement (NAFTA), which removed trade restrictions between the United States, Canada and Mexico. The gay rights movement had grown over the 1980s and 90s, and Clinton in response, instituted the "don't ask don't tell" policy in the military—the first governmental action on gay rights.

Clinton was followed by George W. Bush (the son of the first Bush president), and the election of 2000 made history when the Supreme Court intervened in the vote recount in Florida. The US Constitution states that the President is the winner of the Electoral College votes, and all Electoral College votes are given to the winner of a state. In the state of Florida, it appeared that Al Gore had beaten

George Bush, but because of inconsistencies among the various districts in the state, in how they counted the marked ballots (the hanging chad controversy), the state election commission conducted a recount. The case was rapidly taken to the Supreme Court, which ruled that the recount must be stopped, because different standards were being used to count the votes, and the State Secretary of Florida declared Bush as the winner. This was a controversial decision in the United States at the time, and many Democrats who had voted for Al Gore continued to debate the decision for much of Bush's term.

George W. Bush was followed by another history-making president—Barack Obama became the first African American to ascend to the White House in 2008. Many saw this as the end to a long struggle for civil rights.

The Technology Revolution

The 1980s saw the start of a technology revolution that sowed the seeds for the Information Age of the 21st century. The industrial age of the early and mid-twentieth century had given way to a new kind of technology—portable, personal, and adaptable. Many of the most popular consumer products today saw their origin in the 1980s. To see just how much happened in this decade, here are a dozen technologies that became popular in the 1980s: personal computers, CDs, walkmans, VCRs, camcorders, video game consoles, cable television, answering machines, and fax machines all became popular during this time.

Cable television became the standard in many homes, and ushered in a plethora of channels—two famous ones were MTV and CNN. MTV became the first music video channel, and their early slogan "I want my MTV" still resonates today. A new generation of kids grew up watching their rock stars on videos and not just listening to music on the radio or records. Walkmans, CD, and headphones, allowed music to become portable. The Cable News Network (CNN) earned its stripes by broadcasting Desert Storm I in 1991—live on TV. Millions watched as US tanks drove into Kuwait City and liberated Kuwait. The age of live and portable media had started.

Apple and IBM unveiled the personal computer in the early 1980s, which started a computing revolution in American homes. Now, word processing, spreadsheet calculations, and even games like chess and ping-pong could be played on a computer. California's Silicon Valley was at the heart of a venture investing phenomena that would see numerous start-ups in the next few decades that would personalize the information revolution and bring communications to phones, tablets, and TV's.

The growth in technology for personal and business use also led to economic booms. Inflation and unemployment dropped though the years, and United States saw annual economic growth rates of 2% to 5%. Around the world, China

Key Concept 9.2

Moving into the 21st century, the nation experienced significant technological, economic, and demographic changes.

and India also grew their economies exponentially at 7% to 9% annually, as they joined the information age with their billion plus populations.

The world became interconnected in a myriad of ways—now Facebook, Twitter, and other social media sites allowed the young, the disenfranchised, and the revolutionaries to connect around their social causes. The Arab spring—the activist revolutions in Tanzania, Egypt, and Turkey—were citizen uprisings that arose independently and spread across the Arab world in 2011. The movement originated in Tunisia in December 2010 and quickly took hold in Egypt, Libya, Syria, Yemen, Bahrain, Saudi Arabia, and Jordan. It was the first time that social media had been used on a mass scale to call for protests in the Middle East.

Economic Growth and Crashes

Several key events shaped the economic growth of the post 1980s decades. The stock market grew exponentially, but also suffered huge losses in 1987, 2001, and 2008. The savings and loan (S&L) crises of the 1990s showed that small banks were investing people's savings and retirement funds in risky bonds and investment. The S&Ls had issued long-term loans at fixed interest rates that were lower than the interest rate at which they could borrow. The government bailout of the banks cost almost $150 billion.

Through the 1990s and 2000s, white-collar crime became rampant as companies and individuals mismanaged savings and retirement accounts. People like Michael Milken, Charles Keating, the Enron Corporation, Bernie Ebbers, and Bernard Maddoff became the villains of the "wild west" of stock trading. The stock market became a sign of a burgeoning economy, where wealth was made by speculating on futures, and globally connected markets made tracking and monitoring difficult. The stock market created many new mechanisms of trading—margins, junk bonds, futures, and mutual funds—than in the previous years. As the stock market and investing phenomena unveiled its dark side, government regulation and oversight caught up with more reporting requirements.

In the post-2010 years, cybercrime has had a major effect on the economy. Phishing, hacking, denial of service, stealing financial information, credit card losses, and spoofing are causing economic fluctuations in national growth. It is too early to understand the impact this will have as more and more players from Eastern Europe, Asia, and the Middle East join the cyber world for financial gain.

Immigration

Immigration to the United States changed in the 1980s and 1990s. While immigrants moved to the United States for work and opportunity, an increasing number came for higher education. The Immigration and Naturalization Act of 1965 had abolished an earlier quota system based on national origin and established a new immigration policy based on reuniting immigrant families and attracting skilled labor to the United States. This began to change the makeup of the emigrating populations with a greater number coming from Asia and Latin America, than from Europe.

In the 2000 census, Asian Americans were 3.6 percent of the population of 281 million, and Latinos and Hispanics reported in at 12.6 percent of the population. Over the last two decades, two issues have dominated the political discourse on immigration—the granting of H1-B visas for skilled labor entrants and the illegal migration across the southern US border from Mexico. Both have been issues in congressional and national elections. A report in early 2009 by the DHS's Office of Immigration Statistics estimated the number of "unauthorized immigrants" in the United States at 10.7 million, down from 11.6 million in 2008.

The demographic changes in the last few decades have contributed to the economic growth of the country, and brought diversity to the forefront of the national agenda, as Asian Americans and Hispanics ascended the political and business hierarchies.

End of the Cold War

The Cold War is considered to have lasted from 1947 to 1991. In the 1990s, with the fracturing of the Soviet Union into smaller countries, America's one common enemy of the post-World War II era ceased to exist. With the fall of the Berlin Wall in 1989, the Iron Curtain of the 1950s came down. Now American diplomats sought to create a New World Order based on democracy, free markets, and Western culture. Critical improvements in telecommunications made it possible to stream or broadcast Western culture, media, and goods to previously closed economies. Email and e-commerce entered the lexicon of commonplace words.

Foreign policy involved signing bi-lateral trade agreements for products, manufacturing, and research partnerships. With the breakup of the Soviet Union, many considered the United States the only remaining superpower. The US meanwhile shifted its focus into using its troops to support humanitarian missions in Yugoslavia and Turkey, among many other nations. A new term, "rogue states", was used to refer to nations such as North Korea and Iran, who were seen as violating international laws, humanitarian rules, and possibly developing a nuclear weapons program.

War on Terrorism

The War on Terror started after the September 11, 2001 attacks on the World Trade Center and the Pentagon. Terrorists commandeered four airplanes, and flew three of them into buildings. The fourth crashed into a field in Pennsylvania. This was a strategic and planned attack by a relatively new terror organization calling

Key Concept 9.3

The end of the Cold War and new challenges to US leadership forced the nation to redefine its foreign policy and role in the world.

itself Al Qaeda. Over 3000 innocent Americans died that day. This was the first time since Pearl Harbor that an outside actor had attacked the US on its own soil.

In response, President Bush ordered the attacks on Iraq and Afghanistan, eventually leading to an occupation of the two countries. Several years later, Saddam Hussein was captured and hanged, and Osama Bin Laden was shot, ending the leadership of two rogue actors with heavy anti-US sentiment.

Over the years, the War on Terror also resulted in the establishment of the Department of Homeland Security to safeguard domestic US areas, passage of the Patriot Act, and creation of the Transportation Security Administration to oversee airport security.

The War on Terror also resulted in strong powers given to monitoring and surveilling US citizens and residents. The Patriot Act, in effect, from 2011 to 2015, allowed government agencies to use roving wiretaps, search business records, and conduct surveillance of "lone wolves" — individuals suspected of terrorism-related activities, but not linked to terrorist groups. It also allowed the National Security Agency to monitor communications of ordinary citizens through their email and cell phone accounts. This was seen by many as a trampling of individual freedoms and the right to privacy. After the Edward Snowden revelations in 2013, the Patriot Act was allowed to expire in 2015, and replaced by the USA Freedom Act in June 2015, which reinstated the powers with the exception of the NSA "carte-blanche" surveillance.

Today, terrorism remains an avenue for those with an agenda against the United States or any allied country. The terrorists have built sophisticated information networks in the IT age, to allow them to tap into funding from sympathizers and to recruit new members.

In summary, how does one think about the post-1980 years? One way to look at the three decades after 1980 is as follows: the information age replaced the industrial age, the war on terrorism replaced the cold war, liberal movements for gay rights replaced civil rights movements, social media replaced newspapers, the internet replaced television…. and so on and so forth. It is too early to know the full impacts the decades after 1980 will have on the United States and the world, but suffice to say, that the world is in the midst of its next revolution.

SECTION VI:
Sample Test One

Sample Test One

Instructions

Section I, Part A of this exam contains 55 multiple-choice questions. Fill in only the circles for numbers 1 through 55 on your multiple-choice answer sheet. Because this section offers only four answer options for each question, do not mark the (E) answer circle for any question.

Indicate all of your answers to the multiple-choice questions on the multiple-choice answer sheet. No credit will be given for anything written in this exam booklet, but you may use the booklet for notes or scratch work. After you have decided which of the suggested answers is best, completely fill in the corresponding circle on the multiple-choice answer sheet. Give only one answer to each question. If you change an answer, be sure that the previous mark is erased completely. Here is a sample question and answer.

Sample Quesstion

Chicago is a
  (A) state
  (B) city
  (C) country
  (D) continent

Sample Answer

Ⓐ ● Ⓒ Ⓓ Ⓔ

Use your time effectively, working as quickly as you can without losing accuracy. Do not spend too much time on any one question. Go on to other questions and come back to the ones you have not answered if you have time. It is not expected that everyone will know the answers to all of the multiple-choice questions.

Your total score on the multiple-choice section is based only on the number of questions answered correctly. Points are not deducted for incorrect answers or unanswered questions.

UNITED STATES HISTORY SECTION I, Part A

Time: 55 minutes 55 Questions

Directions: Each of the questions or incomplete statements below is followed by four suggested answers or completions. Select the one that is best in each case and then fill in the appropriate letter in the corresponding space on the answer sheet.

Questions 1–3 refer to the passage below:

> "We think, therefore, that associations may be entered into, the object of which is to adapt measures that may have a tendency to impoverish another, that is, to diminish his gains and profits, and yet so far from being criminal or unlawful, the object may be highly meritorious and public spirited. The legality of such an association will therefore depend upon the means to be used for its accomplishment...."
>
> *Justice Lemard Shaw, Commonwealth v. Hunt, 1842*
> *(portion of the unanimous opinion written by Justice Shaw).*

1. To what does the word "associations" refer to in Justice Shaw's opinion?

    (A) Educational groups
    (B) Immigrant groups
    (C) Workers' groups
    (D) Protestors

2. What group does the court believe may be "impoverished" by joining together of workers?

    (A) The workers
    (B) The labor unions
    (C) Government
    (D) Factory owners

3. What is the significance of the court's decision?

    (A) It precipitated the prison reform movement.
    (B) It explained what a conspiracy was.
    (C) It provided impetus for the women's suffrage movement.
    (D) It made it possible for unions to organize and grow.

Questions 4–6 refer to the passage below:

"…the power of the SEC [Securities Exchange Commission] resided principally in just two provisions, both of them ingeniously simple. The first mandated disclosure of detailed information, such as balance sheets, profit and loss statements, and the names and compensation of corporate officers, about firms whose securities were publicly traded. The second required verification of that information by independent auditors using standardized accounting procedures."

"In the financial and housing sectors, the New Deal built structures of stability by the inventively simple devices of standardizing and promulgating relevant information, and by introducing industry-wide self-insurance schemes that calmed jittery markets and offered dependable safeguards to capital. In many other sectors, the New Deal's technique was somewhat less artful; it was, simply, to suppress competition, or at least to modulate its destructive effects. But everywhere the objective was the same: to create a uniquely American system of risk-reduced, or risk-managed, capitalism."

What the New Deal Did, DAVID M. KENNEDY,
Political Science Quarterly Vol. 124, No. 2 (Summer 2009), p. 256; 259

4. **From reading Kennedy's excerpt above, which of the following was a major driving principle of the Securities Exchange Commission?**

   (A) Capitalism should be replaced by socialism.
   (B) Corporations were believed to operate appropriately and efficiently without interference from regulatory bodies.
   (C) Monopolies on financial investment information should cease, as they were being exploited by individuals.
   (D) Shareholders of publicly traded companies did not need to be transparent in their financial information.

5. **The Glass-Steagall Act was intended to solve the problems started by which event in early twentieth century US economic history?**

   (A) The Great Chicago Fire
   (B) The "Dust Bowl"
   (C) The Cross of Gold speech, delivered by William Jennings Bryan
   (D) The Wall Street Crash

6. Which of the following factors did not contribute to reduced unemployment and a changing labor market during the Second World War?

   (A) Revenue Acts passed during the War that resulted in increased federal tax collections
   (B) The Labor Management Relations Act (a.k.a. Taft–Hartley Act)
   (C) Conscription resulted in fewer men working in the country
   (D) Creation of the Fair Employment Practice Committee (FEPC)

Questions 7–9 refer to the passage below:

> If you were to see, for a moment, one of the streams in the great current which is always pouring through New York, go down a Summer afternoon to the North River wharves…As you approach the end you come upon a noisy crowd of strange faces and stranger costumes…Some are just welcoming an old face,…some are letting down the huge trunks, some swearing…at the endless noise and distractions. They bear the plain marks of the Old World. Healthy, stout frames, and low, degraded faces with many stamps of inferiority…It is a new world to them—oppression, bitter poverty behind—here, hope, freedom, and a chance to work, and food to the laboring man…Everyone in the great City who can make a living from the freshly arrived immigrant, is here…Very many…will start tomorrow at once for the far West. Some will hang about the German boarding-houses, each day losing their money,… until they at last seek a refuge in Ward's island, or settle down in the eleventh Ward, to add to the great mass of foreign poverty and misery there gathered…
>
> *Article published in the* New York Daily Times *in 1853.*

7. What was the intent of this writer?

   (A) To show that America welcomed the immigrants
   (B) To explain cities were having problems handling the flood of migration
   (C) To describe the wharf scene for the paper's readers
   (D) To explain that immigrants often began a westward trek after arriving in New York

8. Why does the article refer to the German boarding houses?

   (A) Fewer German immigrants arrived during the 1850s than immigrants from other nations.
   (B) The Germans maintained the best boarding houses in the city at that time.
   (C) The German boarding house owners were more interested in taking money from the boarders than providing places to stay.
   (D) The ship that was arriving carried primarily German immigrants.

9. Which group or person might have been least likely to be on the dock at the arrival of the immigrant ship?

   (A) A young German peddling strawberries or other fruit
   (B) A moustached peasant in a Tyrolean hat
   (C) A runner from a German hotel
   (D) A young peasant girl with a bare head, a colored headdress, or fringed coat

Questions 10–12 refer to the passage below:

> In order to live a religious and moral life worthy of the name, they feel it is necessary to come out in some degree from the world, and to form themselves into a community of property, so far as to exclude competition and the ordinary rules of trade; while they reserve sufficient private property, or the means of obtaining it, for all purposes of independence, and isolation at will.
>
> *Elizabeth Peabody, writing about Brook Farm in 1843.*

10. What is the writer trying to explain?

    (A) The reasons why Andrew Jackson's campaign was successful
    (B) The reasons for utopian societies
    (C) The reasons why Southerners settled Texas
    (D) The reasons why employers established employer-owned towns

11. What was the goal of utopian community of Brook Farm?

    (A) Creating a religious community
    (B) Establishing a community for freed slaves
    (C) Establishing a socialist community based on political ideas
    (D) Creating a society where community goals were more important than self-interest

12. In the time period between 1840 and 1848, in which parts of the United States were most utopian communities established?

    (A) The East and the Midwest
    (B) The East and the South
    (C) The South and the Midwest
    (D) The South and the Southwest

Questions 13–15 refer to the passages below:

> "All men are born free and equal, and have certain natural, essential, and unalienable rights; among which may be reckoned the right of enjoying and defending their lives and liberties; that of acquiring, possessing, and protecting property; in fine, that of seeking and obtaining their safety and happiness."
>
> *Massachusetts 1780 Declaration of Rights, authored primarily by John Adams*

> "We hold these truths to be self-evident, that all men are created equal, that they are endowed by their Creator with certain unalienable Rights, that among these are Life, Liberty and the pursuit of Happiness."
>
> *US Declaration of Independence, 2nd paragraph, authored primarily by Thomas Jefferson*

13. **From the quotes above, what was the primary difference between John Adams and Thomas Jefferson in their expressions of the most fundamental of all rights?**

    (A) Adams thought rights were not inherent but needed to be "acquired," "defended," or "obtained," while Jefferson viewed rights as already being possessed by all men.
    (B) Both of them thought life and liberty were less important than happiness.
    (C) Adams, who did not own slave "property," thought the protection of private property needed to be mentioned and emphasized, while Jefferson emphasized the pursuit of happiness instead.
    (D) There is no difference in their views on rights.

14. **Which of the following would be most likely to disagree with the statements by Adams and Jefferson on rights?**

    (A) A slaveholder in 1861 who supported secession from the union
    (B) An army officer assigned to take charge of a Japanese-American internment camp in Utah during World War II
    (C) An Oklahoma settler who took over a portion of Indian land, but who had never met an Indian
    (D) An American soldier in the Mexican-American War

15. **Both excerpts are most clearly an example of which of the following developments in the late 1700s in America?**

    (A) Expansionism into the western frontier
    (B) Growing sectionalism and contention over slavery
    (C) A defiance of the rule of law and governmental authority
    (D) An expression of the right to rebel as a "law of nature" possessed by all men

Questions 16–18 refer to the passage below:

> "Madison, and to an even greater extent Jefferson, seemed to think that economic policy consisted of getting out of the way to allow the natural laws of economic recovery and growth to proceed. But Hamilton thought the conditions for economic development needed to be created, then enduringly overseen. His model was England, with its national bank, regulated commerce, and powerful finance ministers...Hamilton regarded the national debt as "a national blessing," for it permitted the clustering of resources in the hands of a small group of enterprising men who would invest and not just spend it. For Madison, on the other hand, "a Public Debt is a Public curse."
>
> *Joseph J. Ellis, historian, Founding Brothers:*
> *The Revolutionary Generation (pp. 63–64), published in 2003.*

16. **The thinking of Madison and Jefferson about economic policy most closely correlates to which of the following?**

    (A) "Reaganomics" of the 1980s
    (B) FDR's "New Deal" policies of the 1930s
    (C) Abraham Lincoln's views of the best way to fund the civil war
    (D) The "free silver" movement of the 1890s

17. **Hamilton's belief of the need for a national bank**

    (A) was Hamilton's main financial goal for the country in 1791, followed by his determination that the federal government should avoid assumption of state debts.
    (B) gained sufficient support from Congress for them to establish a permanent national bank in 1791, which has lasted to this day.
    (C) was later adopted by Madison as well.
    (D) included plans for paper money to be printed within the bank itself.

18. **One significant result of the debate over the economic policies between Hamilton on one hand, and Jefferson and Madison on the other, was**

    (A) the creation of open immigration policies by Congress in 1791, as a way to spur economic growth.
    (B) passage of a federal law banning slavery after the year 1808.
    (C) one factor which contributed to creation of the two party system.
    (D) Jefferson's defeat of Adams in the election of 1800.

Questions 19–21 refer to the picture below:

North Carolina bill, 1775.

19. **The image above best demonstrates which of the following?**

    (A) The popularity of paper money after the revolutionary war.
    (B) The unpopularity of paper money after the revolutionary war.
    (C) How paper money greatly increases in value if the government backs it up with gold and silver.
    (D) How Virginia differed from the other states in handling devalued currency.

20. **The high rate of inflation demonstrated by the note above comes closest to which of the following periods?**

    (A) The great depression in the 1930s
    (B) "Reaganomics" in the 1980s
    (C) The 1920s
    (D) The panic of 1837

21. **After the Revolutionary War, use of paper notes such as that shown above was**

    (A) generally considered good for the country.
    (B) encouraged by some states as a way to decrease debt, by enacting laws forcing creditors to accept paper money.
    (C) one of the 3 steps in Hamilton's plan to improve the economy.
    (D) banned in the Northwest Territory.

Questions 22–24 refer to the passage below:

> Mr. Speaker, Mr. President, Members of the Congress:
>
> I speak tonight for the dignity of man and the destiny of democracy. I urge every member of both parties, Americans of all religions and of all colors, from every section of this country, to join me in that cause. At times history and fate meet at a single time in a single place to shape a turning point in man's unending search for freedom. So it was at Lexington and Concord. So it was a century ago at Appomattox. So it was last week in Selma, Alabama. There, long-suffering men and women peacefully protested the denial of their rights as Americans.
>
> *President Lyndon B. Johnson's address "We Shall Overcome", before a joint session of Congress, 1965.*

22. **The speech given by President Johnson refers to his support of the**

    (A) Civil Rights Act.
    (B) Equal Rights Amendment.
    (C) Voting Rights Act.
    (D) Economic Opportunity Act.

23. **The federal voting rights laws passed in the 1950s and 1960s were designed to**

    (A) return control of voting regulations to the state.
    (B) remove racial barriers to voting.
    (C) extend suffrage to American women.
    (D) prevent recent immigrants from voting.

24. **The Voting Rights Act of 1965**

    (A) banned racial discrimination in voting nationwide.
    (B) tried to eliminate poverty through spending on medical programs.
    (C) allowed women to vote.
    (D) provided more federal funding for public education.

Questions 25–27 refer to the passage below:

"This, then, is held to be the duty of the man of Wealth: First, to set an example of modest, unostentatious living, shunning display or extravagance; to provide moderately for the legitimate wants of those dependent upon him; and after doing so to consider all surplus revenues which come to him simply as trust funds, which he is called upon to administer, and strictly bound as a matter of duty to administer in the manner which, in his judgment, is best calculated to produce the most beneficial results for the community—the man of wealth thus becoming the mere agent and trustee for his poorer brethren, bringing to their service his superior wisdom, experience, and ability to administer, doing for them better than they would or could do for themselves."

Andrew Carnegie (June 1889) "Wealth",
North American Review Vol. 148, Issue 391, 653–665

"Millions of property were turned over without consideration to railroad companies… The veto power conferred by the Constitution as a remedy for ill-considered legislation, was turned by him [President Andrew Johnson] into a weapon of offence against Congress and into an instrument to beat down the just opposition which his usurpation had aroused."

Charles Sumner (1868) Expulsion of the President: opinion of
Hon. Charles Sumner, of Massachusetts, in the case of the impeachment
of Andrew Johnson, President of the United States.
Washington Government Printing Office

25. **Which of the following was not a factor of Andrew Carnegie's philosophy, according to the first excerpt?**

(A) Individual intuition and economic success play a large role in justifying one's position in society

(B) A "survival of the fittest" mentality, as proposed by contemporary Social Darwinist thinkers

(C) The philanthropic obligation of the wealthy to distribute their wealth, in order to aid people that are disadvantaged

(D) The belief that a small group of capitalists should not be allowed to provide financial advice to, or control the stocks of, many individual corporations.

26. As the second excerpt describes, there was growing resentment towards the growing power of monopolies, and the land that was being awarded to them. This resentment was particularly due to government corruption, which escalated in the decades following President Johnson's impeachment. What act was signed in 1883 to limit this corruption by requiring government jobs to be awarded on the basis of merit?

(A) Pendleton Civil Service Reform Act
(B) Amnesty Act
(C) Bland-Allison Act
(D) Judiciary Act

27. Cornelius Vanderbilt was the major railroad monopoly owner in the country, thriving due to a wide range of technological and engineering innovations. Which of the following did not contribute to the growth of railroads during this time?

(A) The widespread use of mass-produced, standardized, interchangeable parts
(B) The transition from whale oil to coal-burning power sources
(C) A boost in demand to expand the Underground Railroad network, which had reached its peak in the 1850s
(D) The refinement of lubricating products from petroleum

Questions 28–30 refers to the passage below:

> "During the last quarter of the nineteenth century, public interest in American Indians surged...The movement culminated with the passage of the General Allotment Act of 1887, commonly called the Dawes Act, which authorized the president to allot Native reservations. The participants in this movement to assimilate American Indians...shared a belief that by imposing their culture on America Indian people, they were fulfilling the destiny of their nation and giving American Indians the greatest gift possible—civilization, as they defined it."
>
> *Stremlau, Rose (2005) "To Domesticate and Civilize Wild Indians":*
> *Allotment and the Campaign to Reform Indian Families, 1875–1887.*
> *Journal of Family History, Vol. 30 No. 3, 268*

28. **President Grover Cleveland signed the Dawes Act on February 8th 1887, referring to it as the "Indian Emancipation Act". According to Stremlau, in what sense did he, and others, believe that these reforms were promoting Native emancipation?**

    (A) Native American culture would be preserved and protected through US governmental measures such as the Ghost Dance Movement.
    (B) By assimilating Native Americans and introducing them to American values they would become free from tribal social structures that prevented individualism and progress.
    (C) Native Americans would be allowed to continue their tribal governments on reservations, but with the benefits of the "Gilded Age", such as electricity and department stores.
    (D) Native Americans would be accepted to the American Federation of Labor as unskilled laborers, freeing them from their unemployment problems.

29. **Between 1862 and 1898 a range of factors contributed to Westward expansion. Which of the following did not occur between those years?**

    (A) The merging of the Union Pacific and Central Pacific railroads
    (B) The Massacre at Wounded Knee
    (C) The United States Arizona Territory was established
    (D) The California Gold Rush in the Sierra Nevada

30. **This period was marked by the US government's generally laissez-faire attitude towards corporate expansion and economic affairs. However, in 1886 what case resulted in a Supreme Court decision limited control of interstate commerce to Congress, resulting in the Interstate Commerce Commission being established in 1887?**

    (A) Dred Scott v. Sandford
    (B) Northern Securities Co. v. United States
    (C) Plessy v. Ferguson
    (D) Wabash, St. Louis & Pacific Railway Co. v. Illinois

Questions 31–33 refer to the picture below:

Cigar Makers' International Union of America union label Published in "Cigar Makers' Official Journal," Jan. 15, 1912

31. Urbanization in cities such as New York and Philadelphia—and even more rapidly in the West—provided employment opportunities and a standard of living that attracted people from many countries. However, immigration was not viewed in a positive light by many. What act was signed by President Chester Arthur in 1882 to restrict immigration?

    (A) Chinese Immigration Act
    (B) Alien Contract Labor Law
    (C) Chinese Exclusion Act
    (D) Burlingame-Seward Treaty

32. Two waves of immigrants arrived in American during the 1800s, with the "New Immigrants" arriving mainly from the 1880s onwards. The New Immigrants were

    (A) mainly from Southern and Eastern Europe.
    (B) arriving from democratic countries.
    (C) literate and skilled.
    (D) mainly Protestant.

33. In contrast to developments in urban centers, there was growing resentment in rural environments. Between the 1870s and 1880s the Farmer's Alliance existed, working especially against the crop-lien credit system. Under which name did this alliance become a political party in 1891, following the McKinley Tariff Act that was passed the preceding year?

    (A) Free Soil Party
    (B) Vegetarian Party
    (C) Progressive Party
    (D) People's Party

Questions 34–36 refer to the passage below:

> There is a twofold liberty-natural (I mean as our nature is not corrupt) and civil or federal. The first is common to man with beasts and other creatures. By this, man, as he stands in relation to man simply, hath liberty to what he lists; it is a liberty to evil as well as to good. This liberty is incompatible and inconsistent with authority, and cannot endure the least restraint of the most just authority. The exercise and maintaining of this liberty make men grow more evil, and in time to be worse than brute beasts…This is that great enemy of truth and peace that wild beast, which all the ordinances of God are bent against, to restrain and subdue it.
>
> The other kind of liberty I call civil or federal; it may also be termed moral, in reference to the covenant between God and man, in the moral in reference of the covenant between God and man, in the moral law, and the politic covenants and constitutions, amongst men themselves. This liberty is the proper end and object of authority, and cannot subsist without it; and it is a liberty to that only which is good, just and honest.
>
> *John Winthrop, "City Upon a Hill", 1630.*

34. Winthrop's argument on liberty is most reflective of what major global movement of the 1600s?

(A) A change from cottage industry to industrial economics and mass production
(B) Philosophe arguments in favor of natural rights
(C) Roman Catholic influences from the counter reformation
(D) Protestant beliefs about creating a Biblical City on a Hill

35. Winthrop's argument on the nature of true freedom would have what significant impact on the development of the Northeastern colonies?

(A) The beginnings of a slave cotton economy
(B) Tensions between European settlers and the Native American tribes
(C) The development of the Puritan faith in Massachusetts
(D) The creation of a mercantile trade in timber and fish with England

36. Winthrop's argument about the nature of faith is most similar to which other American historical movement?

(A) The Civil Rights' movement call for racial freedom
(B) The Evangelical movement in the 1970s
(C) The Women's Rights movement of the 1960s
(D) The Progressive movement of the 1920s

Questions 37–39 refer to the passage below:

> On the Island Hispaniola was where the Spaniards first landed, as I have said. Here those Christians perpetrated their first ravages and oppressions against the native peoples. This was the first land in the New World to be destroyed and depopulated by the Christians, and here they began their subjection of the women and children, taking them away from the Indians to use them and ill use them, eating the food they provided with their sweat and toil. The Spaniards did not content themselves with what the Indians gave them of their own free will, according to their ability, which was always too little to satisfy enormous appetites, for a Christian eats and consumes in one day an amount of food that would suffice to feed three houses inhabited by ten Indians for one month. And they committed other acts of force and violence and oppression which made the Indians realize that these men had not come from Heaven. And some of the Indians concealed their foods while others concealed their wives and children and still others fled to the mountains to avoid the terrible transactions of the Christians.
>
> *Bartolome De Las Casas, "Brief Account of the Devastation of the Indies", 1542.*

37. De Las Casas' description of the treatment of the natives in Mexico reflects what major global relationship of the 1600s?

(A) Protestant reformers trying to establish a model Christian community
(B) The introduction of the slave trade for cash crops in the Caribbean
(C) European mercantile nations seeking out raw resources
(D) The consolidation of kingdoms into nation states

38. The treatment of the Native Americans in Mexico was most similar to

(A) the development of the cult of domesticity for women in the 1830s.
(B) the exclusion of the Chinese immigrants in the late 1800s.
(C) the Red Scare of the 1920s against Eastern European immigrants.
(D) the use of African labor in the 1830s for farming cotton.

39. The use of Native American labor by the Spanish in the 1600s led to what major impact on the global economy?

(A) The switch from mercantilism to capitalist economics
(B) The influx of silver into the global economy
(C) The use of indentured servants for agriculture in North America
(D) The development of mercantile wars in the 1700s

Questions 40–42 refer to the passage below:

> "I am not a Know-Nothing. That is certain. How could I be? How can any one who abhors the oppression of negroes, be in favor of degrading classes of white people? Our progress in degeneracy appears to me to be pretty rapid. As a nation, we begin by declaring that "all men are created equal." We now practically read it "all men are created equal, except negroes." When the Know-Nothings get control, it will read "all men are created equal, except negroes, and foreigners, and Catholics." When it comes to this I should prefer emigrating to some country where they make no pretense of loving liberty—to Russia, for instance, where despotism can be taken pure, and without the base alloy of hypocrisy."
>
> *Abraham Lincoln, letter to Joshua F. Speed, August 24, 1855*

40. Who were the Know Nothings?

(A) A political party that promoted the Alien and Sedition laws
(B) Catholic immigrants
(C) An anti-immigrant political party
(D) A group of uneducated farmers who supported slavery

41. What region had the most people who agreed with the Know-Nothing's philosophy?

(A) Northeast
(B) South
(C) Southwest
(D) California

42. All of the following are tenets of the Nativist philosophy EXCEPT

(A) the belief that the increasing numbers of immigrants were gaining too much political influence.
(B) the belief that only people born in the United States should hold elected office.
(C) the belief that Native American tribes should be removed to reservations.
(D) they were in favor of Protestant values and against Catholics.

Questions 43–45 refer to the passage below:

> "We are glad, now that we see the facts with no veil of false pretense about them, to fight thus for the ultimate peace of the world and for the liberation of its peoples, the German peoples included; for the rights of nations great and small and the privilege of men everywhere to choose their way of life and of obedience. The world must be made safe for democracy. Its peace must be planted upon the tested foundations of political liberty. We have no selfish ends to serve. We desire no conquest, no dominion. We seek no indemnities for ourselves, no material compensation for the sacrifices we shall freely make. We are but one of the champions of the rights of mankind. We shall be satisfied when those rights have been made as secure as the faith and the freedom of nations can make them."
>
> *Woodrow Wilson, War Messages, 65th Cong., 1st Sess. Senate Doc. No. 5, Serial No. 7264, Washington, D.C., 1917; pp. 3–8, passim*

43. **From the turn of the century onwards, debates over America's role in world affairs intensified. From reading the excerpt above, which of the following describes Woodrow Wilson's perspective on American foreign policy?**

    (A) Interventionist and imperialist
    (B) Interventionist and anti-imperialist
    (C) Isolationist and imperialist
    (D) Isolationist and anti-imperialist

44. **What conflict in 1898 enabled the United States' economic and military expansion in the Caribbean and Latin America, most significantly in Cuba and the Philippines?**

    (A) Philippine–American War
    (B) Ten Years War
    (C) Boxer Rebellion
    (D) Spanish-American War

45. **Woodrow Wilson's message to Congress about the need for US leadership in global conflicts is most similar to what other event?**

    (A) American isolation during the 1930s before World War II
    (B) American involvement in the Cold War in Southeast Asia
    (C) Washington's Neutrality Proclamation
    (D) American expansion in the 1830s under Manifest Destiny

Questions 46–48 refer to the picture below:

"For the Sunny South. An airship with a "Jim Crow" trailer" (Feb, 26th 1913) Puck Magazine

46. As the above satirical cartoon shows, during the early twentieth century technological innovations and modernization were not enjoyed by everyone equally. Which of the following occurred between 1910 and 1930 as a major consequence of the Jim Crow laws?

(A) The Niagara Movement was active in demanding desegregation and black suffrage

(B) Segregation was reduced in the Southern states, especially in hospitals and federal workplaces

(C) The abolishment of slavery with the ratification of the Thirteenth Amendment

(D) The first "Great Migration" of Africa-American communities from the South to northern industrial cities

47. After the First World War, xenophobic tensions resulted in a tremendous increase in the number of racial riots and labor strikes. Which of the following was not a cause of the period of fear and paranoia during 1919–20 known as the First Red Scare?

(A) Senator Joseph McCarthy's anti-communist campaigns

(B) The Sedition Act

(C) Labor strikes

(D) The Haymarket massacre

48. Which of the following most accurately describes the "Harlem Renaissance"?

   (A) Native American tribes campaigned for their own representatives in the United States government.
   (B) The belief many that the American government had the right to stretch their power over the entire continent, from coast to coast
   (C) Also known as the New Negro Movement, it was a period of cultural expression and a flourishing of the arts for many African-Americans.
   (D) A march of up to 10,000 African Americans in New York City, in opposition to the outbreak of anti-black violence during the East St. Louis massacres

Questions 49–52 refer to the passage below:

> The world beholds the peaceful triumphs of the industry of our emigrants. To us belongs the duty of protecting them adequately wherever they may be on our soil. The jurisdiction of our laws and the benefits of our republican institutions should be extended over them in the distant regions in which they have selected for their homes.
> *James K. Polk's March 4, 1845, inaugural address.*

49. Which view was President Polk expressing in this part of his inaugural address?

   (A) Containment
   (B) Isolationism
   (C) Imperialism
   (D) Expansionism

50. The practice of settling distant lands in the 1840s and 1850 was referred to as

   (A) Encroachment.
   (B) Manifest Destiny.
   (C) Imperialism.
   (D) Squatters' Rights.

51. What is the meaning of the wording "The world beholds the peaceful triumphs of the industry of our emigrants" in the president's address?

   (A) Immigrants have overcome the evils of industrialization in urban areas.
   (B) Immigrants believe their triumphs are related to their being able to settle in America.
   (C) The government approves the accomplishment of settling vast areas that will eventually become American land.
   (D) The government commends the immigrants for being frugal and hard working to attain American citizenship.

52. Which event is most similar to the ideas expressed by President Polk in his address?

   (A) American withdrawal from Vietnam in 1973
   (B) Lincoln's attempt to reunite the country at the beginning of the Civil War
   (C) Franklin Roosevelt's defense of American entry into WWII as the "arsenal of democracy"
   (D) American annexation of Hawaii over sugar tariffs

Questions 53–55 refer to the picture below:

J.E. Farwell & Co., Boston: Published by J. E. Farwell & Co., 1852.
Courtesy of the Library of Congress

53. What does the purpose of this cartoon appear to be?

   (A) Encourage immigrants
   (B) Discouraging foreign labor
   (C) Protesting immigration laws
   (D) Opposing present school laws

54. What conclusion can be reached about the name of the newspaper?

   (A) The paper does not believe that certain groups are patriotic Americans.
   (B) The paper believes taxes are too high because of immigrants.
   (C) Patriots must have always lived in America.
   (D) All immigrants affect the beliefs of patriotism of Americans.

55. **Which of the following does the American Patriot believe Catholic immigrants contribute?**

    (A) Lower taxes
    (B) Increased protection of American workers
    (C) A free school system
    (D) Corruption of morals

SECTION I, Part B

Time: 45 minutes 4 Questions

Directions: Read each question carefully and write your responses in the corresponding boxes on the free-response answer sheet.

Use complete sentences; an outline or bulleted list alone is not acceptable. On the actual test you may plan your answers in the exam booklet, but only your responses in the corresponding boxes on the free-response answer sheet will be scored.

"Under these impressions, my humble opinion is, that there is a call for decision. Know precisely what the insurgents aim at. If they have real grievances, redress them if possible; or acknowledge the justice of them, and your inability to do it in the present moment. If they have not, employ the force of government against them at once. If this is inadequate, all will be convinced that the superstructure is bad, or wants support."

"These are my sentiments. Precedents are dangerous things; let the reins of government then be braced and held with a steady hand, and every violation of the Constitution be reprehended: if defective, let it be amended, but not suffered to be trampled upon whilst it has an existence...."

George Washington to Henry Lee, October 31, 1786 writing about Shays' Rebellion

"I hold it that a little rebellion now and then is a good thing, and as necessary in the political world as storms in the physical... An observation of this truth should render honest republican governors so mild in their punishment of rebellions as not to discourage them too much. It is a medicine necessary for the sound health of government...."

"Let them take arms. The remedy is to set them right as to facts, pardon & pacify them. What signify a few lives lost in a century or two? The tree of liberty must be refreshed from time to time with the blood of patriots & tyrants. It is its natural manure."

Thomas Jefferson to James Madison, January 20th, 1787
Thomas Jefferson to William Smith, November 13th, 1787
Writing about the Shays' Rebellion

1. Using the excerpts above, answer parts A, B, and C.
   A. Briefly explain why Washington advocated a strong government response.

   B. Briefly explain why Jefferson supported exactly the opposite.

C. Provide one example of why the Articles of Confederation, in existence for ten years, were viewed to be too weak to maintain law and order during this rebellion.

The Big Stick in the Caribbean, 1904

2. Use the image above and your knowledge of history to answer A, B, and C.
   A. Explain Theodore Roosevelt's approach to foreign policy as depicted in the image.

B. Explain one similarity between this approach and the Cold War approach to maintaining peace.

C. Give one example of how the point of view you described in Part (a), was used by Theodore Roosevelt during his term.

"To establish such a right, it remains to show the relation of such an institution, to one or more of the specified powers of the Government. Accordingly, it is affirmed, that it has a relation, more or less direct, to the power of collecting taxes; to that of borrowing money; to that of regulating trade between the states; and to those of raising the maintaining fleets and armies. To the two former, the relation may be said to be immediate. And, in the last place, it will be argued, that it is clearly within the provision which authorizes the making of all needful rules and regulations concerning the property of the US, as the same has been practiced upon by the government."

Alexander Hamilton, "Statement on the Constitutionality of the National Bank" 1791.

The Constitution gives Congress the power to make all laws necessary and proper for carrying into execution the enumerated powers. But they can all be carried into execution without a bank. A bank, therefore, is not necessary, and consequently, not authorized by this phrase.

The Constitution allows only the means which are necessary, not those which are merely convenient for effecting the numerated powers. If such a latitude of construction be allowed to this phrase as to give any non enumerate power, it will go to every one…Therefore it was that the constitution restrained them to be necessary means; that is to say to those means, without which the grant of the power would be nugatory."

Thomas Jefferson, Statement on the Constitutionality of the National Bank, 1791.

3. **Based upon the two opinions stated above about the First National Bank of the United States, respond to A, B, C:**
   A. **Briefly explain Hamilton's argument on the National Bank.**

B. Briefly explain Jefferson's argument on the National Bank.

C. What types of freedom are the two leaders advocating for and how do you know this?

"Just as the period of American history from 1933 to the late 1960s… was chiefly one of liberal reform, so the past thirty-five years have been an era of conservatism…Without Reagan, the conservative movement would never have been as successful as it was. In his political personal, as well as his policies, Reagan embodied a new fusion of deeply conservative politics with some of the rhetoric and even a bit of the spirit of Franklin D. Roosevelt's New Deal and of John F. Kennedy's New Frontier…The impact of the sage of Regan is indicated even more strongly by the guiding assumptions and possibilities of American politics and government, and the hold they have on public opinion. Thirty years ago, the proposition that reducing taxes on the rich was the best solution for all economic problems inspired only a few on the right-wing fringe. Today, it drives the national domestic agenda and is so commonplace that it sometimes appears to have become the conventional wisdom.

Sean Wilentz, The Age of Reagan, 2008.

4. Using the excerpts above, answer parts A, B, and C.
   A. **Based upon the historian, Sean Wilentz, argument, explain his point about the significance of Ronald Reagan for American identity in the 1980s.**

B. Provide ONE piece of evidence about the rise of Reagan and his ability to gain American support.

C. What type of freedom did Reagan support and what type of freedom did he criticize?

UNITED STATES HISTORY SECTION II

Total Time: 1 hour, 35 minutes

Question 1 (Document-Based Question)
Suggested reading period: 15 minutes
Suggested writing period: 45 minutes

Directions: Question 1 is based on the accompanying documents. The documents have been edited for the purpose of this exercise. You are advised to spend 15 minutes reading and planning and 45 minutes writing your answer.

Write your responses on the lined pages that follow the question.

In your response you should do the following:
- State a relevant thesis that directly addresses all parts of the question.
- Support the thesis or a relevant argument with evidence from all, or all but one, of the documents.
- Incorporate analysis of all, or all but one, of the documents into your argument.
- Focus your analysis of each document on at least one of the following: intended audience, purpose, historical context, and/or point of view.
- Support your argument with analysis of historical examples outside the documents.
- Connect historical phenomena relevant to your argument to broader events or processes.

DOCUMENT 1

"The First Cotton Gin", an engraving from Harper's Magazine, 1869.
This carving depicts a roller gin, which preceded Eli Whitney's invention

DOCUMENT 2

Assenting to the "self-evident truth" maintained in the American Declaration of Independence, "that all men are created equal, and endowed by their Creator with certain inalienable rights—among which are life, liberty and the pursuit of happiness," I shall strenuously contend for the immediate enfranchisement of our slave population.

"I will be heard" – William Lloyd Garrison (1833?)

DOCUMENT 3

And on the 12th of May, 1828, I heard a loud noise in the heavens, and the Spirit instantly appeared to me and said the Serpent was loosened, and Christ had laid down the yoke he had borne for the sins of men, and that I should take it on and fight against the Serpent, for the time was fast approaching when the first should be last and the last should be first.

"The last shall be first" CONFESSIONS OF NAT TURNER (1831??)

DOCUMENT 4

Without planters there could be no cotton; without cotton no wealth. Without them Mississippi would be a wilderness, and revert to the aboriginal possessors. Annihilate them tomorrow, and this state and every southern state might be bought for a song. I am not advocating this system; but destroy it—and the southern states become at once comparative ciphers in the Union.

"Cotton and Negroes are the constant theme"
Selection from 1835 book The South-West J. H. Ingram

DOCUMENT 5

What would you have if the Union were dissevered? Why, sir, then the severed parts would be independent of each other—foreign countries! Slaves taken from the one into the other would then be like slaves now escaping from the United States into Canada. There would be no right of extradition; no right to demand your slaves; no right to appeal to the courts of justice to demand your slaves which escape, or the penalties for decoying them.

The Compromise of 1850 Henry Clay's address to Congress in February 1850

DOCUMENT 6

It is a great mistake to suppose that disunion can be effected by a single blow. The cords which bind these states together in one common Union are far too numerous and powerful for that. Disunion must be the work of time. It is only through a long process, and successively, that the cords can be snapped, until the whole fabric falls asunder. Already the agitation of the slavery question has snapped some of the most important, and has greatly weakened all the others, as I shall proceed to show.

The cords which bind the states together are not only many, but various in character. Among them, some are spiritual or ecclesiastical; some political; others social. Others pertain to the benefit conferred by the Union, and others to the feelings of duty and obligation.

"[The South] has little left to surrender" John C. Calhoun
Speech given to Congress 1850

DOCUMENT 7

…[W]e must not confound the rights of citizenship which a state may confer within its own limits, and the rights of citizenship as a member of the Union. It does not by any means follow, because he has all the rights and privileges of a citizen of a State, that he must be a citizen of the United States. He may have all of the rights and privileges of the citizen of a State, and yet not be entitled to the rights and privileges of a citizen in any other State. For, previous to the adoption of the Constitution of the United States, every State had the undoubted right to confer on whomever it pleased the character of a citizen, and to endow him with all its rights. But this character, of course, was confined to the boundaries of the State, and gave him no rights or privileges in other States beyond those secured to him by the laws of nations and the comity of States. Nor have the several States surrendered the power of conferring these rights and privileges by adopting the Constitution of the United States.

Dred Scott v. Sandford (1857) Decision: J: Roger B. Taney

1. Analyze how the issue of slavery led to increased sectional tensions between the 1830s-1850s.

Question 2 or Question 3
Suggested writing period: 35 minutes

Directions: Choose EITHER question 2 or question 3. You are advised to spend 35 minutes writing your answer. Write your responses on the lined pages that follow the questions.

In your response you should do the following:
- State a relevant thesis that directly addresses all parts of the question.
- Support your argument with evidence, using specific examples.
- Apply historical thinking skills as directed by the question.

2. Evaluate the extent to which United States involvement in the First World War in 1917–1918 contributed to maintaining continuity as well as fostering change in United States foreign policy and involvement in foreign affairs.

3. Compare and contrast the similarities and differences, as well as the purposes and goals, of Jacksonian democracy in the 1820s and 1830s, with FDR's New Deal programs 100 years later.

Answer Sheet For Sample Test One

1. Ⓐ Ⓑ Ⓒ Ⓓ Ⓔ
2. Ⓐ Ⓑ Ⓒ Ⓓ Ⓔ
3. Ⓐ Ⓑ Ⓒ Ⓓ Ⓔ
4. Ⓐ Ⓑ Ⓒ Ⓓ Ⓔ
5. Ⓐ Ⓑ Ⓒ Ⓓ Ⓔ
6. Ⓐ Ⓑ Ⓒ Ⓓ Ⓔ
7. Ⓐ Ⓑ Ⓒ Ⓓ Ⓔ
8. Ⓐ Ⓑ Ⓒ Ⓓ Ⓔ
9. Ⓐ Ⓑ Ⓒ Ⓓ Ⓔ
10. Ⓐ Ⓑ Ⓒ Ⓓ Ⓔ
11. Ⓐ Ⓑ Ⓒ Ⓓ Ⓔ
12. Ⓐ Ⓑ Ⓒ Ⓓ Ⓔ
13. Ⓐ Ⓑ Ⓒ Ⓓ Ⓔ
14. Ⓐ Ⓑ Ⓒ Ⓓ Ⓔ
15. Ⓐ Ⓑ Ⓒ Ⓓ Ⓔ
16. Ⓐ Ⓑ Ⓒ Ⓓ Ⓔ
17. Ⓐ Ⓑ Ⓒ Ⓓ Ⓔ
18. Ⓐ Ⓑ Ⓒ Ⓓ Ⓔ
19. Ⓐ Ⓑ Ⓒ Ⓓ Ⓔ
20. Ⓐ Ⓑ Ⓒ Ⓓ Ⓔ
21. Ⓐ Ⓑ Ⓒ Ⓓ Ⓔ
22. Ⓐ Ⓑ Ⓒ Ⓓ Ⓔ
23. Ⓐ Ⓑ Ⓒ Ⓓ Ⓔ
24. Ⓐ Ⓑ Ⓒ Ⓓ Ⓔ
25. Ⓐ Ⓑ Ⓒ Ⓓ Ⓔ
26. Ⓐ Ⓑ Ⓒ Ⓓ Ⓔ
27. Ⓐ Ⓑ Ⓒ Ⓓ Ⓔ
28. Ⓐ Ⓑ Ⓒ Ⓓ Ⓔ
29. Ⓐ Ⓑ Ⓒ Ⓓ Ⓔ
30. Ⓐ Ⓑ Ⓒ Ⓓ Ⓔ
31. Ⓐ Ⓑ Ⓒ Ⓓ Ⓔ
32. Ⓐ Ⓑ Ⓒ Ⓓ Ⓔ
33. Ⓐ Ⓑ Ⓒ Ⓓ Ⓔ
34. Ⓐ Ⓑ Ⓒ Ⓓ Ⓔ
35. Ⓐ Ⓑ Ⓒ Ⓓ Ⓔ
36. Ⓐ Ⓑ Ⓒ Ⓓ Ⓔ
37. Ⓐ Ⓑ Ⓒ Ⓓ Ⓔ
38. Ⓐ Ⓑ Ⓒ Ⓓ Ⓔ
39. Ⓐ Ⓑ Ⓒ Ⓓ Ⓔ
40. Ⓐ Ⓑ Ⓒ Ⓓ Ⓔ
41. Ⓐ Ⓑ Ⓒ Ⓓ Ⓔ
42. Ⓐ Ⓑ Ⓒ Ⓓ Ⓔ
43. Ⓐ Ⓑ Ⓒ Ⓓ Ⓔ
44. Ⓐ Ⓑ Ⓒ Ⓓ Ⓔ
45. Ⓐ Ⓑ Ⓒ Ⓓ Ⓔ
46. Ⓐ Ⓑ Ⓒ Ⓓ Ⓔ
47. Ⓐ Ⓑ Ⓒ Ⓓ Ⓔ
48. Ⓐ Ⓑ Ⓒ Ⓓ Ⓔ
49. Ⓐ Ⓑ Ⓒ Ⓓ Ⓔ
50. Ⓐ Ⓑ Ⓒ Ⓓ Ⓔ
51. Ⓐ Ⓑ Ⓒ Ⓓ Ⓔ
52. Ⓐ Ⓑ Ⓒ Ⓓ Ⓔ
53. Ⓐ Ⓑ Ⓒ Ⓓ Ⓔ
54. Ⓐ Ⓑ Ⓒ Ⓓ Ⓔ
55. Ⓐ Ⓑ Ⓒ Ⓓ Ⓔ

Sample Test One Answer Key

Question Number	Correct Answer
1.	C
2.	D
3.	D
4.	C
5.	D
6.	B
7.	A
8.	C
9.	C
10.	B
11.	D
12.	A
13.	C
14.	A
15.	D
16.	A
17.	C
18.	C
19.	B
20.	D
21.	B
22.	C
23.	B
24.	A
25.	D
26.	A
27.	C
28.	B

Question Number	Correct Answer
29.	D
30.	D
31.	C
32.	A
33.	D
34.	D
35.	C
36.	B
37.	C
38.	D
39.	B
40.	C
41.	A
42.	C
43.	B
44.	D
45.	B
46.	D
47.	A
48.	C
49.	D
50.	B
51.	C
52.	C
53.	B
54.	A
55.	D

Sample Test One Explanations

Questions 1–3 refer to the passage below:

> "We think, therefore, that associations may be entered into, the object of which is to adapt measures that may have a tendency to impoverish another, that is, to diminish his gains and profits, and yet so far from being criminal or unlawful, the object may be highly meritorious and public spirited. The legality of such an association will therefore depend upon the means to be used for its accomplishment...."
>
> *Justice 'Lemard Shaw, Commonwealth v. Hunt, 1842 (portion of the unanimous opinion written by Justice Shaw).*

1. To what does the word "associations" refer to in Justice Shaw's opinion?

    (A) Educational groups
    (B) Immigrant groups
    (C) Workers' groups
    (D) Protestors

The correct answer is C.
In the 1842 case Commonwealth v. Hunt, Justice Lemard Shaw of the Massachusetts Supreme Court ruled that workers' groups could organize to benefit members as long as they used legal means to achieve a legal purpose. Therefore, C is the correct answer. A, B and D are not considered "associations" so they are incorrect.

2. What group does the court believe may be "impoverished" by joining together of workers?

    (A) The workers
    (B) The labor unions
    (C) Government
    (D) Factory owners

The correct answer is D.

The "tendency to impoverish" refers to the additional costs incurred by the factory owners when they meet the union's demands, so D is the correct answer. Unions were formed for the benefit of themselves, the workers, so A and B are incorrect. The passage does not mention the government at all so C is also wrong.

3. **What is the significance of the court's decision?**

   (A) It precipitated the prison reform movement.
   (B) It explained what a conspiracy was.
   (C) It provided impetus for the women's suffrage movement.
   (D) It made it possible for unions to organize and grow.

The correct answer is D.

The decision essentially legalized labor unions, so D is the correct answer. It did not precipitate the prison reform, so A is incorrect. It did not B, explain what a conspiracy was, nor D, provide impetus for the women's suffrage movement.

Questions 4–6 refer to the passage below:

> "…the power of the SEC [Securities Exchange Commission] resided principally in just two provisions, both of them ingeniously simple. The first mandated disclosure of detailed information, such as balance sheets, profit and loss statements, and the names and compensation of corporate officers, about firms whose securities were publicly traded. The second required verification of that information by independent auditors using standardized accounting procedures."
>
> "In the financial and housing sectors, the New Deal built structures of stability by the inventively simple devices of standardizing and promulgating relevant information, and by introducing industry-wide self-insurance schemes that calmed jittery markets and offered dependable safeguards to capital. In many other sectors, the New Deal's technique was somewhat less artful; it was, simply, to suppress competition, or at least to modulate its destructive effects. But everywhere the objective was the same: to create a uniquely American system of risk-reduced, or risk-managed, capitalism."
>
> *What the New Deal Did*, DAVID M. KENNEDY, *Political Science Quarterly Vol. 124, No. 2 (Summer 2009), p. 256; 259*

4. From reading Kennedy's excerpt above, which of the following was a major driving principle of the Securities Exchange Commission?

   (A) Capitalism should be replaced by socialism.
   (B) Corporations were believed to operate appropriately and efficiently without interference from regulatory bodies.
   (C) Monopolies on financial investment information should cease, as they were being exploited by individuals.
   (D) Shareholders of publicly traded companies did not need to be transparent in their financial information.

The correct answer is C.
This excerpt from a political science journal discusses the 1933 Banking Act, which was part of the Glass-Steagall Act. It established the Federal Deposit Insurance Corporation (FDIC) and imposed various other banking reforms. It states that its purpose was to "suppress competition, or at least to modulate its destructive effect," indicating that C is the correct answer. The passage does not mention socialism. Therefore, A is incorrect. B is wrong because the first paragraph mandates regulation and oversight of record keeping, which can be seen as promoting "interference." By "mandating disclosure," the passage requires transparency, so D is incorrect.

5. The Glass-Steagall Act was intended to solve the problems started by which event in early twentieth century US economic history?

   (A) The Great Chicago Fire
   (B) The "Dust Bowl"
   (C) The Cross of Gold speech, delivered by William Jennings Bryan
   (D) The Wall Street Crash

The correct answer is D.
The passage clearly deals with financial matters and not A, The Great Chicago Fire or B, the "Dust Bowl." William Jennings Bryan's 1896 Cross of Gold speech, in which he said, "You shall not crucify mankind upon a cross of gold," was an argument against the gold standard. He believed that bimetallism, or making both gold and silver currency would bring prosperity. Therefore, C is incorrect.

6. Which of the following factors did not contribute to reduced unemployment and a changing labor market during the Second World War?

   (A) Revenue Acts passed during the War that resulted in increased federal tax collections
   (B) The Labor Management Relations Act (a.k.a. Taft–Hartley Act)
   (C) Conscription resulted in fewer men working in the country
   (D) Creation of the Fair Employment Practice Committee (FEPC)

The correct answer is B.

B is the correct answer. The Taft-Hartley Act of 1947 restricted the power of labor unions, and since the war ended in 1945, the restrictions could not have influenced the labor market during the war. During World War II unemployment was reduced and the labor market changed due to A, increased taxation, C, conscription (more commonly known as the Draft), and D, the Fair Employment Practice Committee.

Questions 7–9 refer to the passage below:

> If you were to see, for a moment, one of the streams in the great current which is always pouring through New York, go down a Summer afternoon to the North River wharves…As you approach the end you come upon a noisy crowd of strange faces and stranger costumes…Some are just welcoming an old face,… some are letting down the huge trunks, some swearing…at the endless noise and distractions. They bear the plain marks of the Old World. Healthy, stout frames, and low, degraded faces with many stamps of inferiority…It is a new world to them—oppression, bitter poverty behind—here, hope, freedom, and a chance to work, and food to the laboring man…Everyone in the great City who can make a living from the freshly arrived immigrant, is here…Very many…will start tomorrow at once for the far West. Some will hang about the German boarding-houses, each day losing their money,… until they at last seek a refuge in Ward's island, or settle down in the eleventh Ward, to add to the great mass of foreign poverty and misery there gathered…
>
> *Article published in the New York Daily Times in 1853.*

7. **What was the intent of this writer?**

    (A) To show that America welcomed the immigrants
    (B) To explain cities were having problems handling the flood of migration
    (C) To describe the wharf scene for the paper's readers
    (D) To explain that immigrants often began a westward trek after arriving in New York

The correct answer is A.

The article describes a picture of the wharf and its throng of immigrants. His statement "here, hope, freedom, and a chance to work, and food to the laboring man," indicates that America welcomes the new immigrants. Therefore, A is the correct answer. B is incorrect because the writer does not explain any problems incurred by the city. By making predictions about what the new arrivals will do tomorrow, he goes beyond option C, describing the scene. While he does mention that some will go west, the article is not primarily about D, the westward trek.

8. **Why does the article refer to the German boarding houses?**

   (A) Fewer German immigrants arrived during the 1850s than immigrants from other nations.
   (B) The Germans maintained the best boarding houses in the city at that time.
   (C) The German boarding house owners were more interested in taking money from the boarders than providing places to stay.
   (D) The ship that was arriving carried primarily German immigrants.

The correct answer is C.
The article refers to the German boarding houses to highlight the vulnerability of the new immigrants to swindlers, so C is correct. It does not mention any statistics about the number of German immigrants, so A and D are incorrect. By saying that they lose money at the boarding houses, he implies that they are not the best in the city, so B is wrong.

9. **Which group or person might have been least likely to be on the dock at the arrival of the immigrant ship?**

   (A) A young German peddling strawberries or other fruit
   (B) A moustached peasant in a Tyrolean hat
   (C) A runner from a German hotel
   (D) A young peasant girl with a bare head, a colored headdress, or fringed coat

The correct answer is C.
The passage states that the people "bear the plain marks of the Old World." This could include A, B, or D, but not C, a runner from a German hotel.

Questions 10–12 refer to the passage below:

> In order to live a religious and moral life worthy of the name, they feel it is necessary to come out in some degree from the world, and to form themselves into a community of property, so far as to exclude competition and the ordinary rules of trade; while they reserve sufficient private property, or the means of obtaining it, for all purposes of independence, and isolation at will.
>
> *Elizabeth Peabody, writing about Brook Farm in 1843.*

10. **What is the writer trying to explain?**

    (A) The reasons why Andrew Jackson's campaign was successful
    (B) The reasons for utopian societies
    (C) The reasons why Southerners settled Texas
    (D) The reasons why employers established employer-owned towns

The correct answer is B.
Brook Farm was a utopian community founded by George Ripley in Massachusetts in the

1840s. Peabody is explaining why people choose to live there, so B is the correct answer. It does not mention A, Andrew Jackson. Texas was not settled by utopian reformers so C is not correct. Brook Farm was to "exclude competition and the ordinary rules of trade, so D is also incorrect.

11. What was the goal of utopian community of Brook Farm?

(A) Creating a religious community
(B) Establishing a community for freed slaves
(C) Establishing a socialist community based on political ideas
(D) Creating a society where community goals were more important than self-interest

The correct answer is D.
Peabody mentions living a religious life, A, but the primary purpose of utopian communities was for D, creating a society where community goals were more important than self-interest. Political ideas and slavery were not primary goals either so B and C are incorrect.

12. In the time period between 1840 and 1848, in which parts of the United States were most utopian communities established?

(A) The East and the Midwest
(B) The East and the South
(C) The South and the Midwest
(D) The South and the Southwest

The correct answer is A.
Utopian communities were primarily formed in the East and the Midwest, so A is the correct Answer. This indicates that by default, B, C and D are incorrect.

Questions 13–15 refer to the passages below:

> "All men are born free and equal, and have certain natural, essential, and unalienable rights; among which may be reckoned the right of enjoying and defending their lives and liberties; that of acquiring, possessing, and protecting property; in fine, that of seeking and obtaining their safety and happiness."
> *– Massachusetts 1780 Declaration of Rights,*
> *authored primarily by John Adams*

> "We hold these truths to be self-evident, that all men are created equal, that they are endowed by their Creator with certain unalienable Rights, that among these are Life, Liberty and the pursuit of Happiness."
> *– US Declaration of Independence, 2nd paragraph,*
> *authored primarily by Thomas Jefferson*

13. **From the quotes above, what was the primary difference between John Adams and Thomas Jefferson in their expressions of the most fundamental of all rights?**

    (A) Adams thought rights were not inherent but needed to be "acquired," "defended," or "obtained," while Jefferson viewed rights as already being possessed by all men.
    (B) Both of them thought life and liberty were less important than happiness.
    (C) Adams, who did not own slave "property," thought the protection of private property needed to be mentioned and emphasized, while Jefferson emphasized the pursuit of happiness instead.
    (D) There is no difference in their views on rights.

The correct answer is C.
Adams stressed the importance of protecting private property and Jefferson did not, so C is the correct answer. A is not the right choice because by stating that "All men are born free and equal," Adams sees these rights to be inherent. B is incorrect because they do not indicate that happiness is less important. D is incorrect because Adams was a Federalist and Jefferson was a Republican therefore their views were very different.

14. **Which of the following would be most likely to disagree with the statements by Adams and Jefferson on rights?**

    (A) A slaveholder in 1861 who supported secession from the union
    (B) An army officer assigned to take charge of a Japanese-American internment camp in Utah during World War II
    (C) An Oklahoma settler who took over a portion of Indian land, but who had never met an Indian
    (D) An American soldier in the Mexican-American War

The correct answer is A.
A would be the correct answer because it is the only choice in which a person is actually owned for life and not allowed to have fundamental rights. The army officer, B, temporarily detained the Japanese but he did not own them, at the end of the war they set free, they were not his property for life. The settler, C, owned the land but did not on the Native Americans therefore they were not his property. The soldier in the Mexican War, D, did not "own" his prisoners or the enemy, they were not his property. Only A, the slaveholder, would suffer an economic loss if he were forced to follow Adams and Jefferson's words and treat his slaves as equals born to be free and not his property.

15. **Both excerpts are most clearly an example of which of the following developments in the late 1700s in America?**

    (A) Expansionism into the western frontier
    (B) Growing sectionalism and contention over slavery
    (C) A defiance of the rule of law and governmental authority
    (D) An expression of the right to rebel as a "law of nature" possessed by all men

The correct answer is D.

Almost all of the patriot leaders of the independence movement were well versed in the enlightenment writings of John Locke, who emphasized natural rights and the right to rebel against a government that restricted those rights. Therefore, D is the correct answer. The passage is not about A, B or C, so they are incorrect.

Questions 16–18 refer to the passage below:

> "Madison, and to an even greater extent Jefferson, seemed to think that economic policy consisted of getting out of the way to allow the natural laws of economic recovery and growth to proceed. But Hamilton thought the conditions for economic development needed to be created, then enduringly overseen. His model was England, with its national bank, regulated commerce, and powerful finance ministers...Hamilton regarded the national debt as "a national blessing," for it permitted the clustering of resources in the hands of a small group of enterprising men who would invest and not just spend it. For Madison, on the other hand, "a Public Debt is a Public curse."
> – *Joseph J. Ellis, historian, Founding Brothers:*
> *The Revolutionary Generation (pp. 63–64), published in 2003.*

16. The thinking of Madison and Jefferson about economic policy most closely correlates to which of the following?

(A) "Reaganomics" of the 1980s
(B) FDR's "New Deal" policies of the 1930s
(C) Abraham Lincoln's views of the best way to fund the civil war
(D) The "free silver" movement of the 1890s

The correct answer is A.

A is the correct answer. Free market economic ideas expressed by Madison and Jefferson are most exemplified by 1980s President Ronald Reagan's policies of reducing regulation called "Reaganomics." FDR's New Deal expanded regulation, Lincoln supported Henry Clay's "American System" based on Hamilton's ideas, and the "free silver" movement was not about regulation. Therefore, B, C, and D are incorrect.

17. Hamilton's belief of the need for a national bank

(A) was Hamilton's main financial goal for the country in 1791, followed by his determination that the federal government should avoid assumption of state debts.
(B) gained sufficient support from Congress for them to establish a permanent national bank in 1791, which has lasted to this day.
(C) was later adopted by Madison as well.
(D) included plans for paper money to be printed within the bank itself.

The correct answer is C.

Madison established the Second National Bank in 1816 to pay debts from war of 1812, so C is the correct answer. Hamilton's plan for the national bank did assume state debts, so A is incorrect. B is also incorrect because it was established with a 20-year charter and was not a permanent bank, and it struck coins but not paper money so D is incorrect.

18. **One significant result of the debate over the economic policies between Hamilton on one hand, and Jefferson and Madison on the other, was**

    (A) the creation of open immigration policies by Congress in 1791, as a way to spur economic growth.
    (B) passage of a federal law banning slavery after the year 1808.
    (C) one factor which contributed to creation of the two party system.
    (D) Jefferson's defeat of Adams in the election of 1800.

The correct answer is C.

The debate between Hamilton and Jefferson and Madison contributed to the establishment of two parties, Federalist and Democratic Republican, so C is the correct answer. It did not address immigration policies, ban slavery or result in Jefferson's defeat of John Adams in the 1800 election, so A, B and D are incorrect.

Questions 19–21 refer to the picture below:

North Carolina bill, 1775.

19. **The image above best demonstrates which of the following?**

    (A) The popularity of paper money after the revolutionary war
    (B) The unpopularity of paper money after the revolutionary war
    (C) How paper money greatly increases in value if the government backs it up with gold and silver
    (D) How Virginia differed from the other states in handling devalued currency

The correct asnwer is B.

After the revolution, an oversupply of currency caused its value to plummet. It had become so devalued that states stopped issuing currency. Congress passed a resolution backing it with Spanish milled dollars at the rate of forty to one. The one thousand dollar note shown demonstrates this devaluation and its unpopularity, so answer choice B is correct. A and C say the opposite so they are wrong. This Virginia bill is similar to those issued by other states, so D is incorrect also.

20. The high rate of inflation demonstrated by the note above comes closest to which of the following periods?

(A) The great depression in the 1930s
(B) "Reaganomics" in the 1980s
(C) The 1920s
(D) The panic of 1837

The correct answer is D.
During the great depression, prices fell drastically, so A is incorrect. B, "Reaganomics" is incorrect because inflation dropped during the 1980s. C. is incorrect because inflation was not a problem in the 1920s. Money supply also rose from 1833 to 1837, causing similar inflation, so the correct answer is D.

21. After the Revolutionary War, use of paper notes such as that shown above was

(A) generally considered good for the country.
(B) encouraged by some states as a way to decrease debt, by enacting laws forcing creditors to accept paper money.
(C) one of the 3 steps in Hamilton's plan to improve the economy.
(D) banned in the Northwest Territory.

The correct answer is B.
Paper notes like this were controversial, so A is wrong. Hamilton's three steps included paying off state debts, tariffs on imported goods and the establishment of a national bank, so C is incorrect. The Northwest Territory did not issue bank notes, so D is wrong.

Questions 22–24 refer to the passage below:

> Mr. Speaker, Mr. President, Members of the Congress:
>
> I speak tonight for the dignity of man and the destiny of democracy. I urge every member of both parties, Americans of all religions and of all colors, from every section of this country, to join me in that cause. At times history and fate meet at a single time in a single place to shape a turning point in man's unending search for freedom. So it was at Lexington and Concord. So it was a century ago at Appomattox. So it was last week in Selma, Alabama. There, long-suffering men and women peacefully protested the denial of their rights as Americans.
>
> *President Lyndon B. Johnson's address "We Shall Overcome", before a joint session of Congress, 1965.*

22. **The speech given by President Johnson refers to his support of the**

(A) Civil Rights Act.
(B) Equal Rights Amendment.
(C) Voting Rights Act.
(D) Economic Opportunity Act.

The correct answer is C.
This passage is from Lyndon Johnson's famous address to congress in support of C, the Voting Rights Act of 1965. Johnson's Civil Rights Act and the Economic Opportunity Act were signed in 1964, so A and D are incorrect. Congress did not approve the Equal Rights Amendment until 1972, when Johnson was not in office, so B is not correct.

23. **The federal voting rights laws passed in the 1950s and 1960s were designed to**

(A) return control of voting regulations to the state.
(B) remove racial barriers to voting.
(C) extend suffrage to American women.
(D) prevent recent immigrants from voting.

The correct answer is B.
Voting Rights laws passed in the 1950s and 1960s were meant to address B, racial barriers to voting. They were in response to discriminatory state voting regulations, so A is incorrect. American women gained suffrage rights with the Nineteenth Amendment in 1920. Therefore, C is wrong. D is also wrong because it did not prevent recent immigrants from voting.

24. **The Voting Rights Act of 1965**

(A) banned racial discrimination in voting nationwide.
(B) tried to eliminate poverty through spending on medical programs.
(C) allowed women to vote.
(D) provided more federal funding for public education.

The correct answer is A.
The Voting Rights Act of 1965 prohibits racial discrimination in voting nation wide. A is the correct answer. The Social Security amendments of 1965 addressed medical programs, so B is incorrect. C is incorrect because women had the right to vote since 1920. The Voting Rights Act did not provide funding for education, so D is wrong.

Questions 25–27 refer to the passage below:

"This, then, is held to be the duty of the man of Wealth: First, to set an example of modest, unostentatious living, shunning display or extravagance; to provide moderately for the legitimate wants of those dependent upon him; and after doing so to consider all surplus revenues which come to him simply as trust funds, which he is called upon to administer, and strictly bound as a matter of duty to administer in the manner which, in his judgment, is best calculated to produce the most beneficial results for the community—the man of wealth thus becoming the mere agent and trustee for his poorer brethren, bringing to their service his superior wisdom, experience, and ability to administer, doing for them better than they would or could do for themselves."

Andrew Carnegie (June 1889) "Wealth",
North American Review Vol. 148, Issue 391, 653–665

"Millions of property were turned over without consideration to railroad companies... The veto power conferred by the Constitution as a remedy for ill-considered legislation, was turned by him [President Andrew Johnson] into a weapon of offence against Congress and into an instrument to beat down the just opposition which his usurpation had aroused."

Charles Sumner (1868) Expulsion of the President: opinion of
Hon. Charles Sumner, of Massachusetts, in the case of the impeachment
of Andrew Johnson, President of the United States.
Washington Government Printing Office

25. **Which of the following was not a factor of Andrew Carnegie's philosophy, according to the first excerpt?**

(A) Individual intuition and economic success play a large role in justifying one's position in society.

(B) A "survival of the fittest" mentality, as proposed by contemporary Social Darwinist thinkers

(C) The philanthropic obligation of the wealthy to distribute their wealth, in order to aid people that are disadvantaged

(D) The belief that a small group of capitalists should not be allowed to provide financial advice to, or control the stocks of, many individual corporations

The correct answer is D.
D is the correct answer because Carnegie did not agree with this statement, as he would consider it a duty to use his skills to help other corporations. Andrew Carnegie's philosophy is in agreement with A, B, and C. The passage discusses the responsibility of the wealthy to the

community, so A is a factor. Social Darwinists believed that the wealthy were successful because of their "superior wisdom, experience, and ability to administer." Therefore, B would be part of his philosophy. This superiority gives them C, an obligation to aid the disadvantaged.

26. **As the second excerpt describes, there was growing resentment towards the growing power of monopolies, and the land that was being awarded to them. This resentment was particularly due to government corruption, which escalated in the decades following President Johnson's impeachment. What act was signed in 1883 to limit this corruption by requiring government jobs to be awarded on the basis of merit?**

    (A) Pendleton Civil Service Reform Act
    (B) Amnesty Act
    (C) Bland-Allison Act
    (D) Judiciary Act

The correct answer is A.
A, the Pendleton Civil Service Reform Act was passed in 1883 stating that positions within the federal government should be awarded on the basis of merit. B, The Amnesty Act was passed in 1872 and removed voting restrictions and allowed former secessionists to hold government office, with the exception of confederate officers. C, the Bland-Allison Act required the Treasury to purchase and circulate silver dollars. D is also incorrect because there were several different Judiciary Acts, but none addressed awarding government jobs.

27. **Cornelius Vanderbilt was the major railroad monopoly owner in the country, thriving due to a wide range of technological and engineering innovations. Which of the following did not contribute to the growth of railroads during this time?**

    (A) The widespread use of mass-produced, standardized, interchangeable parts
    (B) The transition from whale oil to coal-burning power sources
    (C) A boost in demand to expand the Underground Railroad network, which had reached its peak in the 1850s
    (D) The refinement of lubricating products from petroleum

The correct answer is C.
The growth of railroads in the nineteenth century was due to a number of factors, Including A, improvements in production of parts, B, the use of coal as fuel, and D, petroleum-based lubricants. An increasing population of immigrant labor and a growing steel-refining industry also contributed to the growth of railroads. The Underground Railroad is a figurative term for the network of secret routes and safe houses that helped slaves escape from the southern states. C is the correct answer.

Questions 28–30 refers to the passage below:

> "During the last quarter of the nineteenth century, public interest in American Indians surged…The movement culminated with the passage of the General Allotment Act of 1887, commonly called the Dawes Act, which authorized the president to allot Native reservations. The participants in this movement to assimilate American Indians…shared a belief that by imposing their culture on America Indian people, they were fulfilling the destiny of their nation and giving American Indians the greatest gift possible—civilization, as they defined it."
>
> *Stremlau, Rose (2005) "To Domesticate and Civilize Wild Indians":*
> *Allotment and the Campaign to Reform Indian Families, 1875–1887.*
> *Journal of Family History, Vol. 30 No. 3, 268*

28. President Grover Cleveland signed the Dawes Act on February 8th 1887, referring to it as the "Indian Emancipation Act". According to Stremlau, in what sense did he, and others, believe that these reforms were promoting Native emancipation?

(A) Native American culture would be preserved and protected through US governmental measures such as the Ghost Dance Movement

(B) By assimilating Native Americans and introducing them to American values they would become free from tribal social structures that prevented individualism and progress.

(C) Native Americans would be allowed to continue their tribal governments on reservations, but with the benefits of the "Gilded Age", such as electricity and department stores.

(D) Native Americans would be accepted to the American Federation of Labor as unskilled laborers, freeing them from their unemployment problems.

The correct answer is B.

The Dawes Act divided the tribes into individual families, provided them with land and granted them United States citizenship. The intention was to assimilate Native Americans to the nation, rather than forcibly remove them from the country. The Ghost Dance Movement was a Native American religious movement that aspired to resist settlers that were taking their land. Therefore, A is incorrect. Native Americans were expected to give up their traditional culture—including language and religion, on the reservations, so C is also incorrect. The American Federation of Labor was a union that was relatively elitist, and restricted their membership to only skilled laborers, so D is not right either.

29. **Between 1862 and 1898 a range of factors contributed to Westward expansion. Which of the following did not occur between those years?**

(A) the merging of the Union Pacific and Central Pacific railroads
(B) the Massacre at Wounded Knee
(C) the United States Arizona Territory was established
(D) the California Gold Rush in the Sierra Nevada

The correct answer is D.
A, B, and C all occurred between 1862 and 1988 contributing to westward expansion. A, the Union Pacific and Central Pacific railroads, merged in 1869. B, The last significant battle against Native American tribes was the Massacre at Wounded Knee in 1890. C, the Arizona Territory was established in 1863. D is the correct answer because the California Gold Rush began in 1848 and the gold was largely depleted before 1862.

30. **This period was marked by the US government's generally laissez-faire attitude towards corporate expansion and economic affairs. However, in 1886 what case resulted in a Supreme Court decision limited control of interstate commerce to Congress, resulting in the Interstate Commerce Commission being established in 1887?**

(A) Dred Scott v. Sandford
(B) Northern Securities Co. v. United States
(C) Plessy v. Ferguson
(D) Wabash, St. Louis & Pacific Railway Co. v. Illinois

The correct answer is D.
In 1886, the Wabash Case resulted in a Supreme Court decision that limited control of interstate commerce to Congress. It denied individual states the right to regulate interstate railroads in an effort to combat corruption. This resulted in one of the first federal regulatory bodies, the Interstate Commerce Commission, being established in 1887 to oversee interstate railway practices. A is wrong because Dred Scott v. Sandford was the Supreme Court ruling that determined that slaves were not citizens, Scott does not have a right to sue in federal court, and the Missouri Compromise is unconstitutional. B is incorrect because The Northern Securities Co. v. United States was a 1904 case that broke up the Great Northern and Northern Pacific railroad companies because they had formed a monopoly. Plessy v. Ferguson was a 1896 Supreme Court ruling that upheld racial segregation in public facilities under the doctrine of "separate but equal."

Questions 31–33 refer to the picture below:

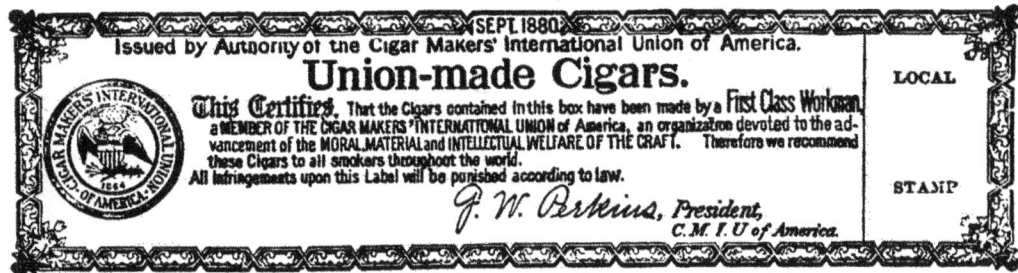

Cigar Makers' International Union of America union label Published in "Cigar Makers' Official Journal," Jan. 15, 1912

31. Urbanization in cities such as New York and Philadelphia—and even more rapidly in the West—provided employment opportunities and a standard of living that attracted people from many countries. However, immigration was not viewed in a positive light by many. What act was signed by President Chester Arthur in 1882 to restrict immigration?

    (A) Chinese Immigration Act
    (B) Alien Contract Labor Law
    (C) Chinese Exclusion Act
    (D) Burlingame-Seward Treaty

The correct answer is C.
The Chinese Exclusion Act was the first time a particular ethnic group was prevented from immigrating to the USA. A is wrong because the Chinese Immigration Act was a Canadian immigration regulation. B is incorrect because The Alien Contract labor Law of 1885 prohibited the importation of foreigners under contract or agreement to perform labor in the United States. D, The Burlingame-Seward Treaty of 1858 established formal friendly relations between the US and China, so it is an incorrect answer.

32. Two waves of immigrants arrived in American during the 1800s, with the "New Immigrants" arriving mainly from the 1880s onwards. The New Immigrants were

    (A) mainly from Southern and Eastern Europe
    (B) arriving from democratic countries
    (C) literate and skilled
    (D) mainly Protestant

The correct answer is A.
The "New Immigrants" came mostly from southern and eastern Europe, including Italy, Greece, Poland, and Russia, so A is the correct Answer. In the 1880s these were not democratic countries, so B is incorrect. They were mostly unskilled, illiterate peasants so C is also wrong. D, is wrong because they were largely Roman Catholic, Greek Orthodox, Russian Orthodox and Jewish.

174   AP US History

33. In contrast to developments in urban centers, there was growing resentment in rural environments. Between the 1870s and 1880s the Farmer's Alliance existed, working especially against the crop-lien credit system. Under which name did this alliance become a political party in 1891, following the McKinley Tariff Act that was passed the preceding year?

(A) Free Soil Party
(B) Vegetarian Party
(C) Progressive Party
(D) People's Party

The correct answer is D.
In 1891, Farmer's Alliance became the People's Party, also known as the Populist Party, a political party that formed to demand inflation to raise the price of crops, a free currency of silver coinage, and the implementation of a graduated income tax. A, the Free Soil Party was formed in 1848 to oppose the expansion of slavery into the western territories. B is also wrong. The Vegetarian Party was a short-lived unsuccessful political party in the 1940s. C, the Progressive Party was formed in the early twentieth century in opposition to "Gilded Age" urbanization, social stratification, segregation, government corruption, immigration, and corporate monopolies.

Questions 34–36 refer to the passage below:

> There is a twofold liberty-natural (I mean as our nature is not corrupt) and civil or federal. The first is common to man with beasts and other creatures. By this, man, as he stands in relation to man simply, hath liberty to what he lists; it is a liberty to evil as well as to good. This liberty is incompatible and inconsistent with authority, and cannot endure the least restraint of the most just authority. The exercise and maintaining of this liberty make men grow more evil, and in time to be worse than brute beasts…This is that great enemy of truth and peace that wild beast, which all the ordinances of God are bent against, to restrain and subdue it.
>
> The other kind of liberty I call civil or federal; it may also be termed moral, in reference to the covenant between God and man, in the moral in reference of the covenant between God and man, in the moral law, and the politic covenants and constitutions, amongst men themselves. This liberty is the proper end and object of authority, and cannot subsist without it; and it is a liberty to that only which is good, just and honest.
>
> *John Winthrop, "City Upon a Hill", 1630.*

34. Winthrop's argument on liberty is most reflective of what major global movement of the 1600s?

(A) A change from cottage industry to industrial economics and mass production
(B) Philosophe arguments in favor of natural rights
(C) Roman Catholic influences from the counter reformation
(D) Protestant beliefs about creating a Biblical City on a Hill

The correct answer is D.
The Protestant Puritans who had been persecuted in Europe aimed to create a biblical "City on a Hill," that could be hidden. A is incorrect because it is in reference to the industrial revolution of the nineteenth century. The Philosophe's movement in favor of natural rights began later in the 1600s, so B is wrong. C is incorrect because the Puritans were not Catholic.

35. Winthrop's argument on the nature of true freedom would have what significant impact on the development of the Northeastern colonies?

(A) The beginnings of a slave cotton economy
(B) Tensions between European settlers and the Native American tribes
(C) The development of the Puritan faith in Massachusetts
(D) The creation of a mercantile trade in timber and fish with England

The correct answer is C.
C is correct because John Winthrop was a Puritan who settled in Massachusetts. A is incorrect because the slave cotton economy rose in the nineteenth century. B is incorrect because Winthrop's argument on the "nature of true freedom" did not have a significant impact on tensions between settlers and Native American tribes. Winthrop's goals were not of a mercantile nature, but a religious one, so D is also incorrect.

36. Winthrop's argument about the nature of faith is most similar to which other American historical movement?

(A) The Civil Rights' movement call for racial freedom
(B) The Evangelical movement in the 1970s
(C) The Women's Rights movement of the 1960s
(D) The Progressive movement of the 1920s

The correct answer is B.
Neither A, C nor D are religious movements about faith. Therefore, B is the correct answer. The Evangelical Movement in the 1970s was a Christian movement that rose in opposition to the counter-culture of the 60s and what was viewed as a loosening of morals.

Questions 37–39 refer to the passage below:

> On the Island Hispaniola was where the Spaniards first landed, as I have said. Here those Christians perpetrated their first ravages and oppressions against the native peoples. This was the first land in the New World to be destroyed and depopulated by the Christians, and here they began their subjection of the women and children, taking them away from the Indians to use them and ill use them, eating the food they provided with their sweat and toil. The Spaniards did not content themselves with what the Indians gave them of their own free will, according to their ability, which was always too little to satisfy enormous appetites, for a Christian eats and consumes in one day an amount of food that would suffice to feed three houses inhabited by ten Indians for one month. And they committed other acts of force and violence and oppression which made the Indians realize that these men had not come from Heaven. And some of the Indians concealed their foods while others concealed their wives and children and still others fled to the mountains to avoid the terrible transactions of the Christians.
>
> *Bartolome De Las Casas, "Brief Account of the Devastation of the Indies", 1542.*

37. De Las Casas' description of the treatment of the natives in Mexico reflects what major global relationship of the 1600s?

(A) Protestant reformers trying to establish a model Christian community
(B) The introduction of the slave trade for cash crops in the Caribbean
(C) European mercantile nations seeking out raw resources
(D) The consolidation of kingdoms into nation states

The correct answer is C.
New Spain forced Aztec and Incan survivors to work in the extraction of silver. Bartolomeo De Las Casas was a Catholic monk and slaveholder. Therefore, C is the correct answer. A, Protestant reformers trying to establish a model Christian community refers to the Puritans. B is about the introduction of the slave trade, so it is incorrect, and D, the consolidation of kingdoms into nation states occurred in the nineteenth century in Europe.

38. The treatment of the Native Americans in Mexico was most similar to

(A) the development of the cult of domesticity for women in the 1830s.
(B) the exclusion of the Chinese immigrants in the late 1800s.
(C) the Red Scare of the 1920s against Eastern European immigrants.
(D) the use of African labor in the 1830s for farming cotton.

The correct answer is D.
The use of African labor in the 1830s was most similar to the treatment of Native Americans in Mexico. A is wrong because the cult of domesticity for women was a movement of the middle and upper classes that emphasized femininity and woman's role in the home. B refers to the Chinese Exclusion act which is not about the treatment of Native Americans, so it is wrong. C is wrong because the Red Scare was about the fear that new immigrants who held communist, socialist, or anarchist beliefs would take over the government.

39. The use of Native American labor by the Spanish in the 1600s led to what major impact on the global economy?

(A) The switch from mercantilism to capitalist economics
(B) The influx of silver into the global economy
(C) The use of indentured servants for agriculture in North America
(D) The development of mercantile wars in the 1700s

The correct answer is B.
B is the correct answer because Native Americans were forced to work in Spanish silver mines. The desire for silver created a worldwide network of trade. A is wrong because the switch from mercantilism to capitalist economics began with the Industrial Revolution. C is incorrect because indentured servants had been used for agriculture since 1617. D is incorrect because there is no strong causal relationship between Native American labor and mercantile wars in the 1700s.

Questions 40–42 refer to the passage below:

> "I am not a Know-Nothing. That is certain. How could I be? How can any one who abhors the oppression of negroes, be in favor of degrading classes of white people? Our progress in degeneracy appears to me to be pretty rapid. As a nation, we begin by declaring that "all men are created equal." We now practically read it "all men are created equal, except negroes." When the Know-Nothings get control, it will read "all men are created equal, except negroes, and foreigners, and Catholics." When it comes to this I should prefer emigrating to some country where they make no pretense of loving liberty—to Russia, for instance, where despotism can be taken pure, and without the base alloy of hypocrisy."
>
> *Abraham Lincoln, letter to Joshua F. Speed, August 24, 1855*

40. Who were the Know Nothings?

(A) A political party that promoted the Alien and Sedition laws
(B) Catholic immigrants
(C) An anti-immigrant political party
(D) A group of uneducated farmers who supported slavery

The correct answer is C.
The Know-Nothing Party was a nativist organization that spread anti-German, anti-Irish, and anti-Catholic propaganda. Most members also opposed slavery. The Alien and Sedition laws were passed during the Adams administration in 1798, so A is incorrect. B is incorrect because the party was against Catholic immigrants because of fears of Papal control or other foreign influence on the US government. The term know-nothing does not imply lack of education. It was dubbed the "Know-Nothing, Party" by newspaper editor Horace Greeley, because they were a secretive group and members claimed to know nothing about the organization, so D is incorrect.

41. What region had the most people who agreed with the Know-Nothing's philosophy?

(A) Northeast
(B) South
(C) Southwest
(D) California

The correct answer is A.
The large numbers of German and Irish immigrants to urban areas in the Northeast drove the concern for foreign influence. Know-Nothings were often reformers, and most detested slavery, so B is incorrect. The American Southwest was not largely settled until the completion of the railroads, so C is not right. D is also incorrect. California was settled and there was anti-Chinese sentiment there, but the majority of Know-Nothing supporters were from the New England and New York.

42. All of the following are tenets of the Nativist philosophy EXCEPT

(A) the belief that the increasing numbers of immigrants were gaining too much political influence.
(B) the belief that only people born in the United States should hold elected office.
(C) the belief that Native American tribes should be removed to reservations.
(D) they were in favor of Protestant values and against Catholics.

The correct answer is C.
The ideology of nativism holds that the native population should be protected over the interest of immigrants, but refers to Anglo-Saxon Protestants born in the United States, not Native American tribes so C is the correct answer. All of the other answers describe beliefs widely held by the Nativist philosophy.

Questions 43–45 refer to the passage below:

> "We are glad, now that we see the facts with no veil of false pretense about them, to fight thus for the ultimate peace of the world and for the liberation of its peoples, the German peoples included; for the rights of nations great and small and the privilege of men everywhere to choose their way of life and of obedience. The world must be made safe for democracy. Its peace must be planted upon the tested foundations of political liberty. We have no selfish ends to serve. We desire no conquest, no dominion. We seek no indemnities for ourselves, no material compensation for the sacrifices we shall freely make. We are but one of the champions of the rights of mankind. We shall be satisfied when those rights have been made as secure as the faith and the freedom of nations can make them."
>
> *Woodrow Wilson, War Messages, 65th Cong., 1st Sess. Senate Doc. No. 5, Serial No. 7264, Washington, D.C., 1917; pp. 3–8, passim*

43. From the turn of the century onwards, debates over America's role in world affairs intensified. From reading the excerpt above, which of the following describes Woodrow Wilson's perspective on American foreign policy?

(A) Interventionist and imperialist
(B) Interventionist and anti-imperialist
(C) Isolationist and imperialist
(D) Isolationist and anti-imperialist

The correct answer is B.

B is the correct answer because by stating that we are glad to fight for "the ultimate peace of the world and for the liberation of its peoples" means that we are willing to intervene against imperialism. This also means that A is wrong because Wilson does not support imperialism. Isolationism means to isolate the United States from foreign affairs rather than intervene, so C and D are incorrect.

44. What conflict in 1898 enabled the United States' economic and military expansion in the Caribbean and Latin America, most significantly in Cuba and the Philippines?

(A) Philippine–American War
(B) Ten Years War
(C) Boxer Rebellion
(D) Spanish-American War

The correct answer is D.

The US victory in the Spanish-American War (1898) resulted in Spain cedimg Cuba, Puerto Rico and the Philippines to the United States. Therefore, D is the correct answer. The 1899–1902 Philippine-American war came about as a result of the Philippines' objection to rule by the United States, so A is incorrect. B is incorrect also because the Ten Years War was part of Cuba's earlier struggle for independence from Spain. The Boxer Rebellion took place in China in 1899 and 1901, so C is incorrect.

45. **Woodrow Wilson's message to Congress about the need for US leadership in global conflicts is most similar to what other event?**

    (A) American isolation during the 1930s before World War II
    (B) American involvement in the Cold War in Southeast Asia
    (C) Washington's Neutrality Proclamation
    (D) American expansion in the 1830s under Manifest Destiny

The correct answer is B.

B is the correct answer because American involvement in Cold War attempts to suppress the expansion of communism was an interventionist policy. A is about isolationism, which is the opposite of the interventionism Wilson supported, so it is the wrong answer. Washington's Neutrality Proclamation was in his Farewell Address which warned of the danger of becoming entangled in foreign alliances. Therefore, C is against the involvement in global conflicts. D, expansion under Manifest Destiny was about acquiring western lands, not global conflicts, so it is incorrect.

Questions 46–48 refer to the picture below:

"For the Sunny South. An airship with a 'Jim Crow' trailer" (Feb, 26th 1913) *Puck Magazine*

46. As the above satirical cartoon shows, during the early twentieth century technological innovations and modernization were not enjoyed by everyone equally. Which of the following occurred between 1910 and 1930 as a major consequence of the Jim Crow laws?

(A) The Niagara Movement was active in demanding desegregation and black suffrage.
(B) Segregation was reduced in the Southern states, especially in hospitals and federal workplaces.
(C) The abolishment of slavery with the ratification of the Thirteenth Amendment
(D) The first "Great Migration" of Africa-American communities from the South to northern industrial cities

The correct answer is D.
Jim Crow laws restricted the rights of African Americans, and poll taxes and literacy tests were imposed to prevent them from voting. The First Great Migration was a period between 1910 and 1930 when thousands of African Americans moved from these harsh conditions in the South to the North and West. Therefore, D is the correct answer. W.E.B. Du Bois and his supporters founded the Niagara Movement in 1905, which became a cornerstone for desegregation and led to the formation of the National Association for the Advancement of Colored People (NAACP) in 1909. Therefore, A is incorrect. B is incorrect because Segregation increased across the Southern States following the Plessy v. Ferguson case in 1896. The Thirteenth Amendment abolishing slavery was signed in 1865, so C is incorrect.

47. After the First World War, xenophobic tensions resulted in a tremendous increase in the number of racial riots and labor strikes. Which of the following was not a cause of the period of fear and paranoia during 1919–20 known as the First Red Scare?

(A) Senator Joseph McCarthy's anti-communist campaigns
(B) The Sedition Act
(C) Labor strikes
(D) The Haymarket massacre

The correct answer is A.
Senator Joseph McCarthy's anti-communist campaigns took place during the late 1950s, not 1919–29, so A is the correct answer. B is incorrect because the 1918 Sedition Act contributed to fear and paranoia. It made it a criminal offense to engage in any activity or communication that was contradictory to America's war efforts. C, labor strikes is wrong because during the Red Scare, those who defended labor unions were sometimes called unpatriotic "radicals." D, The Haymarket massacre, was an early sign of increasing fear and paranoia. In 1886, a group of unionists, socialists and anarchists led a strike at the McCormick Reaper Works and the police fired into a crowd killing and wounding several. Newspapers and the police used the public's fear to support the arrest of labor agitators.

48. Which of the following most accurately describes the "Harlem Renaissance"?

(A) Native American tribes campaigned for their own representatives in the United States government.
(B) The belief many that the American government had the right to stretch their power over the entire continent, from coast to coast
(C) Also known as the New Negro Movement, it was a period of cultural expression and a flourishing of the arts for many African-Americans.
(D) A march of up to 10,000 African Americans in New York City, in opposition to the outbreak of anti-black violence during the East St. Louis massacres

The correct answer is C.
With the first Great Migration, many African Americans settled in the Harlem neighborhood in New York City. This gradually became the cultural center for many African American musicians, writers, poets, scholars and artists, so C is the correct answer. A is incorrect because the Harlem Renaissance was primarily made up of African Americans. B is incorrect because Manifest Destiny is the policy that claimed the continent for the United States from coast to coast. The East St. Louis Riot of 1917 was a result of rising tensions in the competition for jobs between white unions and African Americans newly arrived from the south. The National Guard was sent in but failed to protect African Americans. The recently formed NAACP suddenly grew and mobilized in protest with a silent march of 10,000 people in New York City. Therefore, D did not describe the Harlem Renaissance.

Questions 49–52 refer to the passage below:

> The world beholds the peaceful triumphs of the industry of our emigrants. To us belongs the duty of protecting them adequately wherever they may be on our soil. The jurisdiction of our laws and the benefits of our republican institutions should be extended over them in the distant regions in which they have selected for their homes.
> *James K. Polk's March 4, 1845, inaugural address.*

49. Which view was President Polk expressing in this part of his inaugural address?

(A) Containment
(B) Isolationism
(C) Imperialism
(D) Expansionism

The correct answer is D.
In this excerpt from Polk's inaugural address, he talks about extending the benefits of republican institutions to distant regions. This could include both C, imperialism and D, expansionism. However, if you know that in 1845, the United States was in the process of fulfilling its "Manifest Destiny," or expanding to the west coast, you can deduce that D is the correct answer. A, containment refers to the Cold War policy of working to prevent the spread

of communism, so it is incorrect. B, isolationism refers to the non-involvement in the affairs of other countries.

50. 1840s and 1850 was referred to as

(A) Encroachment.
(B) Manifest Destiny.
(C) Imperialism.
(D) Squatters' Rights.

The correct answer is B.
Manifest Destiny was the belief that the United States was destined to encompass territory from coast to coast, so this is the correct answer. A, encroachment in American history typically refers to the taking of Native American tribal territory, but not specifically to western lands in the 1840s and 50s. C, imperialism is wrong because the term implies colonial acquisition of overseas territories. D, Squatters' Rights refers to the nineteenth century custom that if a farmer lived and improved unoccupied land long enough, he had the right to it.

51. What is the meaning of the wording "The world beholds the peaceful triumphs of the industry of our emigrants" in the president's address?

(A) Immigrants have overcome the evils of industrialization in urban areas.
(B) Immigrants believe their triumphs are related to their being able to settle in America.
(C) The government approves the accomplishment of settling vast areas that will eventually become American land.
(D) The government commends the immigrants for being frugal and hard working to attain American citizenship.

The correct answer is C.
C is correct because Polk favored westward expansion and defeated the Whig candidate Henry Clay, who opposed it. Polk's attention was on defending the Texas and Oregon Territories, and looking to the acquisition of California. A, B & D refer to immigrants but the text refers to emigrants. The people who moved were migrating within the US and the text referred to them as emigrants because they were relocating from one section of the US to another. The two terms are antonyms not synonyms therefore the correct answer has to be C.

52. Which event is most similar to the ideas expressed by President Polk in his address?

(A) American withdrawal from Vietnam in 1973
(B) Lincoln's attempt to reunite the country at the beginning of the Civil War
(C) Franklin Roosevelt's defense of American entry into WWII as the "arsenal of democracy"
(D) American annexation of Hawaii over sugar tariffs

The correct answer is C.
C is the correct answer because FDR's reference to America as the "arsenal of democracy," is

about supporting the allies in defending democracy. A is incorrect because while America went into Vietnam to defend democracy against communism, it withdrew 1973, and South Vietnam fell to the communists soon after. B is wrong because Lincoln's attempt to reunite the country before the Civil War was not about protecting immigrants or defending democracy. The McKinley Tariff of 1890 raised import rates on foreign sugar which depressed the sugar-growing economy of Hawaii. American growers there promoted the annexation to eliminate the tariff costs. Therefore, D is incorrect.

Questions 53–55 refer to the picture below:

J.E. Farwell & Co., Boston: Published by J. E. Farwell & Co., 1852.
Courtesy of the Library of Congress

53. What does the purpose of this cartoon appear to be?

(A) Encourage immigrants
(B) Discouraging foreign labor
(C) Protesting immigration laws
(D) Opposing present school laws

The correct answer is B.
The advertisement states that the group is in favor of "The protection of American Mechanics against Foreign Pauper Labor." Therefore, it clearly discourages foreign labor. This also explains why A is incorrect. It does not encourage immigrants. C is incorrect because it does not discuss any specific immigration laws. D is incorrect because it explicitly states that they are in favor of "Our present Free School System."

54. What conclusion can be reached about the name of the newspaper?

(A) The paper does not believe that certain groups are patriotic Americans.
(B) The paper believes taxes are too high because of immigrants.
(C) Patriots must have always lived in America.
(D) All immigrants affect the beliefs of patriotism of Americans.

The correct answer is A.

It can be concluded that A, the paper believes only certain groups are patriotic Americans, so A is the correct answer. While the paper does assert that they are opposed to "being taxed for the support of Foreign paupers," this cannot be ascertained by only the name of the paper, "American Patriot," so B is incorrect. The name of the paper does not imply that patriots must have always lived in America, nor that immigrant's beliefs affect their patriotis.. Therefore, C and D are incorrect.

55. Which of the following does the American Patriot believe Catholic immigrants contribute?

(A) Lower taxes
(B) Increased protection of American workers
(C) A free school system
(D) Corruption of morals

The correct answer is D.

D is the correct answer because the American Patriot states they are opposed to "Papal Aggression & Roman Catholicism," "Nunneries and the Jesuits," and "Secret Foreign Orders," and concludes that "We are corrupted in the morals of our youth." A is incorrect because it states that, "we are burdened with enormous taxes by foreigners." B is also incorrect because it is in favor of protection against "Foreign Pauper Labor," but doesn't say Catholic immigrants contributed that increased protection. C is wrong because it states that it is in favor of "our present Free School System, but not Catholic Schools.

SECTION I, Part B

Time: 45 minutes 4 Questions

Directions: Read each question carefully and write your responses in the corresponding boxes on the free-response answer sheet.

Use complete sentences; an outline or bulleted list alone is not acceptable. On the actual test you may plan your answers in the exam booklet, but only your responses in the corresponding boxes on the free-response answer sheet will be scored.

> "Under these impressions, my humble opinion is, that there is a call for decision. Know precisely what the insurgents aim at. If they have real grievances, redress them if possible; or acknowledge the justice of them, and your inability to do it in the present moment. If they have not, employ the force of government against them at once. If this is inadequate, all will be convinced that the superstructure is bad, or wants support."
>
> "These are my sentiments. Precedents are dangerous things; let the reins of government then be braced and held with a steady hand, and every violation of the Constitution be reprehended: if defective, let it be amended, but not suffered to be trampled upon whilst it has an existence...."
>
> *George Washington to Henry Lee, October 31, 1786 writing about Shays' Rebellion*

> "I hold it that a little rebellion now and then is a good thing, and as necessary in the political world as storms in the physical... An observation of this truth should render honest republican governors so mild in their punishment of rebellions as not to discourage them too much. It is a medicine necessary for the sound health of government...."
>
> "Let them take arms. The remedy is to set them right as to facts, pardon & pacify them. What signify a few lives lost in a century or two? The tree of liberty must be refreshed from time to time with the blood of patriots & tyrants. It is its natural manure."
>
> *Thomas Jefferson to James Madison, January 20th, 1787*
> *Thomas Jefferson to William Smith, November 13th, 1787*
> *Writing about the Shays' Rebellion*

1. Using the excerpts above, answer parts A, B, and C.
   A. **Briefly explain why Washington advocated a strong government response.**

   Shays' Rebellion was the first major armed rebellion in the newly formed United States. The Massachusetts state government was unresponsive to the rebels and their reasons for discontent. To the rebels, the government (both state and federal) was far away and not responding to their cries for help in very bad economic times. George Washington understood that the actions of the rebels could undermine and even overthrow the young nation's government. He emphasized a position of strength because he realized the underlying forces of discontent and resistance showed the internal conflicts that were existing in the post-Revolutionary period. Washington believed government needed to show its strength and an ability to handle the crisis to avoid the problems similar to the problems the colonists had encountered with England.

   B. **Briefly explain why Jefferson supported exactly the opposite.**

   Thomas Jefferson would have supported a position different from George Washington's because the two had different philosophies about the role of government. Thomas Jefferson believed in republicanism and the common person. He believed in states' rights and the ability of individuals to express themselves. Shays' Rebellion was an example of self-expression and a way for the common people to make the government take notice of their economic plight. Jefferson did not believe that small rebellions would lead to larger revolts against the government, and he believed that rebellions, such as this one, were similar to cyclical events—events that would arise and then go away when the government provided facts to the people and pacified them. Jefferson also believed that actions such as the Shays' Rebellion should not be discouraged because they only made democracy stronger.

   C. **Provide one example of why the Articles of Confederation, in existence for ten years, were viewed to be too weak to maintain law and order during this rebellion.**

   The Articles of Confederation would have been viewed as being too weak to maintain law and order during Shays' Rebellion because the central government was weak. Most of the power was given to the states and there would have been no executive (at the central level of government) to use military force, if necessary to put down the rebellion. Each state retained its sovereignty and independence. While the Articles provided for a "loose" confederation of states, they intended the states to unite for common defense. Shays' Rebellion was a state matter and the Articles of Confederation were not designed to resolve such issues.

The Big Stick in the Caribbean, 1904

2. **Use the image above and your knowledge of history to answer A, B, and C.**
   A. Explain Theodore Roosevelt's approach to foreign policy as depicted in the image.

   Theodore Roosevelt expanded America's role in the world. His policy was to "speak softly and carry a big stick." When European powers attempted to collect debts owed to them by Latin American nations, Roosevelt announced a corollary to the Monroe Doctrine and indicated that they were not to intervene in Latin America, that the U.S. would enforce this policy. President Roosevelt also supported Panama's efforts to secede from Colombia, which led to the construction of the Panama Canal in the area that had once belonged to Colombia. By announcing the Roosevelt Corollary, the President indicated to the world that the U.S. would be willing to back up whatever position it took in foreign affairs.

B. Explain one similarity between this approach and the Cold War approach to maintaining peace.

One similarity between President Theodore Roosevelt's approach to foreign policy and the approach to maintaining peace during the Cold War was President Reagan's attitude toward the Soviet Union. The presidents before Reagan—Carter, Ford, and Nixon—had pursued détente to maintain peaceful co-existence. However, Ronald Reagan believed, like Roosevelt, that peace would be the result of a country's strength. President Reagan built up the supply of our country's weapons and military technology and strengthened the American free-market system. His showing of U.S. strength during the Cold War was similar to the show of strength that Theodore Roosevelt showed in Latin America during the early 1900s.

C. Give one example of how the point of view you described in Part (a), was used by Theodore Roosevelt during his term.

President Roosevelt realized the importance of having a shorter transportation route from the Atlantic Ocean to the Pacific Ocean. Until the Panama Canal was built ships had to travel around South America to reach the opposite ocean. When his administration supported Panama's independence from Colombia, it led the way to negotiations for the building of a canal across the isthmus of Panama. The corollary to the Monroe Doctrine kept European powers out of Latin America and provided an avenue for U.S. dominance in the area and in negotiations for the canal.

"To establish such a right, it remains to show the relation of such an institution, to one or more of the specified powers of the Government. Accordingly, it is affirmed, that it has a relation, more or less direct, to the power of collecting taxes; to that of borrowing money; to that of regulating trade between the states; and to those of raising the maintaining fleets and armies. To the two former, the relation may be said to be immediate. And, in the last place, it will be argued, that it is clearly within the provision which authorizes the making of all needful rules and regulations concerning the property of the US, as the same has been practiced upon by the government."

Alexander Hamilton, "Statement on the Constitutionality of the National Bank" 1791.

The Constitution gives Congress the power to make all laws necessary and proper for carrying into execution the enumerated powers. But they can all be carried into execution without a bank. A bank, therefore, is not necessary, and consequently, not authorized by this phrase.

The Constitution allows only the means which are necessary, not those which are merely convenient for effecting the numerated powers. If such a latitude of construction be allowed to this phrase as to give any non enumerate power, it will go to every one…Therefore it was that the constitution restrained them to be necessary means; that is to say to those means, without which the grant of the power would be nugatory."

Thomas Jefferson, Statement on the Constitutionality of the National Bank, 1791.

3. **Based upon the two opinions stated above about the First National Bank of the United States, respond to A, B, C:**
   A. Briefly explain Hamilton's argument on the National Bank.

   Alexander Hamilton favored the establishment of a National Bank. This excerpt presents his views on why the bank's creation is justified. Hamilton is explaining that the "necessary and proper" clause justifies the creation of the bank. The language of the clause expresses that Congress has implied powers and, that as a result, the creation of a National Bank is justified. Hamilton ties the implied power to specific powers of Congress, i.e., the taxing authority and the borrowing of money. He also relates these powers to even broader powers of regulating trade and raising fleets and maintaining armies.

B. Briefly explain Jefferson's argument on the National Bank.

Thomas Jefferson opposed the creation of a National Bank. Where Hamilton was a Federalist and a supporter of a strong central government, Jefferson was a states' rights advocate. Jefferson believed the "necessary and proper" clause only provided Congress with powers in addition to the enumerated powers that were both necessary and proper. Jefferson believed that the creation / charter of a National Bank was not necessary, therefore an improper power of Congress. He believed that the creation of a National Bank was only because a bank would be "convenient" and that if Congress had within its power to legislate on something that was only "convenient" then its powers could become unlimited.

C. What types of freedom are the two leaders advocating for and how do you know this?

Both men wanted to protect the freedoms that were expressed in the Bill of Rights and also the freedoms identified in the Preamble to the Constitution. They wanted to protect the people from tyranny and from overreaching of government. They wanted to protect the citizens of the new country from all of the types of oppression they experienced during the reign of the British monarchs. However, Jefferson and Hamilton approached the issue of freedom differently. Hamilton believed a strong central government could best protect the Americans, and Jefferson believed that the people themselves and their state governments could protect the freedoms.

"Just as the period of American history from 1933 to the late 1960s… was chiefly one of liberal reform, so the past thirty-five years have been an era of conservatism…Without Reagan, the conservative movement would never have been as successful as it was. In his political personal, as well as his policies, Reagan embodied a new fusion of deeply conservative politics with some of the rhetoric and even a bit of the spirit of Franklin D. Roosevelt's New Deal and of John F. Kennedy's New Frontier…The impact of the sage of Regan is indicated even more strongly by the guiding assumptions and possibilities of American politics and government, and the hold they have on public opinion. Thirty years ago, the proposition that reducing taxes on the rich was the best solution for all economic problems inspired only a few on the right-wing fringe. Today, it drives the national domestic agenda and is so commonplace that it sometimes appears to have become the conventional wisdom.

Sean Wilentz, The Age of Reagan, 2008.

4. Using the excerpts above, answer parts A, B, and C.
   A. **Based upon the historian, Sean Wilentz, argument, explain his point about the significance of Ronald Reagan for American identity in the 1980s.**

   Ronald Reagan became President during the Cold War. His predecessors had followed the policy of détente to keep the Soviet Union contained and to keep a balance of power between the free and communist countries. Wilentz argues that Reagan's guiding assumptions for the American public and his belief in the possibilities for government had a strong hold on the American public. The example that Wilentz provides is that of reducing taxes on the wealthy. He argues that the idea of tax reduction was a way to solve the economic problems of the nation. By reducing taxes, the wealthy could identify with others in the nation and contribute to the economy by increased spending. Another example of Reagan's significance in relation to the American identify is the promotion of conservative values. America shifted from a more liberal approach to problem solving, policy, and public attitudes. As a result, the identify of American society became that of a conservative society, personally and politically.

   B. **Provide ONE piece of evidence about the rise of Reagan and his ability to gain American support.**

   Ronald Reagan had served as governor of California before he was elected President. His rise in popularity occurred because he maintained contact with the American people. He used radio broadcasts to express his views, and he wrote editorials that were published regularly in newspapers across the United States. The vitality he showed at public events countered the issue of his age. He also promoted the principles of the founders of American government and believed these basic ideas, expressed in the 1700s, could be used to solve the problems society was facing. He was called "the great communicator" and people listened to his messages, causing them to vote for him and elect him to the presidency.

C. **What type of freedom did Reagan support and what type of freedom did he criticize?**

President Reagan feared the freedom of achieving success because he thought people could lose their perspective on issues and become lazy and complacent. He believed that people would not appreciate success and would fail to see dangers that may be on the horizon. He also believed that society did not progress after the Vietnam War era because American foreign policy did not prosper, and, as a result Communism was not curtailed. He believed that freedom over Communism could only be accomplished by continuing to resist it and to promote freedom throughout the world.

UNITED STATES HISTORY SECTION II

Total Time: 1 hour, 35 minutes

Question 1 (Document-Based Question)
Suggested reading period: 15 minutes
Suggested writing period: 45 minutes

Directions: Question 1 is based on the accompanying documents. The documents have been edited for the purpose of this exercise. You are advised to spend 15 minutes reading and planning and 45 minutes writing your answer.

Write your responses on the lined pages that follow the question.

In your response you should do the following:
- State a relevant thesis that directly addresses all parts of the question.
- Support the thesis or a relevant argument with evidence from all, or all but one, of the documents.
- Incorporate analysis of all, or all but one, of the documents into your argument.
- Focus your analysis of each document on at least one of the following: intended audience, purpose, historical context, and/or point of view.
- Support your argument with analysis of historical examples outside the documents.
- Connect historical phenomena relevant to your argument to broader events or processes.

DOCUMENT 1

"The First Cotton Gin", an engraving from Harper's Magazine, 1869. This carving depicts a roller gin, which preceded Eli Whitney's invention

DOCUMENT 2

Assenting to the "self-evident truth" maintained in the American Declaration of Independence, "that all men are created equal, and endowed by their Creator with certain inalienable rights— among which are life, liberty and the pursuit of happiness," I shall strenuously contend for the immediate enfranchisement of our slave population.

"I will be heard" – William Lloyd Garrison (1833?)

DOCUMENT 3

And on the 12th of May, 1828, I heard a loud noise in the heavens, and the Spirit instantly appeared to me and said the Serpent was loosened, and Christ had laid down the yoke he had borne for the sins of men, and that I should take it on and fight against the Serpent, for the time was fast approaching when the first should be last and the last should be first.

"The last shall be first" CONFESSIONS OF NAT TURNER (1831??)

DOCUMENT 4

Without planters there could be no cotton; without cotton no wealth. Without them Mississippi would be a wilderness, and revert to the aboriginal possessors. Annihilate them tomorrow, and this state and every southern state might be bought for a song. I am not advocating this system; but destroy it—and the southern states become at once comparative ciphers in the Union.

"Cotton and Negroes are the constant theme"
Selection from 1835 book The South-West J. H. Ingram

DOCUMENT 5

What would you have if the Union were dissevered? Why, sir, then the severed parts would be independent of each other—foreign countries! Slaves taken from the one into the other would then be like slaves now escaping from the United States into Canada. There would be no right of extradition; no right to demand your slaves; no right to appeal to the courts of justice to demand your slaves which escape, or the penalties for decoying them.

The Compromise of 1850 Henry Clay's address
to Congress in February 1850

DOCUMENT 6

It is a great mistake to suppose that disunion can be effected by a single blow. The cords which bind these states together in one common Union are far too numerous and powerful for that. Disunion must be the work of time. It is only through a long process, and successively, that the cords can be snapped, until the whole fabric falls asunder. Already the agitation of the slavery question has snapped some of the most important, and has greatly weakened all the others, as I shall proceed to show.

The cords which bind the states together are not only many, but various in character. Among them, some are spiritual or ecclesiastical; some political; others social. Others pertain to the benefit conferred by the Union, and others to the feelings of duty and obligation.

"[The South] has little left to surrender" John C. Calhoun
Speech given to Congress 1850

DOCUMENT 7

...[W]e must not confound the rights of citizenship which a state may confer within its own limits, and the rights of citizenship as a member of the Union. It does not by any means follow, because he has all the rights and privileges of a citizen of a State, that he must be a citizen of the United States. He may have all of the rights and privileges of the citizen of a State, and yet not be entitled to the rights and privileges of a citizen in any other State. For, previous to the adoption of the Constitution of the United States, every State had the undoubted right to confer on whomever it pleased the character of a citizen, and to endow him with all its rights. But this character, of course, was confined to the boundaries of the State, and gave him no rights or privileges in other States beyond those secured to him by the laws of nations and the comity of States. Nor have the several States surrendered the power of conferring these rights and privileges by adopting the Constitution of the United States.

Dred Scott v. Sandford (1857) Decision: J: Roger B. Taney

1. **Analyze how the issue of slavery led to increased sectional tensions between the 1830s-1850s.**

   The issue of slavery, which began to increase in intensity during the 1820s and 1830s, led to sectional tensions and was not decided until the end of the Civil War and ratification of the Thirteenth Amendment. The economic basis of the South was the plantation system, and the foundation of the plantation system was slave labor. The invention of the cotton gin in the 1790s had increased production in the processing cotton, and ultimately led to an increase of profits, or potential profits, for the landowners. The planters needed the slave labor to develop the wealth cotton could bring the South. (Documents 1 and 4).

   During this time the abolitionist movement also gained momentum. The movement led to the development of the Underground Railroad to provide slaves' escape into freedom. Some of the advocates of freedom for slaves promoted the idea of giving slaves (former slaves) the right to vote and citizenship because all men were created equal. Nat Turner, a slave, led a revolt of slaves to "fight against the serpent" who he likely believes was the slave owner, since slaves were considered personal property. (Documents 2 and 3).

   The issue of slavery was debated in Congress and the Missouri Compromise was an attempt at dividing free and slave areas. The Compromise of 1850 was a further effort at reconciling the differences in thought. The Fugitive Slave Law also provided that slave owners had a right to retrieve their property if the slaves escaped and were found in a non-slave jurisdiction. As the slave issue was debated in the early 1800s, some members of society argued that the Union should continue to exist because it was needed for the protection of slaves. Others argued that any disunion that might occur should be the work of time, rather than the work of individuals because there were too many cords binding the nation. The federal courts also entered the debate and held that slaves could not gain their freedom if they moved to a free state because slaves were not citizens. (Documents 5, 6, and 7).

The issue of slavery began to be debated with intensity in the 1820s. Various groups, ranging from land owners, abolitionists, slaves to legislators and the courts contributed to the raging issue which eventually led to secession of South Carolina and other southern states and the beginning of the Civil War / War Between the States.

Question 2 or Question 3
Suggested writing period: 35 minutes

Directions: Choose EITHER question 2 or question 3. You are advised to spend 35 minutes writing your answer. Write your responses on the lined pages that follow the questions.

In your response you should do the following:
- State a relevant thesis that directly addresses all parts of the question.
- Support your argument with evidence, using specific examples.
- Apply historical thinking skills as directed by the question.

2. Evaluate the extent to which United States involvement in the First World War in 1917–1918 contributed to maintaining continuity as well as fostering change in United States foreign policy and involvement in foreign affairs.

   The United States entered into a period of isolationism after its involvement in World War I. The need for natural resources and the desire for colonies during the early 1900s led to policies of imperialism by many European nations. President Wilson had run his campaign for a second term based on the idea that he had kept the world safe for democracy. American entered World War I, after it could no longer maintain its neutrality. German U-boats began sinking merchant ships and after the ocean liner Lusitania was sunk, America entered the war. At the Paris peace talks, President Wilson proposed the Fourteen Points for lasting world peace. One of the provisions provided for a creation of a League of Nations. The United States Senate failed to ratify the treaty. After the war, American entered a period of isolationism, which it exited when the country declared war on Japan in December 1941.

3. Compare and contrast the similarities and differences, as well as the purposes and goals, of Jacksonian democracy in the 1820s and 1830s, with FDR's New Deal programs 100 years later.

   Jacksonian democracy of the 1820s and 30s was a democracy for the common man. President Jackson showed his loyalty to those who had supported him during the campaign and awarded them with government jobs. During his presidency, the issue of the re-charter of the National Bank was brought before Congress. He opposed the bank because he did not want the wealth of the country in the hands of a few people. He favored internal improvements, such as roads and canals, and he backed cheap land prices while pursuing a program of Indian removal. He tried to gain support of the voters who felt cut off from their government and economic independence. Jacksonian government favored limited government and equality of individuals. The Jacksonian Democrats favored territorial expansion and rights of the common man to have a greater voice in government.

Franklin D. Roosevelt's New Deal was focused on the common person who had been adversely affected by the Great Depression. His goal was to put people back to work and he created many agencies to assist in this effort. The agencies were called the alphabet agencies because many of their names were shortened to letters of the alphabet. For example, the Civil Conservation Corps was the C.C.C. and the Works Progress Administration was the WPA.

Jackson was a Westerner, a war hero and a slave owner but was treated as the "common man." Roosevelt, on the other hand, was from a wealthy New York family and came to the aid of the common person during an economic crisis. Jackson's program of internal improvements was not successful and many of the roads and canals that were begun during the Jackson presidency were not completed because of the Panic of 1837. Roosevelt's plan for the economy began after the stock market crash of 1929 and the closing of banks.

SECTION V:
Sample Test Two

Sample Test Two

Instructions

Section I, Part A of this exam contains 55 multiple-choice questions. Fill in only the circles for numbers 1 through 55 on your multiple-choice answer sheet. Because this section offers only four answer options for each question, do not mark the (E) answer circle for any question.

Indicate all of your answers to the multiple-choice questions on the multiple-choice answer sheet. No credit will be given for anything written in this exam booklet, but you may use the booklet for notes or scratch work. After you have decided which of the suggested answers is best, completely fill in the corresponding circle on the multiple-choice answer sheet. Give only one answer to each question. If you change an answer, be sure that the previous mark is erased completely. Here is a sample question and answer.

Sample Quesstion

Chicago is a
(A) state
(B) city
(C) country
(D) continent

Sample Answer

Ⓐ ● Ⓒ Ⓓ Ⓔ

Use your time effectively, working as quickly as you can without losing accuracy. Do not spend too much time on any one question. Go on to other questions and come back to the ones you have not answered if you have time. It is not expected that everyone will know the answers to all of the multiple-choice questions.

Your total score on the multiple-choice section is based only on the number of questions answered correctly. Points are not deducted for incorrect answers or unanswered questions.

UNITED STATES HISTORY SECTION I, Part A

Time: 55 minutes 55 Questions

Directions: Each of the questions or incomplete statements below is followed by four suggested answers or completions. Select the one that is best in each case and then fill in the appropriate letter in the corresponding space on the answer sheet.

Answer Questions 1–3 using the passage below:

> This case turns upon the constitutionality of an act of the general assembly of the state of Louisiana, . . providing for separate railway carriages for the white and colored races...That it does not conflict with the 13th Amendment, which abolished slavery and involuntary servitude, except as a punishment for crime, is too clear for argument...The object of the 14th amendment was undoubtedly to enforce the absolute equality of the two races before the law,... Laws permitting, and even requiring their separation in places where they are liable to be brought into contact do not necessarily imply the inferiority of either race to the other...Legislation is powerless to eradicate racial instincts or to abolish distinctions based on physical differences...If the civil and political right of both races be equal, one cannot be inferior to the other civilly or politically. If one race be inferior to the other socially, the Constitution of the United States cannot put them upon the same plane.
>
> *Majority opinion written by Justice Henry Billings Brown in Plessy v. Ferguson, 1896*

1. **What is the significance of the Plessy decision?**

   (A) The Thirteenth Amendment is applicable to the issue in the case.
   (B) The Fourteenth Amendment is the basis for eradicating racial instincts.
   (C) The doctrine of equal protection is the basis for the decision.
   (D) The doctrine of separate but equal is the basis for the decision.

2. **The US Supreme Court found that separate facilities were not equal facilities in one area of life. What case was this?**

   (A) Schenk v. United States
   (B) Standard Oil of New Jersey v. United States
   (C) Brown v. Board of Education of Topeka
   (D) Korematsu v. United States

3. Which of the following is NOT an example of a Jim Crow law?

   (A) Citizenship
   (B) Types of schools
   (C) Voting restrictions
   (D) Curfew

Answer Questions 4–6 using the passage below:

> The war had not long been over when cries of alarm from parents, teachers, and moral preceptors began to rend in the air…The dresses that the girls—and for that matter most of the older women—were wearing seemed alarming enough…the hem was now all well of nine inches above the ground…The flappers wore thin dresses, short-sleeved and occasionally (in the evening) sleeveless; some of the wilder young things rolled their stocking below their knees… and many of them were visibly using cosmetics.
>
> *Only Yesterday* by Frederick Lewis Allen (1931)

4. What time period is the focus of the excerpt from this author's work?

   (A) Post World War II
   (B) 1920s
   (C) Progressive Era
   (D) Era of Imperialism

5. Between the conclusion of World War I and the beginning of World War II, there was a Great Migration in the United States. To what does the term "Great Migration" apply?

   (A) A new wave of immigrants coming into the United States
   (B) A movement westward
   (C) The movement to urban areas by blacks to obtain better jobs
   (D) The movement of wildlife into areas that led to the establishment of national parks

6. At the conclusion of World War I, the Senate was asked to ratify which treaty?

   (A) Fourteen Points
   (B) Treaty of Paris
   (C) Treaty of Versailles
   (D) United Nations treaty

Answer questions 7–9 using the picture below:

Poster promoting victory gardens

7. **During what time period were Victory Gardens encouraged?**

   (A) Era of Imperialism
   (B) Progressive Era
   (C) The Civil War
   (D) World War I and II

8. **The Lend Lease Act of 1941 was a program that benefitted which country?**

   (A) England
   (B) Japan
   (C) Italy
   (D) Poland

9. Which leaders signed the Atlantic Charter?

   (A) Joseph Stalin and Franklin D. Roosevelt
   (B) Winston Churchill and Joseph Stalin
   (C) Franklin D. Roosevelt and Winston Churchill
   (D) Joseph Stalin, Winston Churchill, and Franklin D. Roosevelt

Answer Questions 10–12 using the passage below:

> "I have no purpose, directly or indirectly, to interfere with the institution of slavery in the States where it exists. I believe I have no lawful right to do so, and I have no inclination to do so."
>
> *Abraham Lincoln, first inaugural address, March 5, 1861.*

10. **The sentiment expressed above by President Lincoln at his inauguration demonstrates**

    (A) part of his early effort at reconciliation and avoidance of war before shots were fired at Fort Sumter.
    (B) his uncertainty about whether the north should compel the southern states to stay in the union.
    (C) the prevailing sentiment of the more ardent members of the Republican Party at that time.
    (D) how the Thirteenth Amendment was a defiance of the rule of law.

11. **The quote above can most closely be analogized to**

    (A) George Washington's determination to not go to war with France in the 1790s.
    (B) Lyndon Johnson's decision to commit US troops to Vietnam after the Gulf of Tonkin incident.
    (C) Woodrow Wilson's campaign promise in the 1916 presidential election that, if elected, he would continue to keep the US out of the war in Europe.
    (D) James K. Polk's announcement that he would not run for re-election to the presidency in 1848.

12. **Which of the following fits best with the statement "I believe I have no lawful right to do so" in the quote above?**

    (A) The Emancipation Proclamation
    (B) The Thirteenth Amendment
    (C) Constitutional limits on the power of the presidency
    (D) Manifest Destiny

Answer Questions 13–15 using the passage below:

> Not surprisingly, European immigrants did not relish the idea of taking the place of blacks as plantation laborers. One Alabama planter brought in thirty Swedes in 1866, housed them in slave cabins and fed them the usual rations. Within a week the laborers had departed, informing him "they were not slaves."
>
> Eric Foner, *Reconstruction: America's Unfinished Revolution 1863–1877 (1988), p, 213.*

13. **The above quote is a demonstration of**

    (A) Northern efforts at reconstruction of the south after the civil war.
    (B) the beginnings of the labor movement.
    (C) problems resulting from an open immigration policy.
    (D) the challenge of adjusting to a slave-free economy in the south.

14. **A person most likely to agree with the Alabama planter's manner of dealing with his employees would be**

    (A) the owner of a textile factory in Lowell Massachusetts in 1825.
    (B) coal miners in Pennsylvania in 1869.
    (C) the owner of a slaughterhouse in Chicago in the 1880s.
    (D) the manager of an auto assembly line in Detroit in the 1970s.

15. **Based on trends in immigration in the latter half of the nineteenth century, the Swedish immigrants referred to above would most likely have done which of the following after leaving the plantation?**

    (A) Gone back to Sweden
    (B) Gone to another southern plantation to work
    (C) Gone to a city in the north seeking employment
    (D) Gone to the Northwest Territory to take advantage of the Homestead Act

Answer Questions 16–18 using the map below:

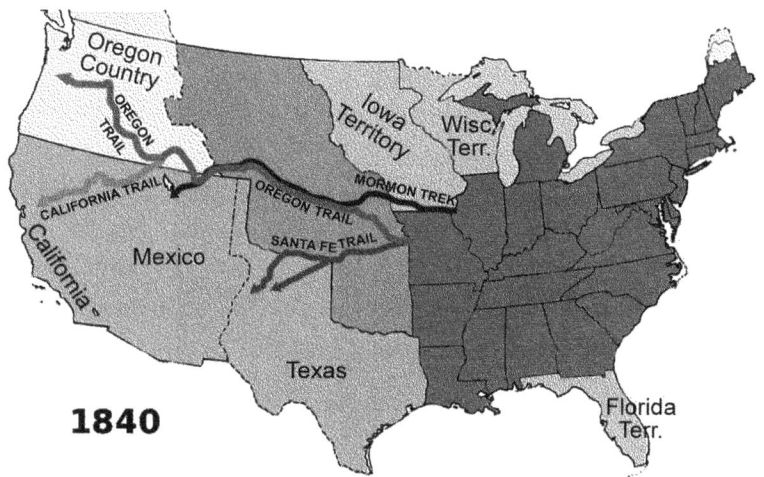

16. According to the map, which westward migration trail ended in United States territory?

    (A) The Oregon Trail
    (B) The Santa Fe Trail
    (C) The Mormon Trek
    (D) None of them did.

17. The westward migration portrayed in the map was most closely analogous to migration and expansion in which other period in American history?

    (A) The 1920s
    (B) The 1860s
    (C) The 1970s
    (D) The colonial era

18. Which of the following was least likely to be a motivation for a settler to use one of the trails identified on the map?

    (A) Gold
    (B) Land
    (C) Cattle ranching
    (D) Religious freedom

Answer Questions 19–21 using the passage below:

> A ton of goods can now be carried on the best managed railroads for a distance of a mile, for a sum so small that outside of China it would be difficult to find a coin of equivalent value to give a boy as a reward for carrying an ounce package across the street.
>
> *David A. Wells, economist, 1884, quoted in Degler's 'The Age of the Economic Revolution 1876–1900' (1977).*

19. **Which of the following persons would most likely think that the low railroad rates described in the quote above actually did more harm than good?**

    (A) A farmer in a remote area previously not serviced by a railroad, but which gains rail service
    (B) The owner of a warehouse next to a major rail line where goods are stored which are to be shipped by rail
    (C) An investor in one of the many railroads that failed in the 1870s due to overbuilding of rail lines
    (D) A ship owner who transports goods up and down the Atlantic coast

20. **The revolution in the cheap shipping of goods created by the great expansion of railroads in America in the latter part of the nineteenth century most closely approximates to which of the following?**

    (A) Building of the interstate highway system in the 1950s and 1960s
    (B) The pony express
    (C) Henry Ford's affordable "Model T," which allowed more common people to own cars
    (D) The increase in the number of luxury cruise ships in the twentieth century

21. **Which of the following would be least likely to benefit from low rail rates as described in the quote?**

    (A) A store owner in a town serviced by a rail line
    (B) The owner of a southern cotton plantation located on the banks of the Mississippi River
    (C) The owner of a new rail line which goes from silver mines in the mountains to major cities in the east
    (D) The owner of a private canal which extends from a rail stop into a remote farm area

210 AP US History

Answer Questions 22–24 using the passage below:

> ...Edison had said laconically: "the machine must talk." Kruesi scratched his head to indicate disbelief. Others present bet the "Old Man" cigars that the contraption would not work. When the thing was completed, it was a solid job of brass and iron, with a three-and-a-half-inch cylinder on a foot-long stylus and a hand crank to turn it...Edison deliberately fixed a sheet of tin foil around the cylinder, began turning the handle of the shaft, and shouted into one of the little diaphragms...Then he turned the shaft backward to the starting point...and once more turned the shaft handle forward. Out of the machine came forth what everyone recognized as the high-pitched voice of Thomas A. Edison himself...Kruesi turned pale and made some pious exclamation German. All the onlookers were dumfounded. Edison declared afterward, "I was never so taken aback in all my life. Everybody was astonished. I was always afraid of things that worked the first time."
>
> Matthew Josephson, *Edison: A Biography*, (1992 ed., p. 163).

22. **The invention of the phonograph described in the quote above would be least likely to benefit which of the following?**

    (A) A wealthy business owner in the north who enjoys listening to music
    (B) A farmer in the Midwest who enjoys listening to music
    (C) A struggling black sharecropper family in the south who enjoy listening to music
    (D) A university music instructor

23. **The invention of the phonograph described above would most closely correlate with which of the following?**

    (A) Alexander Hamilton's idea to form a national bank
    (B) Creation of the internal combustion engine
    (C) Increased economic ties between the United States and China in the late 1800s
    (D) Charles Darwin's theory of evolution

24. **The phonograph was a rare accomplishment that "worked the first time" it was tried. Which other American experiment could be said to be similar?**

    (A) FDR's attempts to stimulate the economy with "New Deal" legislation
    (B) The Wright Brothers' efforts to fly
    (C) Hamilton's national bank
    (D) The Thirteenth Amendment

Answer Questions 25–27 using the chart below:

MAIN SOURCES OF IMMIGRATION TO THE UNITED STATES, 1861–1890

	1861–1870	1871–1880	1881–1890
Europe:			
Austria-Hungary	7,800	72,969	353,719
Denmark	17,094	31,771	88,132
France	35,986	72,206	50,464
Germany	787,468	718,182	1,452,970
Great Britain:			
England	222,277	437,706	644,680
Scotland	38,769	87,564	149,869
Ireland	435,778	436,871	655,482
Italy	11,725	55,759	307,309
Norway	71,631	95,323	176,586
Sweden	37,667	115,922	391,776
Switzerland	23,286	28,293	81,988
USSR	2,512	39,284	213,282
Asia:			
China	64,301	123,201	61,711
America:			
Canada and Newfoundland	153,878	383,640	393,304

25. According to the data above, which nation provided stable rates of immigration to the United States between 1861–1890, which did not fluctuate greatly?

(A) China
(B) France
(C) Norway
(D) None of the above.

26. What was the primary difference between German and Irish migration rates as portrayed in the table?

(A) Irish migration was low to begin with, while German migration was always high.
(B) Immigration from both countries was strong to begin with, but had tapered off for Germany by the end of the century.
(C) Irish immigrants were resented more than German immigrants, no matter where they went.
(D) There was no significant difference between them.

27. Which of the nations providing a large number of immigrants as portrayed above also provided a large number of immigrants in the period prior to the civil war?

(A) Germany
(B) China
(C) Sweden
(D) Ireland

Answer Questions 28–30 using the passage below:

> Freedom has many difficulties and democracy is not perfect, but we have never had to put up a wall to keep our people in, to prevent them from leaving us. I want to say, on behalf of my countrymen, who live many miles away on the other side of the Atlantic, who are far distant from you, that they take the greatest pride that they have been able to share with you, even from a distance, the story of the last eighteen years…
>
> *John F. Kennedy, "Ich bin ein Berliner" speech*
> *June 26, 1963.*

28. Who gave this speech?

(A) President Franklin D. Roosevelt
(B) President Harry S. Truman
(C) President Dwight D. Eisenhower
(D) President John F. Kennedy

29. Why was the speech given in Berlin, Germany?

(A) Berlin was a divided city.
(B) Berlin was a staunch Western supporter.
(C) Berlin needed the encouragement to rebuild after the war.
(D) Berlin was celebrating its reunification.

30. What other aid plan helped the Germans after World War II?

(A) The Celler-Kefauver Act
(B) The Marshall Plan
(C) Lend Lease
(D) The Civil Rights Act of 1964

Answer Questions 31–33 using the following passage below:

> In our success lies the promise of a new life, freed from the heart-stopping fears that now beset the world. The beginning of victory for the great ideals for which millions have bled and died lies in building a workable plan. Now we approach the fulfillment of the aspirations of mankind...The basis of a sound foreign policy, in this new age, for all the nationals here gathered, is that: anything that happens, no matter where or how, which menaces the peace of the world, or the economic stability, concerns each and all of us.
>
> *Bernard Baruch presenting a plan to control atomic energy to the United Nations, 1946.*

31. **What was the reason people believed it was necessary to control atomic energy?**

    (A) It was an unknown source of power.
    (B) It has been used to destroy Asian cities at the end of World War II.
    (C) The Communists had more powerful weapons than the United States.
    (D) An arsenal of arms was needed for the protection of democracies.

32. **What legislation did Congress enact shortly before the end of the war to help Americans better their life and the economy of the United States after World War II?**

    (A) The Fullbright Act
    (B) The GI Bill of Rights
    (C) The Highway Act of 1956
    (D) Title IX

33. **Bernard Baruch's speech was expressing a concern about the period after World War II that was referred to as the**

    (A) Cold War
    (B) Era of the Berlin Wall
    (C) Age of European Recovery
    (D) Era of Neutrality

Answer Questions 34–36 using the passage below:

> "In recent months, the actions of the North Vietnamese regime have become steadily more threatening...
>
> As President of the United States I have concluded that I should now ask the Congress, on its part, to join in affirming the national determination that all such attacks will be met, and that the United States will continue in its basic policy of assisting the free nations of the area to defend their freedom."
>
> *Lyndon B. Johnson's Message to Congress*
> *August 5, 1964*

34. Why was the Vietnam War called "Mr. Johnson's War?"

    (A) The escalation of ground troops war during his administration
    (B) He successfully ended the war.
    (C) People opposed the US involvement in the war during his administration.
    (D) People favored the war during his administration.

35. What policy did Lyndon Johnson follow with regard to American involvement in Vietnam?

    (A) Pull out immediately and declare that the US had achieved its goals.
    (B) Gradually withdraw while asking for United Nations mediation.
    (C) Rapidly send American ground troops in for a massive invasion of North Vietnam.
    (D) Gradually escalate the direct American role in the war.

36. President Nixon's policy in Southeast Asia included all of the following except

    (A) escalation of American bombing of North Vietnam.
    (B) massive increases in American ground troops to invade North Vietnam.
    (C) secret direct negotiations with North Vietnam's foreign minister.
    (D) widening of the war by invading Cambodia.

Answer Questions 37–39 using the passage below:

> "It will be my sincere and constant desire to observe toward the Indian tribes within our limits a just and liberal policy, and to give that humane and considerate attention to their rights and their wants which is consistent with the habits of our Government and the feelings of our people."
>
> *Andrew Jackson, First Inaugural Address, 1829*

37. The statement from President Andrew Jackson addressed which of the following issues?

(A) The annexation of Hawaii for the purposes of trade with the South Pacific

(B) The movement of the Cherokee tribes from Georgia to Oklahoma to access gold and land

(C) The boundary dispute in the Southwest that led to the Mexican American War

(D) The assimilation of Native Americans into the American culture through the Dawes Act

38. Andrew Jackson's statement on Native Americans reinforced which of the following ideas or beliefs of the time period?

(A) The belief in Wilsonian idealism for foreign policy

(B) The ideology of Social Darwinism and racial hierarchies

(C) The ideology of cultural pluralism and multicultural respect for different ethnic groups

(D) The belief in Manifest Destiny and the American obligation to "civilize" the West

39. Andrew Jackson's statement is most similar to what other time period and American political policy?

(A) President McKinley's justification for annexing the Philippines to protect them against the other European powers

(B) President Truman's promise to protect the Western European nations against Communist expansion in the 1940s

(C) President Theodore Roosevelt's belief in protecting American economic and political interests in Latin America

(D) President John F. Kennedy's statement of promoting American beliefs abroad through the Peace Corps

Answer Questions 40–43 using the passage below:

> "The great common people of this country are slaves, and monopoly is the master. The West and South are bound and prostrate before the manufacturing east.
>
> The Parties lie to us and the political speakers mislead us.
>
> We want money, land, and transportation. We want the abolition of the national banks, and we want the power to make loans direct from the government. We want the accursed foreclosure system to be wiped out."
>
> *Mary Lease, lawyer, speech (1890)*

40. **Which of the following best explains the cause of some of the farmers' and workers' problems listed here?**

    (A) Conservation of natural resources
    (B) Racism and the sharecropping system
    (C) Industrialization and mechanization
    (D) Inefficiencies in government bureaucracy

41. **The ideas expressed in the passage reflect which of the following continuities in US History?**

    (A) Conflict over the role of women and gender rights
    (B) Conflict between immigrant and nativist groups
    (C) Conflict over the role of government in the economy
    (D) Conflict over racial justice and citizenship

42. **The statement in the quote is most like which other time period?**

    (A) Martin Luther King, Jr's fight for equal rights for all racial groups
    (B) The American colonists' fight for representation in the British system
    (C) The Evangelical fight in the 1970s for a more Christian American identity
    (D) Franklin Roosevelt's use of the federal government to increase economic power

43. **Which of the following statement explains the conflict over the role of the government in the 1890s?**

    (A) The fight over whether or not the government should provide for more representation
    (B) The fight over whether or not the government should become more active in racial equality
    (C) The fight over whether the government should apply the Bill of Rights to the states
    (D) The fight over whether or not the government should take a leadership role in global politics

Answer Questions 44–46 using the passage below:

> The judicial power of the United States is extended to all cases arising under the constitution.
>
> Thus, the particular phraseology of the constitution of the United States confirms and strengthens the principle, supposed to be essential to all written constitutions, that a law repugnant to the constitution is void, and that courts, as well as other departments, are bound by that instrument.
>
> *William Marbury v. James Madison,*
> *Secretary of State of the United States. Chief Justice Marshall*
> *delivered the opinion of the court. February 10, 1803.*

44. **Chief Justice John Marshall in ruling over Marbury v. Madison established one of the most important tenets of the American judicial system of judicial review, which**

    (A) established that the President had authority to override court decisions in the appointments process.
    (B) made Marbury the first Secretary of State appointed by an outgoing President.
    (C) allowed the Supreme Court to protect the integrity of the presidential appointments process.
    (D) gave the Supreme Court authority to enforce and interpret the Constitution when there is conflict between a law or presidential decision.

45. **Marshall also ruled over Gibbons v. Ogden in 1824, which involved a boat company monopoly operating on the Hudson River, and the States of New York and New Jersey. His ruling enforced which precept?**

    (A) Maritime trade laws within the United States
    (B) Interstate trade is regulated by Congress
    (C) International trade agreements by the states
    (D) A state's ability to grant monopolies in trade

46. **In his many landmark cases, Chief Justice Marshall, a Federalist himself,**

    (A) ruled on the supremacy of federal law over state law.
    (B) ruled in favor of slavery as a Southern economic need.
    (C) protected state rights.
    (D) allowed for equal standing of state and federal law.

Answer Questions 47–49 using the passage below:

> There was indeed a distinctly American approach to manufacturing in the nineteenth century: it was the drive to mass production and mass distribution in every field—from foodstuffs to soap and candles, axes and locomotives, horseshoes, wooden doors, carriage wheels, bedroom furniture, and almost anything else. The nature of the machinery and the underlying technologies varied from product to product—soap making was different from steel-making, and neither had much in common with making guns or clocks. And sometimes, American mass production was all about organization, not machinery, as in the antebellum shoe industry. It was the uniquely American penchant for scale and speed that ultimately created the mass-consumption economy. Mass consumption, the rise of a successful middle class, and a democratized government were all part of the package that was the great American experiment.
>
> *Charles R. Morris. The Dawn of Innovation:*
> *The First American Industrial Revolution. 2012*

47. **Which of the following was NOT an effect of the Industrial Revolution?**

    (A) An increasing number of people worked in factories
    (B) An increasing number of people lived in cities
    (C) An increasing number of people worked on family farms
    (D) An increasing number of people left the family farms

48. **Why was industrialization in the United States primarily concentrated in the Northeast?**

    (A) This region had the greatest supplies of capital and labor.
    (B) The climate of the North favored industrial development.
    (C) Other regions of the country lacked water transportation.
    (D) The Midwest and South had fewer natural resources.

49. **The experiment of industrialization resulted in several problems that were realized several decades after the industrialization had begun. Which policies of the US government allowed such conditions to develop and later led to the growth of labor unions to correct abuses of workers?**

    (A) Laissez faire policies toward big business
    (B) Antitrust policies toward monopolies
    (C) Imperialist policies regarding territorial expansion
    (D) Isolationist policies regarding international alliance

Answer Questions 50–52 using the picture below:

Trail of Tears 1838–1839. Painting by Robert Lindneux, 1942.

50. What does the painting refer to?

(A) Indians crying with joy since they were granted new settlements west of the Mississippi
(B) Indians crying with joy, because the Supreme Court overturned President Jackson's action and they were returning to their settlements
(C) Indians crying in sorrow, because, they were forced to leave their settlements and move west
(D) Indians crying in pain, because, they undertook a migration and the weather turned on them

51. Andrew Jackson's Indian Removal Act of 1830 was condoned by the country because

(A) no one understood the impact the Act would have on the Native Americans.
(B) people wanted the Indians to occupy the West and make it livable for the whites.
(C) they wanted slaves to occupy the vacated Indian settlements in the Eastern states.
(D) many saw the Indians as a morally, economic, and culturally inferior race.

52. Which of the following constitutes a significant change in the treatment of American Indians during the last half of the nineteenth century?

(A) The beginnings of negotiations with individual tribes
(B) The start of a removal policy
(C) The abandonment of the reservation system
(D) The admission of all American Indians to the full rights of United States citizenship

Questions 53–55 refer to the following image:

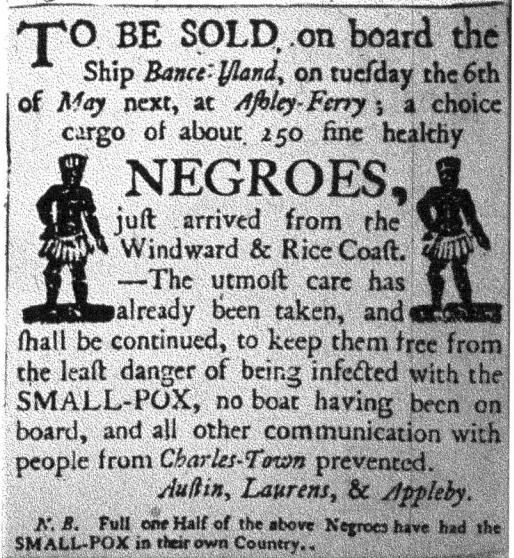

Advertisement, Charleston, South Carolina, 1780s
Image courtesy of the Library of Congress

53. Which of the following BEST reflects the perspective of the above image?

    (A) Slaves represent a public health threat
    (B) The importation of slaves is a legitimate enterprise
    (C) The importation of slaves needs to be halted
    (D) Smallpox was a continuous danger to Charleston

54. Following the American Revolution, many Founding Fathers believed which of the following?

    (A) Slavery would gradually disappear in the United States.
    (B) The freeing of slaves should be outlawed.
    (C) Slavery would be the foundation of the American economy.
    (D) Freed slaves deserved government reparations for their suffering.

55. Which of the following was a reference to slavery in the Constitution?

    (A) Slavery was banned in the Northwest Territory.
    (B) Slavery was outlawed above the Mason-Dixon Line.
    (C) Slavery could not be outlawed.
    (D) A prohibition until 1808 of any law banning the importation of slaves.

SECTION I, Part B

Time: 45 minutes 4 Questions

Directions: Read each question carefully and write your responses in the corresponding boxes on the free-response answer sheet.

Use complete sentences; an outline or bulleted list alone is not acceptable. On the actual test you may plan your answers in the exam booklet, but only your responses in the corresponding boxes on the free-response answer sheet will be scored.

> The conditions which surround us best justify our co-operation; We meet in the midst of a nation brought to the verge of moral, political, and material ruin. Corruption dominates the ballot-box, the legislatures, the Congress, and touches even thee ermine of the bench. The people are demoralized: most of the estates have been compelled to isolate the voters at the polling places to prevent universal intimidation or bribery. The newspapers are largely subsidized or muzzled, public opinion silence, business prostrated, our homes covered with mortgages, labor impoverished and the land concentrating in the hands of the capitalists.
>
> *People's Party Platform, 1892*

1. Using the primary source above, respond to parts A, B, C:
   A. Summarize the point being made by James Weaver, the founder of the Populist or People's Party.

B. What were the economic factors that led to the rise of a People's Party in the late 1800s?

C. What would be a historical example of the late 1800s that would dispute Weaver's argument?

The population shift to the middle-class suburbs and the power shift to the Sunbelt economy requires a new metropolitan framework for political history and public policy that transcends the urban-suburban dichotomy and confronts instead of obscures the pervasive politics of class in the suburban strategies of the volatile center. Surely an honest assessment of the nation's collective responsibility in creating the contemporary metropolitan landscape remains an essential prerequisite for grappling with the spatial fusion of racial and class politics that ultimately produced an underlying suburban consensus in the electoral arena.

Matthew D. Lassiter, "The Silent Majority: Suburban Politics in the Sunbelt South", 2006.

2. Using the secondary source above, respond to parts A, B, C:
   A. Summarize the key issue that Lassiter is arguing about the changing economic demographics in the 2000s.

B. What were the contextual issues of the 1990s and 2000s that led to the changes in class that Lassiter is observing.

C. Give a piece of historical evidence that supports Lassiter's argument.

Under Hanoi's overall direction the Communists have established an extensive machine for carrying on the war within South Vietnam. The focal point is the Central Office for South Vietnam with its political and military subsections and other specialized agencies. A subordinate part of this Central Office is the liberation Front for South Vietnam. The front was formed at Hanoi's order in 1960.
Its principle function is to influence opinion abroad and to create the false impression that the aggression in South Vietnam is an indigenous rebellion against the established Government.

US State Department, 1965.

The US government has committed war crimes, crimes against peace and against mankind. In South Vietnam, half a million US and satellite troops have resorted to the most inhuman weapons and most barbarous methods of warfare, such as napalm, toxic chemicals and gases, to massacre our compatriots, destroy crops, and raze villages to the ground. In North Vietnam, thousands of US aircraft have dropped hundreds of thousands of tons of bombs, destroying towns, villages, factories, schools. In your message, you apparently deplore the sufferings and destruction in Vietnam. May I ask you: Who has perpetrated these monstrous crimes? It is the United States and satellite troops. The US government is entirely responsible for the extremely serious situation in Vietnam.

Ho Chi Minh to Lyndon Johnson, 1967

3. Using the differing primary sources above, respond to parts A, B, C:
   A. Explain the primary difference between the points of view of the two primary sources on the Vietnam War.

B. Explain ONE brief example that would support the point of view of the State Department primary source.

C. Explain ONE brief example that would support the point of view of Ho Chi Minh's letter to President Lyndon Johnson.

4. Using the image above, answer A, B, and C.
   A. Explain how the Great Awakening affected the religious beliefs of the American colonies in the 1730s.

B. Provide ONE brief example of a contrasting idea of the 1730s to the religious beliefs of the Great Awakening.

C. Provide ONE brief example of a similar American movement from another era.

UNITED STATES HISTORY SECTION II

Total Time: 1 hour, 35 minutes

Question 1 (Document-Based Question)
Suggested reading period: 15 minutes
Suggested writing period: 45 minutes

Directions: Question 1 is based on the accompanying documents. The documents have been edited for the purpose of this exercise. You are advised to spend 15 minutes reading and planning and 45 minutes writing your answer.

Write your responses on the lined pages that follow the question.

In your response you should do the following:
- State a relevant thesis that directly addresses all parts of the question.
- Support the thesis or a relevant argument with evidence from all, or all but one, of the documents.
- Incorporate analysis of all, or all but one, of the documents into your argument.
- Focus your analysis of each document on at least one of the following: intended audience, purpose, historical context, and/or point of view.
- Support your argument with analysis of historical examples outside the documents.
- Connect historical phenomena relevant to your argument to broader events or processes.

DOCUMENT 1

> Section 1. Every contract, combination in the form of trust or otherwise, or conspiracy, in restraint of trade of commerce among the several States, or with foreign nations, is hereby declared to be illegal. Every person who shall make any such contract or engage in any such combination or conspiracy, shall be deemed guilty of a misdemeanor, and, on conviction thereof, shall be punished by fine not exceeding five thousand dollars, or by imprisonment not exceeding one year, or by both said punishments, in the discretion of the court.

Section 2. Every person who shall monopolize, or attempt to monopolize, or combine or conspire with any other person or persons, to monopolize any part of the trade or commerce among the several States, or with foreign nations, shall be deemed guilty of a misdemeanor, and, on conviction thereof, shall be punished by fine, not exceeding one year, or by both said punishments, in the discretion of the court.

Sections 1 and 2 of the Sherman Antitrust Act of 1890.

DOCUMENT 2

You are hereby restrained, commanded, and enjoined absolutely to desist and refrain from in any way or manner interfering with, hindering, obstructing, or stopping any of the business of any of the following-named railroads…and from in any way interfering with, hindering, obstructing, or stopping any mail trains, express trains, whether freight or passenger, engaged in interstate commerce, or carrying passengers or freight between or among the States; and from compelling or inducing or attempting to compel or induce, threats, intimidations, persuasion, force, or violence, an of the employees of any of said railroads to refuse or fail to perform any of their duties as employees of any of said railroads in connection with the interstate business or commerce of such railroads, or the transportation of passengers or property between or among the States;…

To Eugene V. Debs and the American Railway Union, from Grover Cleveland.

DOCUMENT 3

The Senate of the United States shall be composed of two Senators from each State, elected by the people thereof, for six years; and each Senator shall have one vote. The electors in each State shall have the qualifications requisite for electors of the most numerous branch of the State legislatures.

Seventeenth Amendment

DOCUMENT 4

Section 3. No person shall on or after the date when the eighteenth amendment to the Constitution of the United States goes into effect, manufacture, sell, barter, transport, import, export, deliver, furnish or possess any intoxicating liquor except as authorized in this Act, and all the provisions of this Act shall be liberally construed to the end that the use of intoxicating liquor as a beverage may be prevented.

Volstead Act, 1919

DOCUMENT 5

Where there had been at the beginning of 1872 twenty-six refining firms in Cleveland, there were but six left. In three months before and during the oil war the Standard had absorbed twenty plants. I was generally charged by the Cleveland refiners that Mr. Rockefeller had used the South Improvement scheme to persuade or compel his rivals to sell to him…[Mr. Rockefeller] was no ordinary man. He had the powerful imagination to see what might be done with the oil business if it could be centered in his hands—the intelligence to analyze the problem into its elements and to find the key to control…

Ida Tarbell, "The Oil War of 1872" McClure's Magazine, 1903.

DOCUMENT 6

One of the striking features of our neighborhood twenty years ago, and one to which we never became reconciled, was the presence of huge wooden garbage boxes fastened to the street pavement in which the undisturbed refuse accumulated day by day…The children of our neighborhood twenty years ago played their games in and around these huge garbage boxes. They were the first objects that the toddling child learned to climb; their bulk afforded a barricade and their contents provided missiles in all the battles of the older boys, and finally they became the seats upon which absorbed lovers held enchanted converse…

Jane Addams, Forty Years of Hull House

DOCUMENT 7

> They tell us that the eight-hour movement cannot be enforced, for the reason that it must check industrial and commercial progress. I say that the history of this country, in its industrial and commercial relations, shows the reverse...They say they can't afford it. Is that true?... In all industries where the hours of labor are long, there you will find the least development of the power of invention. Where the hours of labor are long, men are cheap, and where men are cheap there is no necessity for invention. How can you expect a man to work ten or twelve or fourteen hours at his calling and then devote any tie to the invention of a machine, or discovery of a new principle or force? If he be so fortunate as to be able to read a paper, he will fall asleep before he has read through the second or third line.
>
> Samuel Gompers, "The labor movement is a fixed fact",
> May 1, 1890, Address in Louisville, Kentucky

1. **Analyze to what degree reformers were able to change the economic and political challenges of the period between 1890–1910.**

Question 2 or Question 3
Suggested writing period: 35 minutes

Directions: Choose EITHER question 2 or question 3. You are advised to spend 35 minutes writing your answer. Write your responses on the lined pages that follow the questions.

In your response you should do the following:
- State a relevant thesis that directly addresses all parts of the question.
- Support your argument with evidence, using specific examples.
- Apply historical thinking skills as directed by the question.

2. Analyze how the passage of the Fourteenth and Fifteenth amendments were or were not turning points in the political relationships of race in the United States between 1865 and 1900.

3. Compare and contrast the how the transportation revolutions of the 1820s and the 1920s affected social relationships in the United States.

Answer Sheet For Sample Test Two

1. Ⓐ Ⓑ Ⓒ Ⓓ Ⓔ
2. Ⓐ Ⓑ Ⓒ Ⓓ Ⓔ
3. Ⓐ Ⓑ Ⓒ Ⓓ Ⓔ
4. Ⓐ Ⓑ Ⓒ Ⓓ Ⓔ
5. Ⓐ Ⓑ Ⓒ Ⓓ Ⓔ
6. Ⓐ Ⓑ Ⓒ Ⓓ Ⓔ
7. Ⓐ Ⓑ Ⓒ Ⓓ Ⓔ
8. Ⓐ Ⓑ Ⓒ Ⓓ Ⓔ
9. Ⓐ Ⓑ Ⓒ Ⓓ Ⓔ
10. Ⓐ Ⓑ Ⓒ Ⓓ Ⓔ
11. Ⓐ Ⓑ Ⓒ Ⓓ Ⓔ
12. Ⓐ Ⓑ Ⓒ Ⓓ Ⓔ
13. Ⓐ Ⓑ Ⓒ Ⓓ Ⓔ
14. Ⓐ Ⓑ Ⓒ Ⓓ Ⓔ
15. Ⓐ Ⓑ Ⓒ Ⓓ Ⓔ
16. Ⓐ Ⓑ Ⓒ Ⓓ Ⓔ
17. Ⓐ Ⓑ Ⓒ Ⓓ Ⓔ
18. Ⓐ Ⓑ Ⓒ Ⓓ Ⓔ
19. Ⓐ Ⓑ Ⓒ Ⓓ Ⓔ
20. Ⓐ Ⓑ Ⓒ Ⓓ Ⓔ
21. Ⓐ Ⓑ Ⓒ Ⓓ Ⓔ
22. Ⓐ Ⓑ Ⓒ Ⓓ Ⓔ
23. Ⓐ Ⓑ Ⓒ Ⓓ Ⓔ
24. Ⓐ Ⓑ Ⓒ Ⓓ Ⓔ
25. Ⓐ Ⓑ Ⓒ Ⓓ Ⓔ
26. Ⓐ Ⓑ Ⓒ Ⓓ Ⓔ
27. Ⓐ Ⓑ Ⓒ Ⓓ Ⓔ
28. Ⓐ Ⓑ Ⓒ Ⓓ Ⓔ

29. Ⓐ Ⓑ Ⓒ Ⓓ Ⓔ
30. Ⓐ Ⓑ Ⓒ Ⓓ Ⓔ
31. Ⓐ Ⓑ Ⓒ Ⓓ Ⓔ
32. Ⓐ Ⓑ Ⓒ Ⓓ Ⓔ
33. Ⓐ Ⓑ Ⓒ Ⓓ Ⓔ
34. Ⓐ Ⓑ Ⓒ Ⓓ Ⓔ
35. Ⓐ Ⓑ Ⓒ Ⓓ Ⓔ
36. Ⓐ Ⓑ Ⓒ Ⓓ Ⓔ
37. Ⓐ Ⓑ Ⓒ Ⓓ Ⓔ
38. Ⓐ Ⓑ Ⓒ Ⓓ Ⓔ
39. Ⓐ Ⓑ Ⓒ Ⓓ Ⓔ
40. Ⓐ Ⓑ Ⓒ Ⓓ Ⓔ
41. Ⓐ Ⓑ Ⓒ Ⓓ Ⓔ
42. Ⓐ Ⓑ Ⓒ Ⓓ Ⓔ
43. Ⓐ Ⓑ Ⓒ Ⓓ Ⓔ
44. Ⓐ Ⓑ Ⓒ Ⓓ Ⓔ
45. Ⓐ Ⓑ Ⓒ Ⓓ Ⓔ
46. Ⓐ Ⓑ Ⓒ Ⓓ Ⓔ
47. Ⓐ Ⓑ Ⓒ Ⓓ Ⓔ
48. Ⓐ Ⓑ Ⓒ Ⓓ Ⓔ
49. Ⓐ Ⓑ Ⓒ Ⓓ Ⓔ
50. Ⓐ Ⓑ Ⓒ Ⓓ Ⓔ
51. Ⓐ Ⓑ Ⓒ Ⓓ Ⓔ
52. Ⓐ Ⓑ Ⓒ Ⓓ Ⓔ
53. Ⓐ Ⓑ Ⓒ Ⓓ Ⓔ
54. Ⓐ Ⓑ Ⓒ Ⓓ Ⓔ
55. Ⓐ Ⓑ Ⓒ Ⓓ Ⓔ

Sample Test Two Answers

Question Number	Correct Answer
1.	D
2.	C
3.	A
4.	B
5.	C
6.	C
7.	D
8.	A
9.	C
10.	A
11.	C
12.	C
13.	D
14.	C
15.	C
16.	D
17.	B
18.	A
19.	C
20.	A
21.	C
22.	C
23.	B
24.	D
25.	B
26.	D
27.	D
28.	D

Question Number	Correct Answer
29.	A
30.	B
31.	A
32.	B
33.	A
34.	A
35.	D
36.	B
37.	B
38.	D
39.	A
40.	C
41.	C
42.	B
43.	A
44.	D
45.	B
46.	A
47.	C
48.	A
49.	A
50.	C
51.	D
52.	D
53.	B
54.	A
55.	D

Sample Test Two Explanations

Answer Questions 1–3 using the passage below:

> This case turns upon the constitutionality of an act of the general assembly of the state of Louisiana, … providing for separate railway carriages for the white and colored races…That it does not conflict with the 13th Amendment, which abolished slavery and involuntary servitude, except as a punishment for crime, is too clear for argument…The object of the 14th amendment was undoubtedly to enforce the absolute equality of the two races before the law,… Laws permitting, and even requiring their separation in places where they are liable to be brought into contact do not necessarily imply the inferiority of either race to the other…Legislation is powerless to eradicate racial instincts or to abolish distinctions based on physical differences…If the civil and political right of both races be equal, one cannot be inferior to the other civilly or politically. If one race be inferior to the other socially, the Constitution of the United States cannot put them upon the same plane.
>
> *Majority opinion written by Justice Henry Billings Brown in Plessy v. Ferguson, 1896*

1. **What is the significance of the Plessy decision?**

    (A) The Thirteenth Amendment is applicable to the issue in the case.
    (B) The Fourteenth Amendment is the basis for eradicating racial instincts.
    (C) The doctrine of equal protection is the basis for the decision.
    (D) The doctrine of separate but equal is the basis for the decision.

The correct answer is D.
In the 1896 Plessy v. Ferguson Case separate-but-equal facilities were announced as being constitutional. This would lead to the Jim Crow Laws, which restricted access of African-Americans to federal employment and public services. A is wrong because the passage says, "That it does not conflict with the Thirteenth Amendment." B is also wrong because Fourteenth

Amendment cannot be the basis for eradicating racial instincts. The passage states, "Legislation is powerless to eradicate racial instincts or to abolish distinctions based on physical differences." C is incorrect because the doctrine of equal protection was established in the Fourteenth Amendment and the passage indicates that requiring separation of races does "not necessarily imply the inferiority of either race."

2. The US Supreme Court found that separate facilities were not equal facilities in one area of life. What case was this?

(A) Schenk v. United States
(B) Standard Oil of New Jersey v. United States
(C) Brown v. Board of Education of Topeka
(D) Korematsu v. United States

The correct answer is C.
Brown v. Board of Education determined that "separate but equal" does not apply to educational facilities. A is wrong because Schenk v. United States concluded that distributing leaflets to encourage resistance to the draft violated the Espionage act during WWI. B is incorrect because it refers to the case that broke up the Standard Oil monopoly. D, Korematsu v. United States, ordered Japanese Americans into internment camps during World War II.

3. Which of the following is NOT an example of a Jim Crow law?

(A) Citizenship
(B) Types of schools
(C) Voting restrictions
(D) Curfew

The correct answer is A.
Jim Crow laws did not address citizenship so A is the correct answer. B is wrong because Jim Crow laws were state-sanctioned segregation, which included separate schools. C is incorrect because poll taxes and literacy tests were imposed to prevent African Americans from voting. Many cities imposed a curfew of 10 pm in which African Americans could not leave their homes, so D is also incorrect.

Answer Questions 4–6 using the passage below:

> The war had not long been over when cries of alarm from parents, teachers, and moral preceptors began to rend in the air…The dresses that the girls—and for that matter most of the older women—were wearing seemed alarming enough…the hem was now all well of nine inches above the ground…The flappers wore thin dresses, short-sleeved and occasionally (in the evening) sleeveless; some of the wilder young things rolled their stocking below their knees… and many of them were visibly using cosmetics.
>
> *Only Yesterday by Frederick Lewis Allen (1931)*

238 AP US History

4. **What time period is the focus of the excerpt from this author's work?**

   (A) Post World War II
   (B) 1920s
   (C) Progressive Era
   (D) Era of Imperialism

The correct answer is B.
During the 1920s, women began wearing lighter dresses and shorter skirts in contrast to heavy, floor length ones worn in previous eras. Therefore B is the correct answer. The passage is dated 1931, therefore it cannot be A, post World War II. The Progressive era of the early twentieth century introduced legislation against monopolies, child labor and unsafe working conditions, and was unrelated to women's fashion, so D is incorrect..

5. **Between the conclusion of World War I and the beginning of World War II, there was a Great Migration in the United States. To what does the term "Great Migration" apply?**

   (A) A new wave of immigrants coming into the United States
   (B) A movement westward
   (C) The movement to urban areas by blacks to obtain better jobs
   (D) The movement of wildlife into areas that led to the establishment of national parks

The correct answer is C.
The Great Migration refers to the movement to urban areas by African Americans. A is not correct because the "Great Migration" refers to domestic population movements and not immigration. The westward movement occurred in the latter half of the nineteenth century, not between World War I and II, so B is incorrect. D is also incorrect because the national parks began being established in the nineteenth century.

6. **At the conclusion of World War I, the Senate was asked to ratify which treaty?**

   (A) Fourteen Points
   (B) Treaty of Paris
   (C) Treaty of Versailles
   (D) United Nations treaty

The correct answer is C.
The Senate was asked to ratify the Treaty of Versailles in 1919. Although they did not actually ratify the Treaty of Versailles this is the only one of the four answers that could be correct due to the time frame restriction of after World War I. President Woodrow Wilson's Fourteen Points was a plan for peace after World War I, but not a treaty, so A is an incorrect answer. B is also incorrect because the Treaty of Paris could refer to the one in 1763 ending the French and Indian War, another treaty in 1783, which ended the Revolutionary War, or the 1898 Treaty of Paris which ended the Spanish-American War. D is incorrect because The United Nations Charter was a treaty signed after World War II.

Answer Questions 7–9 using the picture below:

Poster promoting victory gardens

7. **During what time period were Victory Gardens encouraged?**

   (A) Era of Imperialism
   (B) Progressive Era
   (C) The Civil War
   (D) World War I and II

The correct answer is D.
Americans were encouraged to help in the war effort by growing their own fruits and vegetables so more commercial crops could be exported to allies' soldiers. D is the correct answer. A is incorrect because the United States' focus on imperialism was in the late 1800s and early 1900s, and is not related to Victory Gardens. B, The Progressive Era, was a time in the early 1900s when the government took a greater part in regulating the affairs of the nation. C is incorrect because during the Civil War Victory Gardens were not promoted.

8. **The Lend Lease Act of 1941 was a program that benefitted which country?**

   (A) England
   (B) Japan
   (C) Italy
   (D) Poland

The correct answer is A.
The Lend Lease Act of 1941 was a program in which the United States loaned weapons to England as a way to stay out of the war while helping the Allied powers, so A is the correct answer. Japan, Italy and Poland were not allies, so B, C, and D are incorrect.

9. **Which leaders signed the Atlantic Charter?**

   (A) Joseph Stalin and Franklin D. Roosevelt
   (B) Winston Churchill and Joseph Stalin
   (C) Franklin D. Roosevelt and Winston Churchill
   (D) Joseph Stalin, Winston Churchill, and Franklin D. Roosevelt

The correct answer is C.
The Atlantic Charter was a post WWII plan, between Churchill and Roosevelt, regarding collective security, disarmament, self-determination, economic cooperation and freedom of the seas. So C is the correct answer. Joseph Stalin was not included in the deal, so A, B, and D are incorrect.

Answer Questions 10–12 using the passage below:

> "I have no purpose, directly or indirectly, to interfere with the institution of slavery in the States where it exists. I believe I have no lawful right to do so, and I have no inclination to do so."
> *Abraham Lincoln, first inaugural address, March 5, 1861.*

10. **The sentiment expressed above by President Lincoln at his inauguration demonstrates**

    (A) part of his early effort at reconciliation and avoidance of war before shots were fired at Fort Sumter.
    (B) his uncertainty about whether the north should compel the southern states to stay in the union.
    (C) the prevailing sentiment of the more ardent members of the Republican Party at that time.
    (D) how the Thirteenth Amendment was a defiance of the rule of law.

The correct answer is A.
This 1861 passage was A, part of Lincoln's attempt to avoid civil war. His statement that he believes he has "no lawful right to do so," does not imply uncertainty so B is incorrect. C is also incorrect because most Republicans at the time were opposed to slavery. D is incorrect because

the Thirteenth Amendment was passed in 1865 so it could not apply to a passage written in 1861.

11. The quote above can most closely be analogized to

(A) George Washington's determination to not go to war with France in the 1790s.
(B) Lyndon Johnson's decision to commit US troops to Vietnam after the Gulf of Tonkin incident.
(C) Woodrow Wilson's campaign promise in the 1916 presidential election that, if elected, he would continue to keep the US out of the war in Europe.
(D) James K. Polk's announcement that he would not run for re-election to the presidency in 1848.

The correct answer is C.
Lincoln stated that he had no inclination to end slavery, and attempted to avoid war, but ultimately war came and he did free the slaves. Woodrow Wilson campaigned as an anti-war candidate but we were ultimately drawn into WWI. Therefore, C is the correct answer. George Washington's Neutrality Proclamation was followed, and the US did not get involved in the war in Europe in the 1790s, so it is not closely analogous to Lincoln's first inaugural address. Therefore, A is incorrect. B is also wrong because the Gulf of Tonkin Resolution gave Lyndon Johnson authorization to use military force in Vietnam, not to remain neutral. D is an incorrect answer because James K. Polk promised not to run for re-election and kept his promise.

12. Which of the following fits best with the statement "I believe I have no lawful right to do so" in the quote above?

(A) The Emancipation Proclamation
(B) The Thirteenth Amendment
(C) Constitutional limits on the power of the presidency
(D) Manifest Destiny

The correct answer is C.
C is the correct answer because a President did not have a lawful right to interfere with state laws regarding slavery. The Emancipation Proclamation was an executive order that Lincoln believed he had a right to issue. Therefore, A is incorrect. The Thirteenth Amendment was also passed within constitutional boundaries, so B is incorrect. Manifest Destiny was a widely held belief, but not codified in lawful rights, so D is incorrect.

Answer Questions 13–15 using the passage below:

> Not surprisingly, European immigrants did not relish the idea of taking the place of blacks as plantation laborers. One Alabama planter brought in thirty Swedes in 1866, housed them in slave cabins and fed them the usual rations. Within a week the laborers had departed, informing him "they were not slaves."
>
> Eric Foner, *Reconstruction: America's Unfinished Revolution 1863–1877* (1988), p, 213.

13. The above quote is a demonstration of

    (A) Northern efforts at reconstruction of the south after the civil war.
    (B) the beginnings of the labor movement.
    (C) problems resulting from an open immigration policy.
    (D) the challenge of adjusting to a slave-free economy in the south.

The correct answer is D.
The passage describes a Southern planter's difficulty in hiring workers to replace slaves after the Civil War. A is incorrect because reconstruction efforts did not include providing labor for Southern planters. B is incorrect because the Swedish workers chose to depart rather than form a union to work for better conditions. C is incorrect because the passage is not about immigration policy.

14. **A person most likely to agree with the Alabama planter's manner of dealing with his employees would be**

    (A) the owner of a textile factory in Lowell Massachusetts in 1825.
    (B) coal miners in Pennsylvania in 1869.
    (C) the owner of a slaughterhouse in Chicago in the 1880s.
    (D) the manager of an auto assembly line in Detroit in the 1970s.

The correct answer is C.
Slaughterhouse owners paid very low wages and forced workers to work under abhorrent conditions because they had a virtually unlimited supply of new immigrants to replace them. A is incorrect because early nineteenth century textile mills employed young girls who worked long hours, but they lived in boarding houses and had strict codes of behavior to protect them. Many young girls saw these as good jobs. They were cared for better than the Alabama planter's employees. Coal miners formed unions in response to exploitation by owners, so they would not agree with the conditions the Alabama planter expected his employees to work under. Therefore, B is incorrect. D is incorrect because managers in the auto industry were union labor, so they would not agree with the abuse of employees.

15. **Based on trends in immigration in the latter half of the nineteenth century, the Swedish immigrants referred to above would most likely have done which of the following after leaving the plantation?**

    (A) Gone back to Sweden
    (B) Gone to another southern plantation to work
    (C) Gone to a city in the north seeking employment
    (D) Gone to the Northwest Territory to take advantage of the Homestead Act

The correct answer is C.
Most immigrants in the latter half of the nineteenth century went to work in northern cities, so C is the correct answer. Some immigrants returned home, therefore A is a plausible answer just not the best one in response to the wording of this question. B is incorrect because if they went

to work on another plantation, they would likely have found the same conditions. D is incorrect because the Northwest Territory had been divided into states by the time the Homestead Act was passed in 1862.

Answer questions 16–18 using the map below:

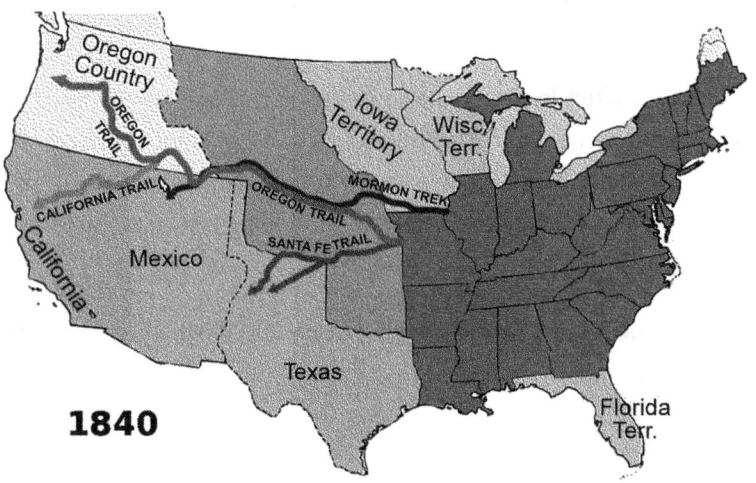

16. **According to the map, which westward migration trail ended in United States territory?**

    (A) The Oregon Trail
    (B) The Santa Fe Trail
    (C) The Mormon Trek
    (D) None of them did

The correct answer is D.
The key is to notice that the map is dated 1840. Oregon was ceded to the United States by Britain in 1846. The Santa Fe Trail ended in Texas, which was an independent nation from 1836 to 1845 when it became a state. The Mormon Trek ended in California, which was among the territory Mexico ceded to the United States in 1848.

17. **The westward migration portrayed in the map was most closely analogous to migration and expansion in which other period in American history?**

    (A) The 1920s
    (B) The 1860s
    (C) The 1970s
    (D) The colonial era

The correct answer is B.
Migration westward was most similar during the 1860s, so B is the correct answer. A is incorrect because the Great Migration in the 1920s was made up of African Americans moving to northern cities. C is incorrect because there was not a large migration westward at that time. D is also incorrect because settlement remained near the east coast during the colonial era.

18. Which of the following was least likely to be a motivation for a settler to use one of the trails identified on the map?

    (A) Gold
    (B) Land
    (C) Cattle ranching
    (D) Religious freedom

The correct answer is A.
A is the correct answer because the Gold Rush did not begin until gold was discovered at Sutter's Mill in 1848. B is incorrect because settlers went west mainly for land. C is incorrect because those using the Sante Fe Trail were mainly cattle ranchers. Mormons sought religious freedom so D is also incorrect.

Answer Questions 19–21 using the passage below:

> A ton of goods can now be carried on the best managed railroads for a distance of a mile, for a sum so small that outside of China it would be difficult to find a coin of equivalent value to give a boy as a reward for carrying an ounce package across the street.
> *David A. Wells, economist, 1884, quoted in Degler's*
> *'The Age of the Economic Revolution 1876–1900' (1977).*

19. Which of the following persons would most likely think that the low railroad rates described in the quote above actually did more harm than good?

    (A) A farmer in a remote area previously not serviced by a railroad, but which gains rail service
    (B) The owner of a warehouse next to a major rail line where goods are stored which are to be shipped by rail
    (C) An investor in one of the many railroads that failed in the 1870s due to overbuilding of rail lines
    (D) A ship owner who transports goods up and down the Atlantic coast

The correct answer is C.
The large supply of rail lines would decrease the demand for new railroads. A is incorrect because a farmer would be pleased to pay less to transport his crops to market. B is incorrect because he would get more business from the low rates of transport. D is incorrect because a ship owner would have more goods to transport because of the low cost of getting goods to the coast.

20. **The revolution in the cheap shipping of goods created by the great expansion of railroads in America in the latter part of the nineteenth century most closely approximates to which of the following?**

    (A) Building of the interstate highway system in the 1950s and 1960s
    (B) The pony express
    (C) Henry Ford's affordable "Model T," which allowed more common people to own cars
    (D) The increase in the number of luxury cruise ships in the twentieth century

The correct answer is A.
The Interstate Highway system also accelerated transportation and reduced shipping costs. B is incorrect because the Pony Express was a system of transporting mail, not large amounts of goods. C, the "Model T," made transportation for individuals less expensive. It did not affect the "cheap shipping of goods," as the question asks. D is also incorrect because luxury cruise ships are not for shipping goods either.

21. **Which of the following would be least likely to benefit from low rail rates as described in the quote?**

    (A) A store owner in a town serviced by a rail line
    (B) The owner of a southern cotton plantation located on the banks of the Mississippi River
    (C) The owner of a new rail line which goes from silver mines in the mountains to major cities in the east
    (D) The owner of a private canal which extends from a rail stop into a remote farm area

The correct answer is C.
C is the correct answer because the owner of a new rail line would not be able to make as much for his service because of the low rates. A is incorrect because a storeowner's shipment of goods would be less expensive and increase his profits. B is incorrect because the cotton could be transported for less money on rail than on the river. D is also incorrect because the rail line could increase the need for transport on his canal to and from the remote area.

Answer Questions 22–24 using the passage below:

> ...Edison had said laconically: "the machine must talk." Kruesi scratched his head to indicate disbelief. Others present bet the "Old Man" cigars that the contraption would not work. When the thing was completed, it was a solid job of brass and iron, with a three-and-a-half-inch cylinder on a foot-long stylus and a hand crank to turn it...Edison deliberately fixed a sheet of tin foil around the cylinder, began turning the handle of the shaft, and shouted into one of the little diaphragms...Then he turned the shaft backward to the starting point...and once more turned the shaft handle forward. Out of the machine came forth what everyone recognized as the high-pitched voice of Thomas A. Edison himself...Kruesi turned pale and made some pious exclamation German. All the onlookers were dumfounded. Edison declared afterward, "I was never so taken aback in all my life. Everybody was astonished. I was always afraid of things that worked the first time."
>
> *Matthew Josephson, Edison: A Biography, (1992 ed., p. 163).*

22. **The invention of the phonograph described in the quote above would be least likely to benefit which of the following?**

    (A) A wealthy business owner in the north who enjoys listening to music
    (B) A farmer in the Midwest who enjoys listening to music
    (C) A struggling black sharecropper family in the south who enjoy listening to music
    (D) A university music instructor

The correct answer is C.
C is the correct answer because the struggling sharecropper could not likely afford the new invention. A and B are examples of people who might purchase a phonograph, so neither is the correct choice. D, a music instructor, could use the phonograph in his lessons so that is also incorrect.

23. **The invention of the phonograph described above would most closely correlate with which of the following?**

    (A) Alexander Hamilton's idea to form a national bank
    (B) Creation of the internal combustion engine
    (C) Increased economic ties between the United States and China in the late 1800s
    (D) Charles Darwin's theory of evolution

The correct answer is B.
The internal combustion engine is the only one that actually describes an invention. The other three answers describe concepts only; therefore B is the best answer.

24. **The phonograph was a rare accomplishment that "worked the first time" it was tried. Which other American experiment could be said to be similar?**

   (A) FDR's attempts to stimulate the economy with "New Deal" legislation
   (B) The Wright Brothers' efforts to fly
   (C) Hamilton's national bank
   (D) The Thirteenth Amendment

The correct answer is D.
A, B, and C, are all examples of things that had many trials and errors before success. A, FDR's new deal had many programs that failed. B, the Wright Bros. plane went through many trials and errors before it flew. C, Hamilton's national bank was repealed in 1811. D is the correct answer because although the Thirteenth Amendment freed the slaves that were not freed by the Emancipation Proclamation. The Fourteenth and Fifteenth Amendments were passed to ensure their rights and citizenship, but were not further attempts to free slaves.

Answer Questions 25–27 using the chart below:

MAIN SOURCES OF IMMIGRATION TO THE UNITED STATES, 1861–1890

	1861–1870	1871–1880	1881–1890
Europe:			
Austria-Hungary	7,800	72,969	353,719
Denmark	17,094	31,771	88,132
France	35,986	72,206	50,464
Germany	787,468	718,182	1,452,970
Great Britain:			
England	222,277	437,706	644,680
Scotland	38,769	87,564	149,869
Ireland	435,778	436,871	655,482
Italy	11,725	55,759	307,309
Norway	71,631	95,323	176,586
Sweden	37,667	115,922	391,776
Switzerland	23,286	28,293	81,988
USSR	2,512	39,284	213,282
Asia:			
China	64,301	123,201	61,711
America:			
Canada and Newfoundland	153,878	383,640	393,304

25. According to the data above, which nation provided stable rates of immigration to the United States between 1861–1890, which did not fluctuate greatly?

    (A) China
    (B) France
    (C) Norway
    (D) None of the above

The correct answer is B.
France is the correct answer because the immigration numbers fluctuated the least. A is incorrect because immigration from China went up significantly in 1871–1880 and then went down. Immigration from Norway rose continually so D is wrong. Since B is correct, D cannot be true.

26. What was the primary difference between German and Irish migration rates as portrayed in the table?

    (A) Irish migration was low to begin with, while German migration was always high.
    (B) Immigration from both countries was strong to begin with, but had tapered off for Germany by the end of the century.
    (C) Irish immigrants were resented more than German immigrants, no matter where they went.
    (D) There was no significant difference between them.

The correct answer is D.
D is the correct answer because both German and Irish migration remained steady from 1861–1880 and then rose sharply. A is incorrect because Irish migration was lower than German, but not low compared to others on the table. B is incorrect because immigration from both countries went up and did not taper off. C is incorrect because the table does not show any information about resentment of any particular group.

27. Which of the nations providing a large number of immigrants as portrayed above also provided a large number of immigrants in the period prior to the civil war?

    (A) Germany
    (B) China
    (C) Sweden
    (D) Ireland

The correct answer is D.
The Irish potato famine in the mid-1840s brought thousands of Irish to the East Coast. While the German revolution of 1848 resulted in a large number of immigrants before the Civil War, it was only a fraction of the number of Irish immigrants, so A is incorrect. B is incorrect because the number of Chinese immigrants did not rise until the 1871–1880 period. C is also incorrect because of the lower number of Swedish immigrants before 1861.

Answer Questions 28–30 using the passage below:

> Freedom has many difficulties and democracy is not perfect, but we have never had to put up a wall to keep our people in, to prevent them from leaving us. I want to say, on behalf of my countrymen, who live many miles away on the other side of the Atlantic, who are far distant from you, that they take the greatest pride that they have been able to share with you, even from a distance, the story of the last eighteen years...
>
> *John F. Kennedy, "Ich bin ein Berliner" speech*
> *June 26, 1963.*

28. Who gave this speech?

(A) President Franklin D. Roosevelt
(B) President Harry S. Truman
(C) President Dwight D. Eisenhower
(D) President John F. Kennedy

The correct answer is D.
The source tells us the speech was given by John F. Kennedy. Therefore D is the correct answer and A, B, and C are not.

29. Why was the speech given in Berlin, Germany?

(A) Berlin was a divided city.
(B) Berlin was a staunch Western supporter.
(C) Berlin needed the encouragement to rebuild after the war.
(D) Berlin was celebrating its reunification.

The correct answer is A.
The speech was given in Berlin because it was a divided city that represented the division between the Soviet east and the democratic west in Europe. Being a divided city, it cannot be said that Berlin was a staunch Western supporter, so B is incorrect. C is incorrect because Kennedy is remarking on the pride that his countrymen feel to have helped rebuild after the war. D is incorrect because the reunification of Germany didn't take place until 1990.

30. What other aid plan helped the Germans after World War II?

(A) The Celler-Kefauver Act
(B) The Marshall Plan
(C) Lend Lease
(D) The Civil Rights Act of 1964

The correct answer is B.
B is the correct answer because the Marshall Plan established how the United States would help rebuild Europe and Japan after the war. A is incorrect because Celler-Kefauver Act was anti-trust legislation passed in 1950. C is wrong because the Lend Lease Act of 1941 was a program in which the United States loaned weapons to England as a way to stay out of the war while helping the Allied powers. D is wrong because the Civil Rights Act of 1964 stated that public accommodations cannot be segregated and no one could be denied access to public accommodation on the basis of race.

Answer Questions 31–33 using the following passage below:

> In our success lies the promise of a new life, freed from the heart-stopping fears that now beset the world. The beginning of victory for the great ideals for which millions have bled and died lies in building a workable plan. Now we approach the fulfillment of the aspirations of mankind…The basis of a sound foreign policy, in this new age, for all the nationals here gathered, is that: anything that happens, no matter where or how, which menaces the peace of the world, or the economic stability, concerns each and all of us.
>
> *Bernard Baruch presenting a plan to control atomic energy to the United Nations, 1946.*

31. What was the reason people believed it was necessary to control atomic energy?

(A) It was an unknown source of power.
(B) It has been used to destroy Asian cities at the end of World War II.
(C) The Communists had more powerful weapons than the United States.
(D) An arsenal of arms was needed for the protection of democracies.

The correct answer is A.
Baruch's plan, presented to the United Nations Atomic Energy Commission, was an effort to regulate international use of atomic energy to control proliferation of nuclear power. While B is true, the real reason for the plan was to work toward using atomic energy for peaceful purposes, so it is not correct. C is also incorrect because the United States had a nuclear monopoly. D is wrong because the plan stipulated that the United States begin destroying its nuclear arsenal.

32. What legislation did Congress enact shortly before the end of the war to help Americans better their life and the economy of the United States after World War II?

(A) The Fullbright Act
(B) The GI Bill of Rights
(C) The Highway Act of 1956
(D) Title IX

The correct answer is B.

After the war, congress passed bills to improve infrastructure, increase jobs, and strengthen the economy. The GI Bill was one of these acts. A is incorrect because the Fullbright Act of 1945 stipulated that funds acquired from sale of US property in other countries to be used for international educational exchange programs. C is incorrect because the Highway Act of 1958 began the construction of the Interstate Highway System. Title IX stated that federal education programs could not discriminate on the basis of sex in 1972, so D is also incorrect.

33. Bernard Baruch's speech was expressing a concern about the period after World War II that was referred to as the

(A) Cold War.
(B) Era of the Berlin Wall.
(C) Age of European Recovery.
(D) Era of Neutrality.

The correct answer is A.

The Cold War was a geopolitical, ideological, economic, and cultural battle fought between the United States and the USSR. B is a component of the Cold War, however the Berlin Wall was not built until 1961, so it is an incorrect choice. C is incorrect because the Age of European Recovery was not a concern of Baruch's speech. D is also wrong. Franklin Roosevelt signed four different Neutrality Acts in the years preceding WWII, and the speech is discussing concerns about the period after the war.

Answer Questions 34–36 using the passage below:

> "In recent months, the actions of the North Vietnamese regime have become steadily more threatening...
>
> As President of the United States I have concluded that I should now ask the Congress, on its part, to join in affirming the national determination that all such attacks will be met, and that the United States will continue in its basic policy of assisting the free nations of the area to defend their freedom."
>
> *Lyndon B. Johnson's Message to Congress*
> *August 5, 1964*

34. Why was the Vietnam War called "Mr. Johnson's War?"

(A) The escalation of ground troops war during his administration
(B) He successfully ended the war
(C) People opposed the US involvement in the war during his administration
(D) People favored the war during his administration

The correct answer is A.

The Vietnam War was called Mr. Johnson's War because after the Gulf of Tonkin resolution,

Congress gave him a "blank check" to conduct the war as he wanted, and he chose to escalate the conflict. Therefore, A is the correct answer. B is incorrect because US involvement in Vietnam ended with the Paris Peace Accords in 1973, not during the Johnson administration. C and D are wrong because the term "Mr. Johnson's War," does not refer to opposition to or support for the war.

35. **What policy did Lyndon Johnson follow with regard to American involvement in Vietnam?**

    (A) Pull out immediately and declare that the US had achieved its goals.
    (B) Gradually withdraw while asking for United Nations mediation.
    (C) Rapidly send American ground troops in for a massive invasion of North Vietnam.
    (D) Gradually escalate the direct American role in the war.

The correct answer is D.
D is the correct answer because Johnson escalated the war over the course of his term of office. A and B are incorrect because Johnson did not pull out of or withdraw from the war. C is incorrect because he gradually sent troops and did not order a massive invasion.

36. **President Nixon's policy in Southeast Asia included all of the following except**

    (A) escalation of American bombing of North Vietnam.
    (B) massive increases in American ground troops to invade North Vietnam.
    (C) secret direct negotiations with North Vietnam's foreign minister.
    (D) widening of the war by invading Cambodia.

The correct answer is B.
B is the correct answer because Nixon began withdrawal of troops. He A, escalated the bombing of North Vietnam as he began troop withdrawal. He also sent Secretary of State Kissinger to negotiate with North Vietnam, so C is incorrect. Nixon also began bombing enemy supply depots in Cambodia, so D is incorrect.

Answer Questions 37–39 using the passage below:

> "It will be my sincere and constant desire to observe toward the Indian tribes within our limits a just and liberal policy, and to give that humane and considerate attention to their rights and their wants which is consistent with the habits of our Government and the feelings of our people."
>
> *Andrew Jackson, First Inaugural Address, 1829*

37. **The statement from President Andrew Jackson addressed which of the following issues?**

   (A) The annexation of Hawaii for the purposes of trade with the South Pacific
   (B) The movement of the Cherokee tribes from Georgia to Oklahoma to access gold and land
   (C) The boundary dispute in the Southwest that led to the Mexican American War
   (D) The assimilation of Native Americans into the American culture through the Dawes Act

The correct answer is B.
You should be able to connect the source and date of the passage with the Indian Removal Act of 1830 that Andrew Jackson signed leading to the Trail of Tears. The annexation of Hawaii did not take place until 1898, so A is incorrect. C is incorrect because the boundary dispute that led to the Mexican-American war did not become an issue until the 1840s. D is incorrect because the Dawes Act was signed in 1887 and divided the tribes into individual families, provided them with land and granted them citizenship in attempt to assimilate them into United States culture.

38. **Andrew Jackson's statement on Native Americans reinforced which of the following ideas or beliefs of the time period?**

   (A) The belief in Wilsonian idealism for foreign policy
   (B) The ideology of Social Darwinism and racial hierarchies
   (C) The ideology of cultural pluralism and multicultural respect for different ethnic groups
   (D) The belief in Manifest Destiny and the American obligation to "civilize" the West

The correct answer is D.
The Indian Removal Act was a part of the idea of Manifest Destiny, the belief that it was America's destiny to explore and settle the west. A is incorrect because the passage is dated 1827, and Woodrow Wilson's foreign policy did not come into play until the twentieth century. Charles Darwin's *On the Origin of Species by Means of Natural Selection* was not published until 1859, so B is also an issue later than 1827. C is incorrect because the ideology of cultural pluralism has roots in the nineteenth century transcendentalist movement, and did not become widely accepted until the twentieth century.

39. Andrew Jackson's statement is most similar to what other time period and American political policy?

(A) President McKinley's justification for annexing the Philippines to protect them against the other European powers
(B) President Truman's promise to protect the Western European nations against Communist expansion in the 1940s
(C) President Theodore Roosevelt's belief in protecting American economic and political interests in Latin America
(D) President John F. Kennedy's statement of promoting American beliefs abroad through the Peace Corps

The correct answer is A.
President McKinley felt that the Philippines were incapable of self-government and it was the responsibility of the US to instill in them American values, therefore A is the correct answer. B is incorrect because Western European nations were not considered to be uncivilized in the 1940s. C is incorrect because Roosevelt had specifically economic and political interests in Latin America. D is also incorrect because JFK's Peace Corps did not include annexing territory.

Answer Questions 40–43 using the passage below:

> "The great common people of this country are slaves, and monopoly is the master. The West and South are bound and prostrate before the manufacturing east.
>
> The Parties lie to us and the political speakers mislead us.
>
> We want money, land, and transportation. We want the abolition of the national banks, and we want the power to make loans direct from the government. We want the accursed foreclosure system to be wiped out."
>
> *Mary Lease, lawyer, speech (1890)*

40. Which of the following best explains the cause of some of the farmers' and workers' problems listed here?

(A) Conservation of natural resources
(B) Racism and the sharecropping system
(C) Industrialization and mechanization
(D) Inefficiencies in government bureaucracy

The correct answer is C.
Lease asserts that the "manufacturing east" is in control because industrialization and mechanization is more advanced there. A is incorrect because the passage is not about natural resources. B is also incorrect because she is talking about economic and labor issues that affect all races. D is incorrect because she is calling for more government intervention.

41. The ideas expressed in the passage reflect which of the following continuities in US History?

(A) Conflict over the role of women and gender rights
(B) Conflict between immigrant and nativist groups
(C) Conflict over the role of government in the economy
(D) Conflict over racial justice and citizenship

The correct answer is C.
C is the correct answer because Lease states that "monopoly is the master," and she wants the government to step in. A and B are incorrect because she is discussing economic and labor issues that cover both men and women and immigrants and natives. D, racial justice is also not included.

42. The statement in the quote is most like which other time period?

(A) Martin Luther King, Jr's fight for equal rights for all racial groups
(B) The American colonists' fight for representation in the British system
(C) The Evangelical fight in the 1970s for a more Christian American identity
(D) Franklin Roosevelt's use of the federal government to increase economic power

The correct answer is B.
The statement is most like B, the American colonists' fight for representation because she is asking for representation for poor workers and farmers. A and C are incorrect because neither issues of race or religion is included in the issue discussed. D is incorrect because while she is encouraging more government representation and regulation, she isn't calling for an increase in federal economic power.

43. Which of the following statement explains the conflict over the role of the government in the 1890s?

(A) The fight over whether or not the government should provide for more representation
(B) The fight over whether or not the government should become more active in racial equality
(C) The fight over whether the government should apply the Bill of Rights to the states
(D) The fight over whether or not the government should take a leadership role in global politics

The correct answer is A.
Mary Lease was a leader in the Populist Movement in the 1890's, which sought more representation and control of economic conditions. They wanted direct election of Senators. While B, C, and D may have been controversial at the time, the Populist Movement was the most prominant.

Answer Questions 44–46 using the passage below:

> The judicial power of the United States is extended to all cases arising under the constitution.
>
> Thus, the particular phraseology of the constitution of the United States confirms and strengthens the principle, supposed to be essential to all written constitutions, that a law repugnant to the constitution is void, and that courts, as well as other departments, are bound by that instrument.
>
> *William Marbury v. James Madison, Secretary of State of the United States. Chief Justice Marshall delivered the opinion of the court. February 10, 1803.*

44. **Chief Justice John Marshall in ruling over Marbury v. Madison established one of the most important tenets of the American judicial system of judicial review, which**

    (A) established that the President had authority to override court decisions in the appointments process.
    (B) made Marbury the first Secretary of State appointed by an outgoing President.
    (C) allowed the Supreme Court to protect the integrity of the presidential appointments process.
    (D) gave the Supreme Court authority to enforce and interpret the Constitution when there is conflict between a law or presidential decision.

The correct answer is D.
The case of Marbury v. Madison established that one of the checks and balances built into the constitution is the power of the judiciary to review decisions by the legislative and executive branches. The case did not establish that Madison had the authority to override outgoing President John Adams' appointment of William Marbury as Justice of the Peace, so A is incorrect. Marbury had been appointed Justice of the Peace, not Secretary of State, so B is incorrect. And C is incorrect because it did not give the Supreme Court the authority over the presidential appointments process.

45. **Marshall also ruled over Gibbons v. Ogden in 1824, which involved a boat company monopoly operating on the Hudson River, and the States of New York and New Jersey. His ruling enforced which precept?**

    (A) Maritime trade laws within the United States
    (B) Interstate trade is regulated by Congress
    (C) International trade agreements by the states
    (D) A state's ability to grant monopolies in trade

The correct answer is B.
Gibbons v. Ogden established that interstate trade, including navigation, is controlled

by congress. While the case was about navigation, it did not cover maritime trade laws, international trade agreements or monopolies. Therefore A, C, and D are incorrect.

46. In his many landmark cases, Chief Justice Marshall, a Federalist himself,

(A) ruled on the supremacy of federal law over state law.
(B) ruled in favor of slavery as a Southern economic need.
(C) protected state rights.
(D) allowed for equal standing of state and federal law.

The correct answer is A.
Federalists, like Alexander Hamilton, James Madison, and John Adams, believed in a strong central government. B is incorrect because Marshall did not rule on whether slavery was economically necessary. C and D cannot be correct because a Federalist would not be very concerned about states' rights or of equality of state and federal government because they believed in a strong national government that had more power than the state government.

Answer Questions 47–49 using the passage below:

> There was indeed a distinctly American approach to manufacturing in the nineteenth century: it was the drive to mass production and mass distribution in every field—from foodstuffs to soap and candles, axes and locomotives, horseshoes, wooden doors, carriage wheels, bedroom furniture, and almost anything else. The nature of the machinery and the underlying technologies varied from product to product—soap making was different from steel-making, and neither had much in common with making guns or clocks. And sometimes, American mass production was all about organization, not machinery, as in the antebellum shoe industry. It was the uniquely American penchant for scale and speed that ultimately created the mass-consumption economy. Mass consumption, the rise of a successful middle class, and a democratized government were all part of the package that was the great American experiment.
> *Charles R. Morris. The Dawn of Innovation:*
> *The First American Industrial Revolution. 2012*

47. Which of the following was NOT an effect of the Industrial Revolution?

(A) An increasing number of people worked in factories.
(B) An increasing number of people lived in cities.
(C) An increasing number of people worked on family farms.
(D) An increasing number of people left the family farms.

The correct answer is C.
The Industrial Revolution and the accompanying increase in factories drew people from the

countryside to the cities to work for wages rather than farming. Therefore, A, B and D were all effects of the Industrial Revolution and are wrong answers.

48. **Why was industrialization in the United States primarily concentrated in the Northeast?**

   (A) This region had the greatest supplies of capital and labor.
   (B) The climate of the North favored industrial development.
   (C) Other regions of the country lacked water transportation.
   (D) The Midwest and South had fewer natural resources.

The correct answer is A.
Larger supplies of capital and labor found in the Northeast were crucial for the Industrial Revolution, which is why A is the correct answer. B is incorrect because climate was not a factor. C and D are incorrect because water transportation and natural resources were abundant in many other areas of the United States.

49. **The experiment of industrialization resulted in several problems that were realized several decades after the industrialization had begun. Which policies of the US government allowed such conditions to develop and later led to the growth of labor unions to correct abuses of workers?**

   (A) Laissez faire policies toward big business
   (B) Antitrust policies toward monopolies
   (C) Imperialist policies regarding territorial expansion
   (D) Isolationist policies regarding international alliance

The correct answer is A.
Laissez Faire policies allowed businesses to operate with minimal regulation from the federal government, which allowed for industries to prioritize profits over wages, working conditions, and safety. B is the correct answer because anti-trust policies were a reaction to the expansion of monopolies due to Laissez Faire policies. C and D are incorrect because industrialization was not directly related to foreign policy.

Answer Questions 50–52 using the picture below:

Trail of Tears 1838–1839. Painting by Robert Lindneux, 1942.

50. What does the painting refer to?

(A) Indians crying with joy since they were granted new settlements west of the Mississippi
(B) Indians crying with joy, because the Supreme Court overturned President Jackson's action and they were returning to their settlements
(C) Indians crying in sorrow, because, they were forced to leave their settlements and move west
(D) Indians crying in pain, because, they undertook a migration and the weather turned on them

The correct answer is C.
The Trail of Tears is the term given to the forced migration of thousands of Cherokees from Georgia to Oklahoma in the Indian Removal Act. Therefore, C is the correct answer. A and B are incorrect because Native American tribes were not happy about being forced to leave their homelands. They resisted and won a Supreme Court case in their favor, but President Andrew Jackson nevertheless ordered federal troops to force their removal. Nearly a quarter of them died along the way, and it was unlikely that the weather was a primary reason for their tears, so D is incorrect.

51. Andrew Jackson's Indian Removal Act of 1830 was condoned by the country because

(A) no one understood the impact the Act would have on the Native Americans.
(B) people wanted the Indians to occupy the West and make it livable for the whites.
(C) they wanted slaves to occupy the vacated Indian settlements in the Eastern states.
(D) many saw the Indians as a morally, economic, and culturally inferior race.

The correct answer is D.

Jackson's primary supporters favored his plan to remove the Indian tribes to western lands because they believed Native Americans to be an inferior race. Therefore, D is correct. Most were unconcerned about the affect it would have on the tribes, so A is not correct. The intention was not to have the Indians prepare the west for whites so B is incorrect. Gold was found on their land, which was a part of the motivation to remove them, but not to move slaves into the vacated settlements, so C is incorrect.

52. Which of the following constitutes a significant change in the treatment of American Indians during the last half of the nineteenth century?

(A) The beginnings of negotiations with individual tribes
(B) The start of a removal policy
(C) The abandonment of the reservation system
(D) The admission of all American Indians to the full rights of United States citizenship

The correct answer is D.

There was a movement to "civilize" Native Americans with the ultimate goal of assimilation and citizenship so D is correct. A is incorrect because negotiations with individual tribes began in the early years of the colonial period. Andrew Jackson's Indian Removal policy began in 1830, which was not the last half of the century, so B is incorrect. C is incorrect because the reservation system was not abandoned.

Questions 53–55 refer to the following image:

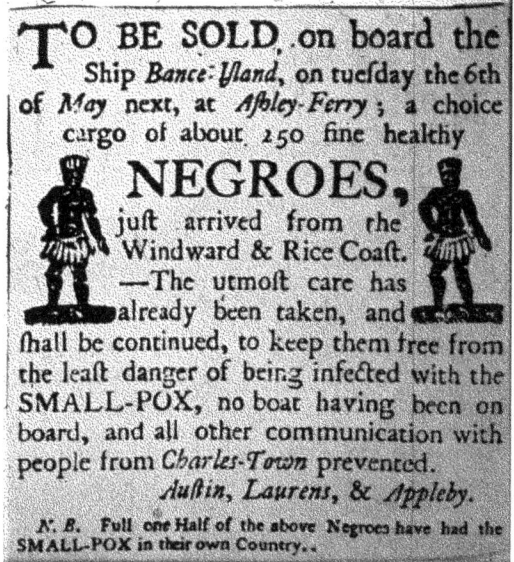

Advertisement, Charleston, South Carolina, 1780s
Image courtesy of the Library of Congress

53. Which of the following BEST reflects the perspective of the above image?

(A) Slaves represent a public health threat.
(B) The importation of slaves is a legitimate enterprise.
(C) The importation of slaves needs to be halted.
(D) Smallpox was a continuous danger to Charleston.

The correct answer is B.
The advertisement does not attempt to hide the fact that they are selling people just abducted from Africa. A is incorrect because it states that care has been taken to ensure that they are not infected with smallpox. While smallpox was a danger, it is not the primary perspective of the advertiser, so D is incorrect also. C is incorrect because it does not imply that importation needs to be halted.

54. Following the American Revolution, many Founding Fathers believed which of the following?

(A) Slavery would gradually disappear in the United States.
(B) The freeing of slaves should be outlawed.
(C) Slavery would be the foundation of the American economy.
(D) Freed slaves deserved government reparations for their suffering.

The correct answer is A.
The founders hoped that slavery would ultimately end on its own, or that some solution would present itself to future generations of Americans. They were not in agreement that slaves should not be freed, so B is incorrect. C is also incorrect because they did not believe that the economy would ever be based on slavery. D is incorrect because there was no prominent movement at the time for reparations to former slaves.

55. Which of the following was a reference to slavery in the Constitution?

(A) Slavery was banned in the Northwest Territory.
(B) Slavery was outlawed above the Mason-Dixon Line.
(C) Slavery could not be outlawed.
(D) A prohibition until 1808 of any law banning the importation of slaves.

The correct answer is D.
Article 1, section 9 of the Constitution reads, "The Migration or Importation of such Persons as any of the States now existing shall think proper to admit, shall not be prohibited by the Congress prior to the Year one thousand eight hundred and eight, but a Tax or duty may be imposed on such Importation, not exceeding ten dollars for each Person." This means that D is the correct answer. Neither A, B, or C was stipulated in the Constitution.

SECTION I, Part B

Time: 45 minutes 4 Questions

Directions: Read each question carefully and write your responses in the corresponding boxes on the free-response answer sheet.

Use complete sentences; an outline or bulleted list alone is not acceptable. On the actual test you may plan your answers in the exam booklet, but only your responses in the corresponding boxes on the free-response answer sheet will be scored.

> The conditions which surround us best justify our co-operation; We meet in the midst of a nation brought to the verge of moral, political, and material ruin. Corruption dominates the ballot-box, the legislatures, the Congress, and touches even thee ermine of the bench. The people are demoralized: most of the estates have been compelled to isolate the voters at the polling places to prevent universal intimidation or bribery. The newspapers are largely subsidized or muzzled, public opinion silence, business prostrated, our homes covered with mortgages, labor impoverished and the land concentrating in the hands of the capitalists.
>
> *People's Party Platform, 1892*

1. Using the primary source above, respond to parts A, B, C:
   A. **Summarize the point being made by James Weaver, the founder of the Populist or People's Party.**

   James Weaver is making the point that the two major political parties have failed the common person and that the Populist Party (the People's Party) can solve the moral, political, and economic problems of the country by implementing free coinage of silver, public ownership of railroads, and instituting a graduated federal income tax.

   B. **What were the economic factors that led to the rise of a People's Party in the late 1800s?**

   The economic factors that led to the rise of the People's Party focused on the Panic of 1893 and on the farmers' suffering. Farming was becoming less profitable because of several factors: declining prices, high interest rates, bad crop years, chronic debt, and the unpredictability of domestic and international markets. The Panic of 1893 was a serious economic depression. Crop prices declined, unemployment increased, banks collapsed, and there were problems with the money supply.

C. What would be a historical example of the late 1800s that would dispute Weaver's argument?

Examples of events that took place in the late 1800s that would dispute Weaver's arguments that the nation was on the verge of moral, political, and material ruin include: the arrest of Boss Tweed, the establishment of the first national park, oil discovery in Oklahoma, and the enactment of the Sherman Anti-Trust Act.

The population shift to the middle-class suburbs and the power shift to the Sunbelt economy requires a new metropolitan framework for political history and public policy that transcends the urban-suburban dichotomy and confronts instead of obscures the pervasive politics of class in the suburban strategies of the volatile center. Surely an honest assessment of the nation's collective responsibility in creating the contemporary metropolitan landscape remains an essential prerequisite for grappling with the spatial fusion of racial and class politics that ultimately produced an underlying suburban consensus in the electoral arena.

Matthew D. Lassiter, "The Silent Majority: Suburban Politics in the Sunbelt South", 2006.

2. **Using the secondary source above, respond to parts A, B, C:**

   A. Summarize the key issue that Lassiter is arguing about the changing economic demographics in the 2000s.

   The key issue is how the American people, collectively, must decide how to deal with the changes in the metropolitan composition after the shift of population to the Sunbelt and to the suburbs.

   B. What were the contextual issues of the 1990s and 2000s that led to the changes in class that Lassiter is observing.

   There were several issues during the 1990s early 2000s that led to the changes Lassiter is observing. The Midwest area became known as the rust belt because factories closed and new manufacturing did not replace the steel mills and other industries that left the area. The economic conditions affected the housing market and the renewed threat of terrorism and the bombing of New York on 9/11 added to the movement to the suburbs and the Sunbelt.

   C. Give a piece of historical evidence that supports Lassiter's argument.

   One obvious piece of evidence to support Lassiter's argument is the census numbers that showed the increase and decrease of populations. The increase of U.S. Representatives in the Sunbelt areas and the decrease in states such as Indiana are also examples. The "Brain Drain" from metropolitan areas and the decrease in land values throughout the country are other examples. Also, there were major shifts in manufacturing centers. Manufacturers left the U.S. to construct plants in Mexico and other areas where they benefitted from the country's tax assessments, where labor was less expensive., and where production of items was cheaper.

> Under Hanoi's overall direction the Communists have established an extensive machine for carrying on the war within South Vietnam. The focal point is the Central Office for South Vietnam with its political and military subsections and other specialized agencies. A subordinate part of this Central Office is the liberation Front for South Vietnam. The front was formed at Hanoi's order in 1960.
> Its principle function is to influence opinion abroad and to create the false impression that the aggression in South Vietnam is an indigenous rebellion against the established Government.
> US State Department, 1965.

> The US government has committed war crimes, crimes against peace and against mankind. In South Vietnam, half a million US and satellite troops have resorted to the most inhuman weapons and most barbarous methods of warfare, such as napalm, toxic chemicals and gases, to massacre our compatriots, destroy crops, and raze villages to the ground. In North Vietnam, thousands of US aircraft have dropped hundreds of thousands of tons of bombs, destroying towns, villages, factories, schools. In your message, you apparently deplore the sufferings and destruction in Vietnam. May I ask you: Who has perpetrated these monstrous crimes? It is the United States and satellite troops. The US government is entirely responsible for the extremely serious situation in Vietnam.
> Ho Chi Minh to Lyndon Johnson, 1967

3. **Using the differing primary sources above, respond to parts A, B, C:**
   A. **Explain the primary difference between the points of view of the two primary sources on the Vietnam War.**

   The primary difference between the points of view is which country is creating the problems in Vietnam. The State Department memo blames Hanoi and the North Vietnamese and indicates that the North Vietnamese leadership has set up a front in Saigon to stage the attacks. The letter from Ho Chi Minh to President Johnson blames the United States for the problems in Vietnam, especially North Vietnam.

B. **Explain ONE brief example that would support the point of view of the State Department primary source.**

On New Year's Eve in 1964, the Viet Cong blew up the Brink Hotel where American officers were staying. The explosion filled two Americans and more than 50 South Vietnamese. In 1968, during the celebration of the lunar new year, the North Vietnamese attacked South Vietnam provinces. The Americans responded to this attack and Communist losses were significant.

C. **Explain ONE brief example that would support the point of view of Ho Chi Minh's letter to President Lyndon Johnson.**

The My Lai Offensive Massacre is an example that Ho Chi Minh would have used to support his argument. My Lai was an area of South Vietnam where the Viet Cong were entrenched. The "search and destroy" mission by the American forces resulted in the killing of more than 300 unarmed individuals.

4. Using the image above, answer A, B, and C.
   A. **Explain how the Great Awakening affected the religious beliefs of the American colonies in the 1730s.**

   The Great Awakening had a tremendous impact on religious beliefs during the 1730s and 40s. The evangelistic preaching of Jonathan Edwards and George Whitefield focused on those who were church members. The sermons helped people gain greater senses of conviction and redemption and made religion more personal. Some of the rituals were changed and people had more of a self-awareness. Another result was that there became more of a demand for religious freedom. Church membership increased and African Americans began taking part in religion in greater numbers. There were also new religious movements that developed. Examples were the Baptists and the Methodists. The Great Awakening also led to the Anglican Church having less influence in the colonies.

   B. **Provide ONE brief example of a contrasting idea of the 1730s to the religious beliefs of the Great Awakening.**

   The Enlightenment was an example of a contrasting idea to the Great Awakening. The Enlightenment was an intellectual idea that began in Europe. The Great Awakening was a religious idea that began in America. The Enlightenment focused on reason and science and the discovery of natural laws through the process of observation. The Great

Awakening focused on individual salvation, redemption, and self-awareness. Leaders of the Enlightenment included Isaac Newton, Copernicus, John Locke, and Benjamin Franklin. George Whitefield and Jonathan Edwards were preachers during the Great Awakening of the 1730s.

C. Provide ONE brief example of a similar American movement from another era.

The evangelism and preaching of Billy Sunday in the late 1800s and early 1900s is a similar example. His evangelical preaching encouraged many to accept Christ. He was also influential in the Prohibition movement. That movement promoted the idea that drinking, saloons, and the manufacture, sale, and consumption to alcoholic beverages were detrimental to society. The fervor of the Prohibition Movement could be compared to the fervor of the Great Awakening. The tent meetings and the religious revivals of the 1950s are another example. During the late nineteenth and early twentieth centuries the Chautauqua movement gained popularity. This movement focused on betterment of individuals through education. Chautauquas were held at lakeside and mountain settings and other areas where people could hear concerts, speakers, educational programs, and other cultural programs. The formation of the Utopian communities during the mid-1800s was also a movement to lead a better life. Communities, such as Brook Farm, Oneida, New Harmony, the Amanas, and Zoar Village promoted communal living and the focus on an ideal life. Many were religious-based. Brook Farm was a transcendentalist society.

UNITED STATES HISTORY SECTION II

Total Time: 1 hour, 35 minutes

Question 1 (Document-Based Question)
Suggested reading period: 15 minutes
Suggested writing period: 45 minutes

Directions: Question 1 is based on the accompanying documents. The documents have been edited for the purpose of this exercise. You are advised to spend 15 minutes reading and planning and 45 minutes writing your answer.

Write your responses on the lined pages that follow the question.

In your response you should do the following:
- State a relevant thesis that directly addresses all parts of the question.
- Support the thesis or a relevant argument with evidence from all, or all but one, of the documents.
- Incorporate analysis of all, or all but one, of the documents into your argument.
- Focus your analysis of each document on at least one of the following: intended audience,

purpose, historical context, and/or point of view.
- Support your argument with analysis of historical examples outside the documents.
- Connect historical phenomena relevant to your argument to broader events or processes.

DOCUMENT 1

Section 1. Every contract, combination in the form of trust or otherwise, or conspiracy, in restraint of trade of commerce among the several States, or with foreign nations, is hereby declared to be illegal. Every person who shall make any such contract or engage in any such combination or conspiracy, shall be deemed guilty of a misdemeanor, and, on conviction thereof, shall be punished by fine not exceeding five thousand dollars, or by imprisonment not exceeding one year, or by both said punishments, in the discretion of the court.

Section 2. Every person who shall monopolize, or attempt to monopolize, or combine or conspire with any other person or persons, to monopolize any part of the trade or commerce among the several States, or with foreign nations, shall be deemed guilty of a misdemeanor, and, on conviction thereof, shall be punished by fine, not exceeding one year, or by both said punishments, in the discretion of the court.

Sections 1 and 2 of the Sherman Antitrust Act of 1890.

DOCUMENT 2

You are hereby restrained, commanded, and enjoined absolutely to desist and refrain from in any way or manner interfering with, hindering, obstructing, or stopping any of the business of any of the following-named railroads…and from in any way interfering with, hindering, obstructing, or stopping any mail trains, express trains, whether freight or passenger, engaged in interstate commerce, or carrying passengers or freight between or among the States; and from compelling or inducing or attempting to compel or induce, threats, intimidations, persuasion, force, or violence, an of the employees of any of said railroads to refuse or fail to perform any of their duties as employees of any of said railroads in connection with the interstate business or commerce of such railroads, or the transportation of passengers or property between or among the States;…

To Eugene V. Debs and the American Railway Union, from Grover Cleveland.

DOCUMENT 3

The Senate of the United States shall be composed of two Senators from each State, elected by the people thereof, for six years; and each Senator shall have one vote. The electors in each State shall have the qualifications requisite for electors of the most numerous branch of the State legislatures.

Seventeenth Amendment

DOCUMENT 4

Section 3. No person shall on or after the date when the eighteenth amendment to the Constitution of the United States goes into effect, manufacture, sell, barter, transport, import, export, deliver, furnish or possess any intoxicating liquor except as authorized in this Act, and all the provisions of this Act shall be liberally construed to the end that the use of intoxicating liquor as a beverage may be prevented.

Volstead Act, 1919

DOCUMENT 5

Where there had been at the beginning of 1872 twenty-six refining firms in Cleveland, there were but six left. In three months before and during the oil war the Standard had absorbed twenty plants. I was generally charged by the Cleveland refiners that Mr. Rockefeller had used the South Improvement scheme to persuade or compel his rivals to sell to him...[Mr. Rockefeller] was no ordinary man. He had the powerful imagination to see what might be done with the oil business if it could be centered in his hands—the intelligence to analyze the problem into its elements and to find the key to control...

Ida Tarbell, "The Oil War of 1872" McClure's Magazine, 1903.

DOCUMENT 6

One of the striking features of our neighborhood twenty years ago, and one to which we never became reconciled, was the presence of huge wooden garbage boxes fastened to the street pavement in which the undisturbed refuse accumulated day by day...The children of our neighborhood twenty years ago played their games in and around these huge garbage boxes. They were the first objects that the toddling child learned to climb; their bulk afforded a barricade and their contents provided missiles in all the battles of the older boys, and finally they became the seats upon which absorbed lovers held enchanted converse...

Jane Addams, Forty Years of Hull House

DOCUMENT 7

They tell us that the eight-hour movement cannot be enforced, for the reason that it must check industrial and commercial progress. I say that the history of this country, in its industrial and commercial relations, shows the reverse…They say they can't afford it. Is that true?… In all industries where the hours of labor are long, there you will find the least development of the power of invention. Where the hours of labor are long, men are cheap, and where men are cheap there is no necessity for invention. How can you expect a man to work ten or twelve or fourteen hours at his calling and then devote any tie to the invention of a machine, or discovery of a new principle or force? If he be so fortunate as to be able to read a paper, he will fall asleep before he has read through the second or third line.

Samuel Gompers, "The labor movement is a fixed fact",
May 1, 1890, Address in Louisville, Kentucky

1. **Analyze to what degree reformers were able to change the economic and political challenges of the period between 1890–1910.**

   Reformers made giant strides during the late 1800s and early 1900s. One of their biggest accomplishments was to curb some of the abuses of big business and monopolization. There were several barons of industry during this time period. Andrew Carnegie owned steel mills. John D. Rockefeller owned Standard Oil. Cornelius Vanderbilt controlled the railroads. Jay Gould and J. Pierpont Morgan were also magnates of industry and Wall Street. The age was one of excess and was called the Gilded Age. The muckrakers and reformers wanted to curb the abuses and raise the living standards for the poor.

   The Sherman Antitrust Act of 1890 was an act passed by Congress to prevent monopolization. President Roosevelt used this act to break up Standard Oil in the early 1900s. As a result he became known as the "trust buster." Ida Tarbell, a writer, had written an expose on Standard Oil and the consolidation of oil interests. This book made people aware of excess and the strength of large monopolies. Her efforts also led to the breaking up of the trusts. (Documents 1 and 5).

   Jane Addams was a reformer who established a settlement house in Chicago. She worked with people in slum neighborhoods to improve their standard of living. Other reformers included Dorothea Dix who tried to make prisons cleaner; Horace Mann who made efforts to improve the educational systems of communities in Massachusetts; and Susan B. Anthony and Elizabeth Cady Stanton who supported women suffrage. (Document 6).

   Carrie Nation and other reformers led the temperance movement. They believed alcohol was an evil that ruined individuals, broke up homes, and tore apart the nation. They led the fight that resulted in the ratification of the Eighteenth Amendment (Prohibition) and the passage of the Volstead Act, which provided means of enforcing Prohibition. (Document 4).

Working conditions in factories were horrible during the late 1800s and early 1900s. The overcrowding of cities and rapid growth of immigrants from southern and Eastern Europe added to the squalor of cities and unsanitary working conditions. Workers began to organize in an attempt to improve working conditions and the first labor unions began to be established. As the workers organized, they began demands for better wages and working conditions. When employers ignored their demands, they began to strike. The Homestead Steel Strike is an example. The Pullman strike is another. President Cleveland feared the railroad strike would disrupt transportation and the flow of interstate commerce, he issued a cease and desist order to Eugene V. Debs. He also sent federal troops to stop the strike. (Documents 2 and 7).

During the Progressive Era, there was a movement to directly elect Senators. The state legislatures had previously elected U.S. Senators. The Seventeenth Amendment, when ratified, made the election of U.S. Senators by popular vote. (Document 3).

Society faced many challenges during the time period between 1890 and 1900. While the challengers were great, reformers made great strides in confronting and resolving the issues even though they did not solve all of the economic and political problems of the time.

Question 2 or Question 3
Suggested writing period: 35 minutes

Directions: **Choose EITHER question 2 or question 3. You are advised to spend 35 minutes writing your answer. Write your responses on the lined pages that follow the questions.**

In your response you should do the following:
- State a relevant thesis that directly addresses all parts of the question.
- Support your argument with evidence, using specific examples.
- Apply historical thinking skills as directed by the question.

2. **Analyze how the passage of the Fourteenth and Fifteenth amendments were or were not turning points in the political relationships of race in the United States between 1865 and 1900.**

   The passage of the Fourteenth and Fifteenth amendments were not turning points in the political relationships of race in the United States between 1865 and 1900 but were stepping stones to turning points that were reached in the 1960s.

   Section 1 of the Fourteenth Amendment provides citizenship to the former slaves. The section also provides that states shall not deny citizens due process of law or equal protection of the laws. The Fifteenth Amendment gave former slaves voting rights. States continued to discriminate against the former slaves. There were the Jim Crow laws that limited the rights of the blacks. Poll taxes and literacy tests kept many of the former slaves from voting. The state legislatures continued to separate the races. They passed laws that provided separate facilities for the races. Louisiana passed a law providing for separate rail cars for the whites and blacks. The law was upheld in the U.S. Supreme Court in the case of Plessey v. Ferguson in 1896. The federal and state government continued to segregate the races in this time period and the two Constitutional Amendments did not serve as a turning point in race relations.

3. **Compare and contrast the how the transportation revolutions of the 1820s and the 1920s affected social relationships in the United States.**

   There were similarities and differences in the transportation revolutions of the 1820s and 1920s but both affected social relationships in the United States.

   During the early 1800s many pioneers were moving west. The Conestoga wagon was the best means of transportation for the settlers because the covered wagon protected its passengers from rains and bad weather. Stagecoaches were also a way people traveled between cities. During this time there was also river traffic that people used to get products to market and to get themselves from one location to another. However, with the advent of the turnpike, transportation because easier. States began building roads and tolls were charged to help pay for construction and maintenance. The National Road was built between Maryland and Illinois. The more than 500 mile distance later became part of U.S. Highway 40 and, later, Interstate 70.

   Steamboats were also used in the 1800s to carry people and products. The Clermont, called Clinton's Folly, and other steamboats became a popular mode of transportation because they linked the East and West. Boats on the Erie Canal transported agricultural goods to market and the Erie Canal was a financial success. The railroad was part of the transportation revolution of the 1820s. Routes connect parts of the industrial Northeast and various cities in the East coast area. There were also some rail lines in the South but there were no long lines.

   In the 1920s, the transportation revolution was the result of the Model T automobile and the growth of the automobile industry. Henry Ford has developed the use of the assembly line and the cars could be purchased by the middle class person.

   Both transportation revolutions opened up areas of the country. The earlier revolution opened up western lands for development and agricultural and industrial markets. The later transportation revolution made areas outside metropolitan areas accessible to people. As a result, suburbs began to develop. There was further road expansion and people began taking vacations in automobiles, resulting in the development of new commercial ventures. Rail travel became more luxurious in the 1920s. The Pullman cars provided a way for people to travel in luxury. Charles Lindbergh's solo flight across the Atlantic Ocean in the late 1920s opened the way for the construction of airports and air travel for people throughout the country.

   While the types of transportation developed in each era were different, they all accomplished the goal of opening up parts of the United States to more people, industry, and agricultural products and improved the quality of life for the people.

Appendix: Timeline of Important Dates, Key Figures, and Significant Events

This XAMonline timeline is an outline of important dates, key figures and significant events in the history of the United States. It is to be used as a supplement to the AP US History study guide and is not meant as a comprehensive list of material covered in the AP US History Course.

Period 1: 1491–1585

1513 ■ **Ponce de Leon** claims Florida for Spain.

1524 ■ **Verrazano** explores North American Coast.

1539-1542 ■ **Hernando de Soto** explores the Mississippi River Valley.

1540-1542 ■ **Coronado** explores what will be the Southwestern United States.

1565 ■ Spanish found the city of **St. Augustine** in Florida.

1579 ■ **Sir Francis Drake** explores the coast of California.

1585 ■ **Sir Walter Raleigh** establishes "Lost Colony" of **Roanoke**

Colonial Period

Significant Events

Europeans Explore North America

Lost Colony of Roanoke

Period 2: 1585–1750

Important Events

Jamestown, Plymouth, and Massachusetts Bay Colonies founded

Colonial Period

1607	British establish **Jamestown Colony** in Virginia.
1614	**John Rolfe** introduces tobacco cultivation in Virginia.
1619	First **African slaves** brought to British America. Virginia begins representative assembly.
1620	**Plymouth Colony** founded. **Mayflower Compact** signed.
1624	**New Amsterdam** (Renamed New York under British rule) founded by Dutch.
1629	Puritans arrive and found **Massachusetts Bay Colony,** led by **John Winthrop**.
1634	**Roger Williams** banished from Massachusetts Bay Colony. **Maryland** founded as a Catholic settlement by George Calvert, the first Lord Baltimore.
1635	**Connecticut** founded.
1636	**Roger Williams** exiled and founds Rhode Island. Harvard College founded.
1638	**Anne Hutchinson** excommunicated for challenging Puritan authority.
1638	**Delaware** founded.
1650–1696	The **Navigation Acts** are enacted by Parliament.
1670	Charles II grants charter for **Carolina** colonies.

Colonial Period

1676 ■ **Bacon's Rebellion** becomes the first uprising against the British.

1682 ■ Pennsylvania founded by William Penn.

1689-1713 ■ **King William's War** (The War of the League of Augsburg).

1692 ■ The **Salem Witchcraft Trials**

1700s ■ **The Enlightenment Period**

1702-1713 ■ **Queen Anne's War** (War of the Spanish Succession)

1720-1740 ■ **Great Awakening**

Influential Ministers: George Whitefield, Jonathan Edwards

1732 ■ **Georgia** founded as a penal colony.

1735 ■ **Zenger Trial**

1740-1748 ■ **King George's War** (War of the Austrian Succession)

Key Figures
- John Rolfe
- John Winthrop
- Roger Williams
- Anne Hutchinson
- William Penn
- George Whitefield
- Jonathan Edwards

Period 3: 1751–1799

Significant Events
French and Indian War
Treaty of Paris
Boston Massacre
Treaty of Paris signed
Shay's Rebellion

Major Legislation
Royal Proclamation Act
Currency Act
Sugar Act
Stamp Act
Quartering Act
Townshend Acts
The Tea Act

Colonial Period

1754-1763 ■ The **French and Indian War**

General George Washington defeated at Fort Necessity.

1754 ■ Albany Plan of Union fails to unify the Thirteen Colonies.

1763 ■ **Treaty of Paris** ends the French and Indian War.

Paxton Boys Rebellion against Native Americans.

Royal Proclamation Act

Pontiac's Rebellion: Native American tribes organize against British movement.

Salutatory Neglect ends and the British Government begins enforcing parliamentary laws in the colonies.

1764 ■ **Currency Act**

Sugar Act

1765 ■ The **Stamp Act**

"**Sons of Liberty**" formed to oppose British efforts of tighter control of colonies.

1766 ■ **Quartering Act**

1767 ■ The **Townshend Acts**

1770 ■ **Boston Massacre**

British Parliament repeals all Townshend duties except for the one on tea.

1772 ■ Samuel Adams organizes the **Committees of Correspondence**.

Colonial Period

Gaspee Incident

1773 ■ **The Tea Act**

Boston Tea Party

1774 ■ **The Intolerable Acts**
- Boston Port Act
- Massachusetts Government Act

The First Continental Congress convenes in Philadelphia.

1775 ■ **Battles of Lexington and Concord.**

Battles of Bunker Hill

The Second Continental Congress convenes

War for Independence

1776 ■ **Second Continental Congress** adopts **American Declaration of Independence** written largely by **Thomas Jefferson.**

Thomas Paine writes *Common Sense*.

Battles of Long Island and Trenton

1777 ■ Battle of Saratoga

Congress adopts the **Articles of Confederation.**

1778 ■ **Treaty of Alliance:** France sends navy and army to aid colonists.

1779 ■ Spain declares war on England.

1781 ■ **British surrender at Yorktown.**

1783 ■ **Treaty of Paris** signed.

1785 ■ Land Ordinance of 1785

Treaty of Hopewell ends hostilities with the Cherokee.

1786 ■ **Shays' Rebellion**

1787 ■ **Constitutional Convention in Philadelphia.**

Constitution written with principles developed by **James Madison.**

Federalist Papers written by **James Madison, Alexander Hamilton** and **John Jay**.

Key Figures
Thomas Jefferson
Thomas Paine
James Madison
Alexander Hamilton
George Washington
Eli Whitney
John Adams

Significant Events

Constitutional Convention in Philadelphia

Federalist Papers Written

Whiskey Rebellion

XYZ Affair

Major Legislation

Constitution

Bill of Rights

Alien and Sedition Acts

Logan Act

George Washington

- **1788** — **Constitution** ratified
- **1789** — **George Washington** inaugurated first President.
  Judiciary Act establish courts beneath Supreme Court.
- **1790** — Residence Act approves creation of Washington D.C. on the Potomac River.
- **1791** — **The Bill of Rights** ratified.
  First Bank of the United States is established.
- **1793** — **Eli Whitney** invents the Cotton Gin.
- **1794** — **The Whiskey Rebellion**
- **1795** — Jay Treaty with Britain
  Pinckney's Treaty with Spain
- **1796** — Washington's Farewell Address
  John Adams (Federalist) elected President.

John Adams

- **1797** — **XYZ Affair** leads to Quasi-war with France.
- **1798** — **Alien and Sedition Acts**
- **1798–1799** — **Virginia and Kentucky Resolutions** against Alien and Sedition Acts.
- **1799** — **John Fries Rebellion**
  Logan Act

Period 4: 1800–1843

Thomas Jefferson

1800 ■ Convention of 1800 ends the **Quasi-war** with France

Thomas Jefferson (Democratic Republican) elected president.

1803 ■ **Louisiana Purchase**

Marbury v. Madison establishes that the Supreme Court can declare laws unconstitutional.

1804 ■ **Twelfth Amendment**: Establishes separate ballots for President and Vice President.

Essex Junto: Federalist organization in New England attempts to secede.

1804–1806 ■ **Lewis and Clark Expedition**.

1805 ■ Tripoli war ends, Barbary pirates are defeated.

1807 ■ **Robert Fulton** builds his first steamboat.

Embargo Act

1808 ■ **African Slave Trade** ends.

James Madison elected president.

James Madison

1809 ■ Non-Intercourse Act

1810 ■ *Fletcher v. Peck* establishes that action of a state can be declared unconstitutional.

1811 ■ Charter for Bank of US rejected

Battle of Tippecanoe: William Henry Harrison defeats Indian Tecumseh who made alliance with Indians for defense.

Key Figures
Thomas Jefferson
James Madison

Important Events
Louisiana Purchase
Lewis and Clark Expedition
African Slave Trade Ends

Major Legislation
Marbury v. Madison
Twelfth Amendment
Embargo Act
Nonintercourse Act
Fletcher v. Peck

SECTION III: Time Period Summaries

Key Figures

James Monroe
John Quincy Adams
Andrew Jackson
Cyrus McCormick

Major Legislation

Land Act
National Road Bill
Tariff of Abominations
Factory Act

James Madison

1812–1814 ■ **The War of 1812**
- Trade issues with Great Britain
- British impressment of sailors
- British support of Native American attacks on the frontier.

1814 ■ Hartford Convention

Treaty of Ghent ends the war with *status quo*.

Era of Good Feelings begins.

1815 ■ **Battle of New Orleans**, Andrew Jackson defeats British before getting word that the war was over.

1816 ■ **American Colonization Society** founded to relocate free African Americans to Liberia.

American Anti-Slavery Society formed.

Henry Clay's **American System**

Second Bank of US created.

First protective tariffs passed.

James Monroe (Democratic Republican) elected president.

1817 ■ President Madison vetoes **Bonus Bill** for domestic improvements.

James Monroe

1818 ■ Convention of 1818: US and Britain settle boundary dispute, agreeing on the 49th parallel.

1819 ■ **Adams-Onís Treaty** (Transcontinental Treaty) Spain cedes Florida to the US.

Panic of 1819

McCulloch v. Maryland: Establishes the principle that federal law took priority over state law.

1820 ■ **Missouri Compromise:** Maine admitted as free state and Missouri as a slave state but allowed no slave states north of Missouri.

Land Act

1821 ■ Americans begin settling in Texas.

James Monroe

1822 ■ National Road Bill

1823 ■ **Monroe Doctrine** declared.

1824 ■ Election of **John Quincy Adams** (Democratic Republican) Contested election, Jackson calls it a "Corrupt Bargain."

Gibbons v. Ogden: Establishes that interstate trade, including navigation, is controlled by congress.

1825 ■ **Erie Canal** opened.

1828 ■ **Andrew Jackson** (Democrat) elected president.

Tariff of Abominations passed

Andrew Jackson

1830s ■ The Second Great Awakening

1830 ■ Baltimore and Ohio Railroad begins operation.

1831 ■ Abolitionist newspaper, the Liberator begins publication.

Nat Turner Rebellion

Cyrus McCormick invents the reaper.

1831-1838 ■ The Trail of Tears

1832 ■ Tariff of 1832

Force Bill passed, allowing president to do what is necessary to enforce tariff.

Ordinance of Nullification: South Carolina nullifies tariff, Henry Clay negotiates and reduces tariff.

National Bank recharter is vetoed.

Department of Indian affairs established.

Seminole War begins.

1833 ■ Factory Act

1835-1836 ■ **Texas Revolution** seeks independence from Mexico.

1836 ■ **Battle of the Alamo:** Mexican General Santa Anna crushes small band of Texans defending the Alamo Mission in San Antonio.

Significant Events

War of 1812

Treaty of Ghent

Battle of New Orleans

Adams-Onís Treaty

Missouri Compromise

Erie Canal opened

Second Great Awakening

Nat Turner Rebellion

Trail of Tears

Texas Revolution

Major Legislation

Independent Treasury
Act Repealed

Tariff Bill

Significant Events

Battle of the Alamo

Specie Circular

Oregon Trail

Andrew Jackson

The Gag Rule prevents discussions of slavery in congress.

Specie Circular: western land must be purchased from the federal government with hard currency.

Martin Van Buren (Democrat) elected president.

1837 — US recognizes the **Republic of Texas**.

Oberlin College enrolls its first women students.

Panic of 1837

1838–1839 — Aroostook "War": bloodless boundary dispute between Maine and New Brunswick.

1840s — Large numbers of immigrants begin arriving from Germany, France and Ireland.

1840 — Independent Treasury System: Public funds must be retained by the Treasury.

William Henry Harrison (Whig) elected president.

William Henry Harrison

1841 — After one month in office, Harrison dies and Vice President **John Tyler** (Independent) becomes president.

Independent Treasury Act Repealed.

President Tyler vetoes recharter National Bank.

John Tyler

1842 — **Tariff Bill** raises tariffs back to 1832 status.

Dorr Rebellion against land qualifications for voting in Rhode Island.

Webster-Ashburton Treaty ends boundary dispute between Maine and New Brunswick.

Massachusetts court rules that workers have the right to form associations.

1843 — **Oregon Trail**

Period 5: 1844–1865

James K. Polk

1844 — **Samuel Morse** sends first telegraph between Washington, D.C. and Baltimore, Maryland.

James K. Polk (Democrat) elected president.

1845 — **Annexation of Texas**

Florida and Texas become states.

Publication of **Fredrick Douglass'** *Narrative of the Life of Frederick Douglass, An American Slave.*

1846 — Elias Howe invents the sewing machine.

Treaty with Britain: Britain gives up its claims south of the 49th parallel. Oregon Territory ceded to the United States.

1846-1848 — **Mexican-American War**

- Mexican Government rejects President Polk's offer to purchase disputed land.
- Gen. Zachary Taylor provokes Mexicans by moving into disputed territory between the Rio Grande and the Neuces River.

1846-1847 — **Wilmont Proviso** provides that slavery be prohibited in new states formed on prior Mexican land was rejected by Congress.

Independent Treasury System reestablished.

Frederick Douglass begins publishing anti-slavery paper *The North Star.*

1848 — **Treaty of Guadalupe Hidalgo**

Key Figures
Frederick Douglass
Gen. Zachary Taylor

Important Events
Annexation of Texas
Mexican-American War
Wilmont Proviso

SECTION III: Time Period Summaries

Key Figures

Lucretia Mott

Elizabeth Cady Stanton

Harriet Tubman

Commodore Matthew Perry

Dred Scott

John Brown

Ulysses S. Grant

Jefferson Davis

Robert E. Lee

Susan B. Anthony

James K. Polk

- US gains territories of Arizona, California, Colorado, Nevada, New Mexico, Utah, and Wyoming.

Gold is discovered at **Sutter's Mill**.

Women's Suffrage Convention held in Seneca Falls, NY, headed by **Lucretia Mott** and **Elizabeth Cady Stanton.**

Zachary Taylor (Whig) elected president.

1849 — California Gold Rush

Zachary Taylor

1850s — **Underground Railroad** reaches peak activity.

Millard Fillmore

1850 — Vice President **Millard Fillmore** becomes president upon President Taylor's death.

Clay's Compromise of 1850

Clayton-Bulwer Treaty: US and Britain agree to neutral control of a Proposed canal in Nicaragua.

Treaty of Fort Laramie sets precedent for Native Americans to be moved to certain territories.

1852 — **Commodore Matthew Perry** opens Japan to US trade.

Benjamin Franklin Pierce (Democrat) elected president.

Fugitive Slave Act passed.

1853 — **Gadsden Purchase:** US buys portions of present-day Arizona and New Mexico from Mexico to build a railroad.

Publication of *Uncle Tom's Cabin* by Harriet Beecher Stowe.

1854 — **The Kansas-Nebraska Act** passed to create states for railroad to go to west.

1854-1859 — **Bleeding Kansas:** caused by popular sovereignty clause in the newly formed state of Kansas.

- **Potawatomi Massacre**: John Brown kills four pro-slavery settlers.

1856 — **James Buchanan** (Democrat) elected president.

James Buchanan

1857 ■ *Dred Scott v. Sandford*: The Supreme Court rules that slaves were not citizens and that Scott does not have a right to sue in federal court and that the Missouri Compromise is unconstitutional.

Panic of 1857.

1858 ■ **Lincoln-Douglas Debates**

Abraham Lincoln gives speech, "A House Divided."

1859 ■ **John Brown's Raid on Harpers Ferry**

1860 ■ Crittenden Compromise

Industrial Revolution begins in the US.

Abraham Lincoln (Republican) elected president.

South Carolina secedes from the Union.

Abraham Lincoln

1861 ■ The **Civil War begins** at Fort Sumter.

Confederacy established with **Jefferson Davis** as president.

Confederate Constitution adopted.

Kansas admitted as a free state.

First Battle of Bull Run

1862 ■ **Pacific Railroad Act**

Homestead Act

Second Battle of Bull Run

Morrill Act

1863 ■ **Battle at Antietam**

Banking Acts (1863, 1864) establish federally charted banks.

Draft Riot in New York City

The Emancipation Proclamation

Battle of Gettysburg

Lincoln announces "10 Percent Reconstruction Plan."

Woman's National Loyal League founded by Susan B. Anthony and Elizabeth Cady Stanton.

1864 ■ **Wade-Davis Bill**

Significant Events

Treaty of Guadalupe Hidalgo

Gadsden Purchase

Lincoln-Douglas Debates

The Civil War begins at Fort Sumpter

New York Draft Riots

Major Legislation

Kansas-Nebraska Act

Dred Scott v Sanford

Pacific Railroad Act

Homestead Act

Morrill Act

Banking Acts

Significant Events

Sand Creek Massacre

Civil War Ends

Freedmen's Bureau established

Abraham Lincoln

Pullman Car and refrigerated car invented.

Sand Creek Massacre: Chivington attacks defenseless Cheyenne and Arapaho village

1865

Civil War Ends: Lee surrenders to Grant at Appomattox Courthouse, VA

Thirteenth Amendment abolishes slavery.

President Lincoln assassinated by John Wilkes Booth and Vice President **Andrew Johnson** becomes president.

President Johnson's **Amnesty Plan** pardons almost all Confederates.

Freedmen's Bureau established.

Andrew Johnson

Period 6: 1866–1899

Andrew Johnson

1866 ■ **Civil Rights Act of 1866** is passed over President Johnson's veto giving African Americans equal rights.

National Labor Union formed.

Fetterman Massacre: During Red Cloud's War, Federal troops lost battle against Lakota, Cheyenne, and Arapaho Indians.

1867 ■ **Alaska** purchased from Russia.

Reconstruction Acts

Tenure of Office Act states that the president cannot remove any appointed official without the Senate's consent, later declared unconstitutional.

1868 ■ **Fourteenth Amendment** ratified, granting equal protection under the law to African Americans.

Ku Klux Klan begins.

Battle of Washita River: Gen. George Armstrong Custer destroys Cheyenne village.

Carnegie Steel Company formed.

President Andrew Johnson impeached.

Ulysses S. Grant (Republican) elected.

Ulysses S. Grant

1869 ■ **Transcontinental Railroad** completed from Union Pacific and Central Pacific.

Knights of Labor formed.

National Woman Suffrage Association formed by **Susan B. Anthony.**

National Prohibition Party formed.

Important Events

Federman Massacre

Impeachment of Andrew Jackson

Completion of Transcontinental Railroad

Major Legislation

Wade-Davis Bill

Thirteenth Amendment

Civil Rights Act of 1866

Reconstruction Acts

Tenure of Office Act

Fourteenth Amendment

SECTION III: Time Period Summaries

Key Figures

Mark Twain

Alexander Graham Bell

Rutherford B. Hayes

Thomas Edison

Booker T. Washington

Helen Hunt Jackson

Grover Cleveland

Ulysses S. Grant

1870 — **Fifteenth Amendment** is ratified stating that the right to vote can't be determined by race, color, or previous condition of servitude.

Force Acts passed to protect the constitutional rights guaranteed to blacks by the Fourteenth and Fifteenth Amendments.

Standard Oil Company formed.

1871 — New Immigrants begin arriving from Southern and Eastern Europe.

1872 — **Credit Mobilier Scandal:** Stock holders of Railroad construction company overcharge government.

1873 — **Slaughterhouse Cases:** Fourteenth Amendment doesn't place federal government under obligation to protect basic rights concerning monopolies.

Panic of 1873

Mark Twain calls the period the "Gilded Age."

1874 — **Red River War:** Last Native American attempt to resist removal to reservations.

Women's Christian Temperance Union founded.

1875 — **Civil Rights Act of 1875** guarantees African Americans equal treatment in public accommodations, public transportation, and prohibits exclusion from jury service.

Pearl Harbor acquired.

Farmers Alliance developed.

Whiskey Ring Scandal

1876 — **Battle of Little Bighorn:** Custer killed in overwhelming defeat by Chief Crazy Horse in the **Great Sioux War.**

US v. Reese: allows voting qualifications like literacy tests and poll taxes.

Alexander Graham Bell invents the telephone.

1877 — *Munn v. Illinois:* US Supreme Court upholds the power of federal government to regulate private industries.

Compromise of 1877: **Rutherford B. Hayes** (Republican) becomes president, reconstruction ends.

Rutherford B. Hayes

Redeemer governments in the south pass Jim Crow laws.

Nez Perce War

1879 ■ **Thomas Edison** invents the electric light.

1880s ■ **Dust Bowl** begins.

1880-1910 ■ **Panama Canal** Built

1880 ■ **James Garfield** (Republican) elected president, six months later Garfield dies and Vice President **Chester Arthur** becomes president.

James Garfield

1881 ■ **Tuskegee Institute** founded by **Booker T. Washington**.

Helen Hunt Jackson writes *A Century of Dishonor*

1882 ■ **Chinese Exclusion Act**

European Restriction Act

Chester Arthur

1883 ■ **Brooklyn Bridge** completed.

Pendleton Civil Service Reform Act

Five civil rights cases disable the 1875 Civil Rights Act in the Supreme Court

1884 ■ **Grover Cleveland** (Democrat) elected president.

1884 ■ First **Skyscraper** built in Chicago

1886 ■ **The American Federation of Labor** is founded by Samuel Gompers

Interstate Commerce Act

Haymarket Incident

Wabash Case

Grover Cleveland

1887 ■ **Interstate Commerce Commission** established

American Protective Association established

Dawes Act

1888 ■ **Benjamin Harrison** (Republican) elected president.

1889 ■ **Jane Addams** founds Hull House.

Significant Events
Red River War
Battle of Little Bighorn
Compromise of 1877
Dust Bowl
Haymarket Incident

Major Legislation
Fifteenth Amendment
Civil Rights Act of 1875
US v. Reese
Munn v. Illinois
Chinese Exclusion Act
Interstate Commerce Act
Dawes Act

Key Figures

Jane Addams

Booker T. Washington

Significant Events

Wounded Knee Massacre

Pullman Strike

Coxey's Army

Spanish-American War

Benjamin Harrison

1890-1900 — African Americans are deprived of the vote in the South.

1890 — **National American Woman Suffrage Association** is founded.

The Sherman Antitrust Act

McKinley Tariff Act

Wounded Knee Massacre: Last showdown between Native Americans and the United States Army.

Sherman Silver Purchase Act requires the Treasury to buy more silver with a special issue of Treasury Notes that could be redeemed for either silver or gold.

1891 — **National Consumers League** founded to protest child labor in factories

1892 — **The Homestead Strike:** At Carnegie Steel, Pinkerton guards and troops put down strike

Coeur d'Alene Miners Strike in Idaho

General Electric Company formed.

Grover Cleveland (Republican) elected president.

Grover Cleveland

1893 — Panic of 1893

Sherman Silver Purchase Act repealed to prevent the depletion of federal gold reserves.

Anti-saloon League formed.

1894 — **The Pullman strike**

Coxey's Army marches to Washington DC by unemployed workers seeking relief.

1895 — *US v. E. C. Knight Company.* Supreme Court establishes that the Anti-Trust Act regulates commerce but not manufacturing.

Pollack v. Farmers' Loan and Trust Co:. Supreme Court rules that income tax is unconstitutional.

Booker T. Washington's "Atlanta Compromise" Speech

Grover Cleveland

1896 — *Plessy v. Ferguson:* Supreme Court upholds racial segregation in public facilities under the doctrine of "separate but equal."

Wabash, St. Louis & Pacific Railway Company v. Illinois (Wabash Case): Supreme Court denies states rights to regulate interstate railroads

William McKinley (Republican) elected president

William McKinley

1897 — **Dingley Tariff Act**

1898 — **Spanish-American War**
- Begun after explosion of battleship USS Maine in Havana Harbor
- Begins US economic and military expansion in the Caribbean and Latin America
- Peace of Paris: Cuba gains independence and US annexes Puerto Rico, Philippines, and Guam.

US annexes Hawaii

1899 — Samoa divided between US and Germany.

Anti-Imperialist League founded.

Open Door Policy: grants equal opportunity for international trade and commerce in China.

Major Legislation

Sherman Antitrust Act
McKinley Tariff Act
Sherman Silver Purchase Act
Plessy v. Ferguson
Wabash Case
Dingley Tariff Act

Period 7: 1900–1945

Important Events

Platt Amendment

Assassination of McKinley

Coal Strike of 1902

Wright Brothers' first flight

World War I begins

William McKinley

1900 — **National Negro Business League** founded by Booker T. Washington

Gold Standard Act: Gold becomes the only standard for paper money.

Progressive Era begins.

1901 — **US Steel Corporation** formed.

Platt Amendment ends the Spanish-American war.

Insular Cases: Series of Supreme Court cases that establish that full constitutional rights do not automatically extend to all places under American control.

President McKinley assassinated and **Theodore Roosevelt** (Republican) becomes president.

Theodore Roosevelt

1902 — **Coal Strike** by United Mine Workers of America

1903 — **Department of Commerce and Labor** created

Wright Brothers fly the first airplane, The Kittyhawk.

Elkins Act

1904 — **Panama Canal Zone** acquired.

The National Child Labor Committee formed.

Roosevelt Corollary added to the Monroe Doctrine.

1905 — **Industrial Workers of the World** formed.

1906 — **Upton Sinclair** writes *The Jungle* which led to Meat Inspection Act.

Theodore Roosevelt receives Nobel Prize for negotiating Treaty of Portsmouth, ending Russo-Japanese War.

Theodore Roosevelt

Hepburn Act

Pure Food and Drug Act

1907 ■ Bank Panic

1908 ■ *Muller v. Oregon:* upheld restrictions on the working hours of women as justified by the need to protect women's health.

Root-Takahira Agreement stipulates that Japan will honor the US Open Door Policy.

William Howard Taft (Republican) elected president.

William Howard Taft

1909 ■ **NAACP** founded.

President Taft begins implementation of **Dollar Diplomacy** to further the interests of the United States abroad by encouraging the investment of US capital in foreign countries.

Payne-Aldrich Tariff Act

1911 ■ *Standard Oil Co. v. US:* Standard Oil Co. broken up.

1912 ■ **Woodrow Wilson** (Democrat) elected president.

1913 ■ **The Sixteenth Amendment** authorizes income taxes.

The Seventeenth Amendment directs popular election of Senate.

Underwood Tariff

Federal Reserve Act creates federal reserve system.

Woodrow Wilson

1914 ■ **World War I** begins out in Europe.

Federal Trade Bill establishes The Federal Trade Commission.

United States invades Veracruz in Mexico and US soldiers arrested.

Clayton Antitrust Act

1915 ■ The **USS Lusitania** is sunk by a German submarine

After Haitian president assassinated United States Marines sent in to restore order and maintain political and economic stability; occupation continues until 1934.

Women's Peace Party founded by Jane Addams.

Key Figures
Upton Sinclair

Major Legislation
Pure Food and Drug Act

Sixteenth Amendment

Seventeenth Amendment

Federal Reserve Act

Clayton Antitrust Act

Significant Events

USS Lusitania sunk

Great Migration

Harlem Renaissance

Armistice Day

Treaty of Versailles

Red Scare and Palmer Raids

Washington Disarmament Conference

Teapot Dome Scandal

Woodrow Wilson

1916 ■ **Adamson Act**

Troops sent to Dominican Republic to prevent the coming to power of a strongman or caudillo, Desiderio Arias.

War Industries Board established to coordinate production and mobilize.

Food Administration headed by Herbert Hoover to provide food reserves to Allies in WWI.

Lever Act sets prices for agricultural products.

Fuel Administration established to manage the use of fuel and coal.

1917 ■ **US enters WWI.**

Selective Service Act passes.

Great Migration begins: Many African Americans move from rural south to northern cities.

Harlem Renaissance

Marcus Garvey leads first movement of African American working class and promotes Back-to-Africa movement.

Committee on Public Information (Creel Committee) formed **Liberty Leagues.**

1918 ■ **Espionage and Sedition Act**

National War Labor Board to arbitrate disputes to avoid strikes during the war.

Armistice Day: Secession of hostilities on the Western front.

Wilson's speech to Congress, "**Fourteen Points.**"

1919 ■ **Treaty of Versailles** establishes peace between Germany and Allied forces.

The Red Scare and **Palmer Raids** begin.

Schenck v. US determines that there is no freedom of speech when it presents a "clear and present" danger.

American Protective League works with government to counteract the activities of radicals, anarchists, anti-war activists, and left-wing labor and political organizations.

Woodrow Wilson

Senate rejects Versailles Treaty and League of Nations.

Eighteenth Amendment ratifies prohibiting alcoholic beverages.

Volstead Act enforces Eighteenth Amendment.

Race riots in Chicago

1920 ■ **Nineteenth Amendment** grants Women's Suffrage.

Francis Perkins becomes the first female Cabinet Member as US Secretary of Labor.

First radio station established (KDKA in Pittsburgh).

Sinclair Lewis writes *Main Street*.

Warren G. Harding (Republican) elected president.

1921 ■ **Margaret Sanger** founds the **American Birth Control League.**

Revenue Act decreases taxes.

Washington Disarmament Conference limits naval arms.

Post War Depression begins.

Immigration Act restricts immigration.

Teapot Dome Scandal

1922 ■ Sinclair Lewis writes *Babbit*.

Fordney-McCumber Tariff raises tariffs in support of American farmers.

Warren G. Harding

1923 ■ President Warren G. Harding dies and **Calvin Coolidge** (Republican) becomes president.

1924 ■ **Dawes Plan** helps Germany with reparation.

Peak of KKK.

1925 ■ The Scopes "Monkey" Trial

Great Gatsby written by F. Scott Fitzgerald.

The New Negro by Alain LeRoy Locke.

1926 ■ "Weary Blues" written by Langston Hughes.

1927 ■ **Charles Lindbergh** flies solo from New York to Paris.

Key Figures

Marcus Garvey

Francis Perkins

Margaret Sanger

Major Legislation

Selective Service Act

Espionage and Sedition Act

Schenck v. US

Eighteenth Amendment

Volstead Act

Nineteenth Amendment

Revenue Act

Immigration Act

Appendix: US History Timeline

Key Figures

F. Scott Fitzgerald
Alain LeRoy Locke
Langston Hughes
Charles Lindbergh
Sacco and Vanzetti

Calvin Coolige

Sacco and Vanzetti executed.

The Jazz Singer becomes first full length movie with dialog audio.

1928 ■ **Herbert Hoover** (Republican) elected president.

1929 ■ **Kellogg-Briand Pact**: international agreement to avoid war

The Great Stock Market Crash: Great Depression begins.

Agricultural Market Act

Tax Cut

Young Plan reduces reparation payments to Germany.

1930 ■ **The Smoot-Hawley Tariff:** High protective tariff

London Naval Treaty decreases shipbuilding among United Kingdom, Japan, France, Italy, and the US.

1931 ■ Japan invades Manchuria.

Jane Addams becomes first woman to be awarded the Nobel Peace Prize.

Herbert Hoover

1932 ■ **Stimpson Doctrine**

Federal Home Loan Bank Act

The **Reconstruction Finance Corporation** formed

Bonus Army marches on DC to receive veterans bonus, Hoover sends in troops.

Franklin D. Roosevelt (Democrat) is elected president.

1933 ■ "**Good Neighbor Policy**" repudiates Roosevelt Corollary.

Twentieth Amendment stipulates that presidential term starts on January 20th.

New Deal begins:

- WPA (Works Progress Administration)
- CCC (Civilian Conservation Corps)
- NIRA (National Industrial Recovery Act)
- SEC (Securities and Exchange Commission)
- AAA (Agricultural Adjustment Association)
- TVA (Tennessee Valley Authority)
- CWA (Civil Works Administration)

Franklin D. Roosevelt

- NYA (National Youth Administration)
- HOLC (Home Owners Loan Corp.)
- Glass-Steagall Banking Act

1934 ■ **Nye Committee** investigated the financial and banking interests behind the United States' involvement in World War I.

Indian Reorganization Act restores tribal ownership of lands, recognized tribal constitutions and government, and provided loans for economic development.

Share the Wealth Society founded by Huey Long.

1935 ■ **Wagner Act** set up **National Labor Relations Board**

Fair Labor Standards Act

CIO (Congress of Industrial Organization) labor union formed.

Social Security Acts provided benefits to old and unemployed.

Revenue Act raises taxes on the wealthy.

First Neutrality Act

1936 ■ **Second London Conference on Disarmament**

Second Neutrality Act

1937 ■ **Third Neutrality Act**

FDR's Quarantine Speech opposing neutrality and nonintervention.

USS Panay Incident: Japanese bomb American ship and apologize, claiming it was accidental.

1938 ■ **End of New Deal Reforms.**

John Steinbeck writes *Grapes of Wrath*.

1940 ■ Selective Service begins peacetime draft.

Destroyers for Bases Agreement

Smith Act begins fingerprinting of aliens.

America First Committee started.

Significant Events
Bonus Army march on Washington

Major Legislation
Dawes Plan
Scopes Monkey Trial
Smoot-Hawley Tariff
New Deal
Indian Reorganization Act
Wagner Act
Fair Labor Standards Act
Social Security Acts

Key Figures
John Steinbeck

Significant Events
Peacetime Draft
Atlantic Charter
Attack on Pearl Harbor
Japanese Internment Camps open
US enters WWII
Allied Invasion of Normandy

Major Legislation
Lend Lease Act
GI Bill

Franklin D. Roosevelt

1941 — **Atlantic Charter** drawn up by President Roosevelt and Winston Churchill.

Japanese attack Pearl Harbor.

Lend Lease Act

US enters WWII.

Internment Camps for Japanese Americans open.

1942 — **Congress of Racial Equality** founded.

Revenue Act of 1942.

Bracero Program begins.

1943 — **Office of Price Administration**

Office of War Mobilization created.

Detroit race riots

Casablanca Conference: FDR and Churchill meet in Morocco to settle the future strategy of the Allies.

Cairo Conference: Allied leaders plan for Japan's unconditional surrender.

Tehran Conference: FDR, Stalin, Churchill discuss strategy against Germany.

1944 — **GI Bill** passed.

Allied invasion of Normandy (D-Day)

Renunciation Act

Period 8: 1945–1980

FDR

1945
- **Yalta Conference**: Allies meet to decide on final war plans
- **Battle of Bulge**
- **Battle of Iwo Jima**
- Upon the death of Franklin Delano Roosevelt, **Harry Truman** (Democrat) becomes president.
- The US drops atomic bombs on **Hiroshima and Nagasaki**, Japan.
- **WWII ends.**
- **Potsdam Conference**
- US joins **United Nations.**

Harry Truman

1946
- Cold War begins.
- Kennan policy of **"Containment."**
- **Employment Act**
- **Atomic Energy Act** establishes Atomic Energy Commission.
- **President's Commission on Civil Rights**
- Philippines gain independence.
- Winston Churchill's **"Iron Curtain"** speech in response to Russian aggression.

1947
- **The Marshall Plan** oversees economic aid to Europe after WWII.
- **Taft-Hartley Act**
- **Truman Doctrine** establishes financial commitment to nations fighting Communism.

Important Events
Yalta Conference
Battle of the Bulge
Battle of Iwo Jima
FDR dies
Atomic Bombs dropped
WWII ends
Potsdam Conference
Cold War begins

Major Legislation
Atomic Energy Act

Key Figures

- Jackie Robinson
- Alger Hiss
- George Orwell
- Joseph McCarthy
- Julius and Ethel Rosenberg
- Nikita Khrushchev

Harry Truman

Federal Employee Loyalty Program instituted to eliminate communist influence in the US federal government.

National Security Act creates **CIA.**

Jackie Robinson breaks color barrier in baseball.

1948
Truman convenes **Committee on Civil Rights** and desegregates armed forces.

Berlin Airlift instituted in response to Berlin Blockade.

OAS (Alliance of North America and South America)

Alger Hiss accused of being a Soviet Spy and convicted of perjury.

Nuremberg trials

1949
NATO formed

Chinese Communist leader Mao Zedong declares the creation of the **People's Republic of China** (PRC).

Soviet Union detonates its First Atomic Bomb.

Department of Defense created.

West and East Germany created.

President Truman's "**Fair Deal**" speech

George Orwell writes *1984*.

1950
Korean War begins.

Senator **Joseph McCarthy**'s crusade against communists begins.

McCarren Internal Security Act

National Security Council Memo 68 begins massive defense spending.

1951
Twenty-second Amendment: No president can be elected more than twice or act as president more than ten years.

Catcher in the Rye written by J. D. Salinger.

Treaty of Mutual Cooperation and Security between the United States and Japan allows US military bases in Japan.

Harry Truman

ANZUS Treaty: Australia, New Zealand, and US become allies

President Truman fires **General Douglas MacArthur.**

1952 ■ Truman forms **NSA** (National Security Agency).

Dwight D. Eisenhower (Republican) elected president.

1953 ■ **Julius and Ethel Rosenberg** executed for being Soviet Spies.

Korean Armistice Agreements end Korean War.

1953 Iranian coup d'état: US and the United Kingdom return the **Shah of Iran** to power to keep Iran from becoming Communist.

Nikita Khrushchev becomes Premier of the Soviet Union.

Dwight D. Eisenhower

1954 ■ **Army-McCarthy hearings** bring down Joseph McCarthy.

Brown v. Board of Education determines "separate but equal" does not apply to educational facilities.

SEATO: Alliance between Turkey, US, Iraq, and Iran.

Fall of Dien Bien Phu: French loose in Vietnam.

Geneva Conference reduces nuclear weapons, and divides Vietnam along 17th parallel.

1955 ■ **Montgomery Bus Boycott**

Clear Air Act

AFL and the CIO merge

Warsaw Pact: USSR and Eastern European allies unite to counter NATO.

1956 ■ **Interstate Highway Act**

US puts **Ngo Dinh Diem** in power in South Vietnam.

"Howl" written by Allen Ginsberg.

1957 ■ **Eisenhower Doctrine** extends to Truman Doctrine to Middle East to help resist spread of Communism.

Domino Theory: If one country fell to Communism, others would fall in a domino effect.

Baby Boom peaks.

Significant Events
Marshall Plan
Berlin Airlift
Nuremberg Trials
Department of Defense created
Korean War
Warsaw Pact
Geneva Conference

Major Legislation
Taft-Hartley Act
Twenty-second Amendment
Brown v. Board of Education
Clean Air Act

Key Figures

Ngo Dinh Diem

Allen Ginsberg

Jack Kerouac

Rachel Carson

Lee Harvey Oswald

Martin Luther King, Jr.

Betty Friedan

Major Legislation

Interstate Highway Act

Civil Rights Acts of 1957 and 1960

Dwight D. Eisenhower

Civil Rights Act of 1957 establishes the Civil Rights Commission

School desegregation is enforced in **Little Rock**, Arkansas.

Southern Christian Leadership Conference founded and closely associated with Martin Luther King Jr.

Russians launch **Sputnik**, beginning space race.

World's first **nuclear power plant** opens in Arco, Idaho

On the Road written by Jack Kerouac.

1958 ■ **National Defense Education Act** passes to increase the technological sophistication and power of the United States.

NASA formed.

1959 ■ US Backs **Cuban Revolution**, led by Fidel Castro.

Labor Reform Act

Alaska and Hawaii admitted as states.

1960 ■ **U-2 incident**: US spy plane crashes in USSR, reveals covert operation

Greensboro, North Carolina sit-ins begin.

Civil Rights Act of 1960: Federal government registers black voters.

National Liberation Front forms the **Viet Cong.**

First televised presidential debate.

John F. Kennedy (Democrat) elected president.

1961 ■ **Bay of Pigs Invasion:** failed attempt to overthrow Fidel Castro in Cuba.

Alliance for Progress establishes economic cooperation between the US and Latin American nations.

Berlin Wall built.

Peace Corps founded.

Diem ousted in South Vietnam with support of President Johnson.

John F. Kennedy

OPEC (Organization of Petroleum Exporting Countries) formed by a majority of Arab oil producing nations.

1962 ■ **Cuban Missile Crisis**

Baker v. Carr ends gerrymandering.

Engel v. Vitale: prayer in public schools banned on basis of First Amendment.

Silent Spring Written by Rachel Carson.

Students for a Democratic Society (SDS) condemned anti-Democratic tendencies of large corporations, racism and poverty.

1963 ■ **Nuclear Test Ban Treaty** stops testing in atmosphere or ocean by US, Soviet Union and United Kingdom.

Martin Luther King Jr. leads **March on Washington** and gives "I have a Dream" Speech.

The Feminine Mystique written by Betty Friedan.

President Kennedy assassinated by Lee Harvey Oswald and **Lyndon Johnson** (Democrat) becomes President

1964 ■ **Twenty-fourth Amendment** outlaws poll tax.

US enters **Vietnam War.**

Gulf of Tonkin Resolution passes.

War Powers Act

Economic Opportunity Act: Office of Economic Opportunity establishes Equal Opportunity Laws.

Civil Rights Act of 1964: Public accommodations cannot be segregated and no one could be denied access to public accommodation on the basis of race.

Martin Luther King, Jr. awarded Nobel Peace Prize.

Tax reduction

Great Society: Platform for President Johnson's campaign, it stressed the 5 P's: Peace, Prosperity, anti-Poverty, Prudence and Progress.

1965 ■ Medicare and Medicaid passed.

Higher Education Act

Significant Events

School Desegregation
NASA formed
Bay of Pigs Invasion
Berlin Wall built
OPEC formed
Cuban Missile Crisis
JFK assassinated

Key Figures

Robert F. Kennedy

Neil Armstrong

Spiro Agnew

Major Legislation

Twenty-fourth Amendment

Gulf of Tonkin Resolution

War Powers Act

Medicare and Medicaid begin

Civil Rights Act of 1964

Voting Rights Act

Miranda v. Arizona

Twenty-fifth Amendment

Equal Rights Amendment

Unsafe at any Speed written by Ralph Nader.

Army sent to quell race riots in Watts neighborhood of Los Angeles and Detroit.

Voting Rights Act

Immigration and Naturalization Act

1966 — **Department of Housing and Urban Development** established.

Department of Transportation created.

National Traffic and Motor Vehicle Safety Act

Miranda v. Arizona detained criminal suspects must be informed of their rights before being questioned.

National Organization for Women (NOW) formed.

1967 — Twenty-fifth Amendment allows a Vice President to appoint a new Vice President if he becomes President.

1968 — Robert F. Kennedy assassinated.

Martin Luther King, Jr. assassinated.

Nixon's "New Federalism" returns power to the states.

Vietnamization begins reducing US involvement in war.

TET Offensive: Viet Cong attacks during Vietnamese holiday.

War extended to Laos and Cambodia.

Civil Rights Act of 1968 attempts to provide African Americans with equal-opportunity housing.

Richard M. Nixon (Republican) elected president.

1969 — **Nixon Doctrine** reduces number of troops abroad by helping nations economically and militarily.

Neil Armstrong walks on the moon.

Stonewall Riots in New York City.

1970 — Troops sent to quell protest at Kent State University, four students killed.

1971 — *Reed v. Reed* establishes that the Fourteenth Amendment applies to a law that discriminated against women.

Lyndon B. Johnson

Lyndon B. Johnson

Desegregation of schools begins.

"War on Drugs" begins.

1972 ■ Nixon visits China and eases tensions.

SALT1: Nuclear arms limitation agreement.

Watergate Scandal

Equal Rights Amendment (ERA) passed but not ratified by all states.

1973 ■ Vice President Spiro Agnew resigns and is replaced by **Gerald Ford.**

Paris Peace Accords end US involvement in Vietnam.

Federal Highway Act

Gideon v. Wainwright decides state and local courts must provide counsel for defendants in felony cases.

OPEC Oil Embargo begins.

Roe v. Wade establishes a woman's right to have an abortion after the second trimester

1974 ■ South Vietnam falls and becomes Communist.

Richard Nixon resigns presidency and **Gerald Ford** (Republican) becomes president.

President Ford pardons Richard Nixon.

Richard Nixon

1975 ■ US ship Mayaguez attacked by Cambodia and crew rescued.

1976 ■ James Earl "Jimmy" Carter, Jr. (Democrat) elected president.

1977 ■ President Carter creates **Department of Energy.**

US gives up rights to Panama Canal.

1978 ■ China and US agree to establish diplomatic relations.

1979 ■ Fuel shortage

Camp David Accords: President Carter facilitates peace agreement between Israel and Egypt.

Shah expelled from Iran; **American embassy taken hostage**, Carter's rescue mission fails.

SALT II: Strategic Arms Limitation Treaty with Russia.

Significant Events

US enters Vietnam War

RFK assassination

MLK assassination

TET Offensive

Stonewall Riots

Desegregation

Watergate scandal

Paris Peace Accords

OPEC Oil Embargo

Appendix: US History Timeline

Key Figures
Sandra Day O'Connor
Geraldine Ferraro

Major Legislation
Roe v. Wade

Gerald Ford

Three Mile Island: Nuclear power plant failure in Pennsylvania.

Department of Energy and Department of Education Created.

1980 ■ **Olympic Boycott:** To protest the Soviet invasion of Afghanistan.

Ronald Reagan (Republican) elected president.

Iran hostages released.

Jimmy Carter

Period 9: 1980 to present

Ronald Reagan

1981 ■ **Air Traffic Controllers Strike**

Assassination attempt on Reagan

Economic Recovery Tax Bill

"Reaganomics" program of reducing taxes and spending begins.

Sandra Day O'Connor becomes first woman Supreme Court justice.

First case of **AIDS** reported

1983 ■ **Strategic Defense Initiative** (Star Wars)

Military **Invasion of Grenada**

American peacekeeping force in Lebanon attacked by terrorists.

1984 ■ Taxes increase

Geraldine Ferraro (Democrat) chosen as first female vice presidential candidate.

Congress bans military aid to Contras in Nicaragua.

1985 ■ **Iran-Contra Affair**: Senior administration officials secretly sell weapons to Iran, and use the money to fund the Contras in Nicaragua.

Late 1980s ■ **Savings and Loan Crises** resulted in the bankruptcy of half of the Savings and Loan banks in the United States.

1986 ■ US bombs terrorist targets in Libya.

Space Shuttle Challenger explodes.

1987 ■ **Black Monday**: Stock market crashes.

Important Events

Nixon resigns
Camp David Accords
Three Mile Island
Iran Hostage Crisis
Invasion of Grenada
Iran-Contra Affair
Savings and Loan Crises

Key Figures

Monica Lewinsky

Osama Bin Laden

Saddam Hussein

Major Legislation

Americans with Disabilities Act

Brady Handgun Violence Prevention Act

NAFTA passed

Welfare Reform Act

Patriot Act

Education Reform Bill

George H. W. Bush

1988 — **Intermediate-Range Nuclear Forces Treaty** (INF Treaty) limits intermediate-range missiles in the US and the Soviet Union.

Civil Liberties Act

George H. W. Bush (Republican) elected president.

1989 — **Berlin Wall** torn down.

Exxon Valdez oil spill in Alaska

US invades Panama and overthrows **Manuel Noriega.**

1990 — Economic recession begins.

Americans with Disabilities Act

1991 — Persian Gulf War (Operation Desert Storm).

START (Strategic Arms Reduction Treaty) between US and USSR

Soviet Republics declare independence.

1992 — *Roe v. Wade* upheld by Supreme Court.

Race Riot in Los Angeles in response to acquittal of police accused of **Rodney King** beatings.

William Jefferson "Bill" Clinton (Democrat) elected president.

Bill Clinton

1993 — Recession ends.

World Wide Web goes public

World Trade Center bombed by Middle Eastern Terrorists.

Brady Handgun Violence Prevention Act

1994 — **NAFTA** passed.

"Don't ask, don't tell" policy adopted in the military.

1996 — **Welfare Reform Act**

1998 — **Operation Desert Thunder** in Iraq.

Monica Lewinsky Scandal breaks.

President Clinton is Impeached in the United States House of Representatives.

George W. Bush

1999 ■ President Clinton is acquitted by the United States Senate.

2000 ■ **George W. Bush** (Republican) becomes president amidst vote-count controversy.

2001 ■ **Enron scandal** and bankruptcy

September 11th terrorist attacks led by **Osama Bin Laden**: Attacks on World Trade Center and Pentagon and additional attempt failed when plane crashed in Pennsylvania.

Patriot Act

Operation Enduring Freedom and **War against Terrorism** begins.

United States invades Afghanistan due to reports of Osama Bin Laden being harbored.

Anthrax Attacks: Letters containing poisonous powder mailed to several news media offices and two Democratic US Senators, killing five people and infecting seventeen others.

Education Reform Bill (No Child Left Behind Act) passed.

2002 ■ US withdraws from **Anti-Ballistic Missile Treaty**.

United States **Department of Homeland Security** formed.

Space Shuttle Columbia explodes.

2003 ■ United States, United Kingdom, Australia and Poland invade **Iraq** in response to reports of stockpiles of weapons of mass destruction.

Iraqi leader **Saddam Hussein** captured by US special forces.

2004 ■ **Facebook** launched.

Four deadly hurricanes hit Florida.

2005 ■ **Hurricane Katrina** devastates coastal Louisiana, Mississippi, and Alabama.

2007 ■ **Nancy Pelosi** (Democrat) becomes first woman to become Speaker of the US House of Representatives.

Significant Events

Black Monday

Berlin Wall torn down

Exxon Valdez oil spill

Persian Gulf War

Rodney King race riot

World Trade Center bombing of 1993

Monica Lewinsky scandal

Clinton impeached in the House of Representatives

September 11th attacks on World Trade Center

Invasion of Afghanistan

Invasion of Iraq

Key Figures

Nancy Pelosi

Significant Events

Global Financial Crisis

Affordable Care Act

Deepwater Horizon BP oil spill

Osama bin Laden killed

Withdrawal from Iraq begins

Ferguson, MO protests

US restores diplomatic relations with Cuba

George W. Bush

Virginia Tech Massacre

2008 ■ **Global Financial Crisis:** Bankruptcy of Lehman Brothers, national governments bail out banks to prevent further collapses.

Barack Hussein Obama (Democrat) elected first African American president.

2009 ■ **American Recovery and Reinvestment Act**

Tea Party protests begin.

Barack Obama

2010 ■ **Patient Protection and Affordable Care Act**

Deepwater Horizon BP oil spill in Gulf of Mexico.

Dodd-Frank Wall Street Reform and Consumer Protection Act establishes the Consumer Financial Protection Bureau.

Don't Ask, Don't Tell Repeal Act

New START treaty ratified.

2011 ■ **Osama bin Laden** found and killed by United States Navy Seals.

US Troops begin withdrawal from Iraq according to **Status of Forces Agreement.**

Occupy Wall Street movement begins in New York City.

Largest tornado outbreak in US history occurs in the American Midwest and Southern United States.

Budget Control Act

2013 ■ **Boston Marathon bombings**

Edward Snowden leaks classified information revealing global surveillance programs.

2014 ■ **Protests begin in Ferguson, Missouri** over police shooting of Michael Brown.

Diplomatic relations with Cuba restored.

2015 ■ *Obergefell v. Hodges:* Supreme Court legalizes gay marriage.

AP

The Advanced Placement® program is designed to offer students college credit while still in high school. The more than 30 AP courses culminate in an intensive final exam given every year in May.

Successful completion of a course and a passing score on the exam not only provides students with a deep sense of accomplishment, but also gives them a jumpstart on their college careers. AP credit is almost universally accepted by post-secondary schools, however each school has different guidelines as to what scores they will accept.

AP US History
ISBN 978-1-60787-552-9 $21.99

AP US Government and Politics
ISBN 978-1-60787-601-4 $21.99

AP Biology
ISBN 978-1-60787-553-6 $21.99

AP Calculus
ISBN 978-1-60787-555-0 $21.99

AP Chemistry
ISBN 978-1-60787-554-3 $21.99

AP Psychology
ISBN 978-1-60787-556-7 $21.99

AP English
ISBN 978-1-60787-557-4 $21.99

AP Spanish
ISBN 978-1-60787-558-1 $21.99

AP Macroeconomics/Microeconomics
ISBN 978-1-60787-585-7 $21.99

TO ORDER

XAMonline.com

or **amazon** or **BARNES & NOBLE** BOOKSELLERS

www.ingramcontent.com/pod-product-compliance
Lightning Source LLC
Chambersburg PA
CBHW080917170426
43201CB00016B/2174